MW01140545

Responses

to *Critical Cities Volume 1* , *Volume 2* and *Volume 3*

"*Critical Cities Volume 3* is a compilation of impressive proportion. Working from the starting point of "city as inequality," over 40 contributors from all around the globe offer essays and photo-essays, articles, criticism, reflections, and interviews that strive to answer questions about the emptying of the global countryside and the outcomes for millions of dispossessed rural-to-urban migrants; about the role of the urban industry in this mass migration; and about the future class conflicts that may come as a result of this new urban class order. Coming from a place both within and well beyond the confines of academia, in the end, *Critical Cities Volume 3* is yet another excellent contribution to the process of imagining our post-capitalist urban futures." **John Finn, Book Review Editor, *Human Geography: A New Radical Journal***

"This edition of *Critical Cities* – as well as the previous ones – is of great interest for better understanding the anthropology of cities in the current times; the grade of conflict, and the scale of social unevenness. It investigates the issues challenging the social order in Eastern, in Western countries, and in so-called 'upcoming economies', or in those territories that will lead the world economies soon." **Menene Gras, Director, *House of Asia***

"*Critical Cities Volume 3* is not a university book and doesn't fall into the mainstream of urban or architectural scientific/academic production. Even better, as it speaks about the city in an unusual and refreshing way... The city is usually discussed in a dry and one-dimensional way, ignoring the 'dirt' of human relationships – power, class, politics, money and memory. While the profession was sleeping, while everyone was asleep, the city changed from its roots." **Dominko Blažević, Architectural Critic**

"This is such an important contribution that helps to fill a yawning gap. There is a dearth of critical commentaries examining the changes in cities wrought by neo-liberalism. At last a multi-disciplinary collection of writing that brings together some of the best." **Anna Minton, Author of *Ground Control***

"*Critical Cities Volume 2* is a fascinating, challenging and insightful critique of contemporary urbanism and gives a voice to many who are often overlooked and bypassed in development processes. It is an essential counterweight to the glib assertions of many urban commentators".
Julian Dobson, Co-founder of *New Start Magazine*

"Cities are turbulent masses of contradictions, in which exhilaration can turn to frustration at the turn of a corner. So if I say that this book also has these traits, I mean it as the highest compliment, because in that it reflects the urban condition. A typical academic response to cities is to iron out the mess in order to control the contradictions under the guise of reasoned argument, be it in the commonplaces of 'placemaking' or the doctrines of new urbanism. In contrast, this book dismisses any notion of control or single viewpoint, and instead allows voices from outside and underneath to bubble up."
Professor Jeremy Till, Author of *Architecture Depends*

Published in 2015 by Myrdle Court Press, London, UK
in association with This Is Not A Gateway

ISBN 978-0-9563539-5-5

Myrdle Court Press is an independent
publishing company.

Unit 24 Myrdle Court, Myrdle Street, London E1 1HP
www.myrdlecourtpress.net

Designed by Karolin Schnoor
www.karolinschnoor.co.uk

Printed and bound by Imprint Digital, Exeter, UK

CRITICAL CITIES

IDEAS, KNOWLEDGE AND AGITATION
from
EMERGING URBANISTS

VOLUME 4

edited by
DEEPA NAIK & TRENTON OLDFIELD
THIS IS NOT A GATEWAY

In memory of those who have perished
in the Mediterranean Sea.

THANK YOU

It has been wonderful to work alongside each of the contributors to this book, who are all in their own way forging new means for critical engagement with cities around the world. We are grateful for the opportunity to continue to learn from each and every one of them.

We are also enormously thankful to Barbara Murray for her thoughtful editing, insightful criticism and advice with all aspects of producing the book.
It remains a pleasure and inspiration to work with illustrator and designer Karolin Schnoor. We thank her for proposing ways to translate a festival into a book and for her patience with us and our tight deadlines.

Contents

INTRODUCTION

The Urban Industry

Mass Murder, Theft and Impoverishment

DEEPA NAIK & TRENTON OLDFIELD

How is it possible that just about every single person who has, or provides, a platform to discuss and share knowledge about the so-called 'Urban Age'[1] is an uncritical and unabashed champion, advocate and supporter?

Quite unlike, for example, 'Climate Change', there are almost no books or articles or well-funded organisations that challenge the processes creating urbanisation, particularly the expediential rate of the last 30 years. Library shelves aren't stocked full of books drawing our attention to the emergency of hyper-urbanisation, highlighting the likely consequences. There is no significant percentage of books dedicated to showing ways it can be prevented or giving precedence or even a voice to those most affected. One almost only finds books that promote and 'naturalise' cities; suggesting unreservedly that cities are good for us. So upbeat and well funded are the 'Friends of the Urban Age' that it seems to make them, and most of the people around them, giddy. Very few if any examine the Urban Industry[2], researching, highlighting and pulling apart those with clear vested interests that knowingly and unknowingly are obfuscating the facts and creating, co-ordinating and managing the greatest land clearances and transformation of the human condition in modern times.

There are books that study urban power and politics, some even a little critical. And there are books that seek to improve urban lives by somehow making them 'sustainable' or making them 'liveable' via something called urban design. There are books by academics that eulogise 'Urban Studies', the field that has paid off their holiday home. These books are insular self-referential nonsense that demonstrates nothing more than their distance from the everyday life of the 99% and their desperation to maintain membership to a club nobody cares about but them. There is an abundance of speculative literature and hipster projects that imagine ways to ease the pressures or provide temporary palliatives for the conditions of urbanisation. Without wishing to be unnecessarily alarmist, the majority of existing literature and projects on urbanisation are the equivalent of being invited to participate in a consultation that may lead, at some point, to being able to choose to support a charity that may be allowed to assist you in selecting one of three available colours of paint that may possibly cover the walls of your prison cell! You may choose the colour of paint from these three colours but, whatever you do, don't ask why the walls exist! These projects and theories are nothing more than varieties of paracetamol for an inflicted and painful terminal illness. Perhaps, as with the pharmaceutical industry, there is significantly more profit in medicating the symptoms than in preventing the illness? Just about every government and cities organisation is ruminating and making statements on how to live with what is, in fact, an entirely avoidable disease. Aside from individuals and groups who have been brutalised and forced into urbanisation, there are very few agencies, university urban labs or NGOs working to prevent the processes, and it is very difficult to find anyone working to expose and undermine the false though 'given' logic that 'urbanisation is inevitable'[3].

This fact is as much as a phenomenon as the increasingly efficient herding of the world's population off their lands and into cities. The United Nations Department of Economic and Social Affairs (DESA) suggests over six billion people will be pushed into urban areas by 2045. Currently these urban areas occupy around 2–3% of the earth's land surface. With these statistics and ever decreasing trust in politicians and politics what sort of life will we six billion be living?

Is this really an "offer of enormous promise, with overwhelming potential for innovation and a better life"[4], or should we be honest with ourselves and admit these are the elements for an unprecedented human catastrophe all but set in place? Why are so very few challenging the Urban Industry while, at the same time, there are so many well-funded champions? Who is it that benefits from the overwhelming majority of humans being concentrated in small, highly definable and controllable geographies? Who benefits from the clearing of land? Who benefits from the building, both physical and ideological, of new cities?

The wrong side of history?

It is difficult to think of another current crucial and urgent condition with such profound human consequences that has so many potentially brilliant minds on the so-called 'wrong side of history'. Perhaps the last time this happened was when 'leftist progressive intellectuals/academics' openly championed social Darwinism, eugenics and racial determinism? The consequences of their support and/or silence were the European perpetrated genocides in 'the Americas', in 'Australia' and throughout Africa. The practice of mass-murder made the European holocaust inevitable and the mechanisms used highly efficient – as is well documented.

With this in mind, how is it that 'cities' have garnered such uncritical and undeserved promotion when the facts are demonstrably counter to the universally parroted meta-narrative? Some of the most educated people on this planet have somehow been seduced or mesmerised by one of the greatest untruths, certainly for generations if not a millennium. Is this an unprecedented situation for an unparalleled change in the human condition or is this lack of criticality on par from the educated/educating classes? It should be a concern to everyone that it is difficult to tell the difference between the websites of: a global corporation that sells concrete[5], any university's 'urban lab', and the Pulitzer Prize winning *Guardian* newspaper's 'Cities' section that is sponsored solely by the Rockefellers and their foundation[6]. How do you react when you learn that Shell, one of the world's most reviled oil companies, is pumping money into a PR campaign titled 'The Future of Cities'? Under this campaign Shell is paying for 'sponsored content' on news and other websites that make sweeping claims such as "Urban truths are universal", "the world's future is an urban one", "ultimately, the key currency in the urban future is human capital".[7] Shell also organised and paid for the ignorantly titled 'Escape to City' advert-event held at the deeply problematic[8] Royal Geographic Society in June 2014. What is the logical, critical, rational response when you realise all these profiteering global corporations are key agents in the Urban Industry and in the creation and heavily funded promotion of the Urban Age?

With such hegemonic positioning, it is vital to point out some very simple facts. First, contemporary urbanisation is absolutely not 'natural' or 'inevitable'; second, 'cities' do not equate to social, economic or evolutionary 'progress'; third, cities are creators, incubators and expanders of inequality and social deprivation; and fourth, pronouncements linking innovation and creativity to the 'nature' of cities are entirely vapid and meaningless.

Should there be surprise when the elitists respond with anger?

It feels necessary to point out that we[9] organise the This Is Not A Gateway festivals and publish the *Critical Cities* volumes not to join in academic point scoring nor to scorn extra-educated foolishness but because we[10] have researched and seen with our own eyes how many human tragedies have been created in the processes of urbanisation and how myths and lies about 'cities' have made them central in popular westernised culture. Our collective research shows many more catastrophes are set to unfold as a result of the hyperbole and untruths so many are so very quick to uncritically regurgitate.

Our programme is a sincere, rational (and heartfelt) response to the facts of the matter. From the outset our work has been calling for a cool-headed, robust, critical and urgent focus, not on speculating and mitigating the catastrophes, but on changing the prevailing conditions that facilitate them. We have been echoing and attempting to amplify the calls of those brutalised by urbanisation and calling for an urgent re-focus of attention and redeployment of resources to expose the Urban Industry and undermine the processes of the current Urban Age. It is a difficult endeavour as few narratives are as falsely positive, upbeat and emancipatory as the 'cities' narrative has become.

This situation makes it almost impossible not to 'step on a few toes', upset some people, frustrate and aggravate many more, as we directly or indirectly challenge the real cost of their mortgage and the foundations of their careerising. Anyone who challenges this agreed cheerfulness is liable to being angrily denounced as a killjoy. As we come from studying and working in the Urban Industry and the Academic Industrial Complex, this means people who have known us for a long time, sometimes as friends and colleagues, can feel this about us. We have lost friends and fallen out with ex-colleagues but it is also the case that after a few years people have started working on related issues and have got back in touch. Once they have had the time to read more about the issue(s) that initially frustrated or annoyed them it becomes clear we have only ever been working with the just facts of the matter and the situation really is urgent. Unfortunately some don't reach this realisation, often those who think the personal and the political can or should be separated.

Surely the situation can't be that bad?

It has been difficult to decide on the most effective example for this book's introduction, one that swiftly illustrates just how problematic and deeply entrenched the situation is across all fields, disciplines and agencies. But, even with so many to choose from, it was hard to go past UN–Habitat (the United Nations Human Settlements Programme) and particularly their recently launched World Cities Day and World Urban Campaign manifesto.

Most United Nations (UN) agencies and programmes are so large and globalised and have such a long organisational history that it is difficult to pin down exactly what they do and who and how many work for the agency. UN–Habitat is no different. Those with a keen eye will notice the Masonic symbols in the logo.[11] Established in 1978 in 'Vancouver, Canada', with headquarters in Nairobi, Kenya:

The United Nations Human Settlements Programme, UN–Habitat ... is mandated by the UN General Assembly to promote socially and environmentally sustainable towns and cities with the goal of providing adequate shelter for all. It helps the urban poor by transforming cities into safer, healthier, greener places with better opportunities where everyone, including the urban poor, can live in dignity.[12]

Its website declares:

UN–Habitat has developed a unique position supporting urban development and the planning and building of a better urban future for next generations. This key process supports economic growth and social development, and reduces poverty and inequalities.[13]

Setting aside the overarching structural disfunctionality and Euro-American/ western bias of the United Nations temporarily, it is worth observing what is absent from the 'world's premier global non-governmental organisation'. There are no agencies or programmes within the United Nations that work to prevent urbanisation. UN-Habitat is just one example of a number of its agencies that attempt to 'mop up the mess' or 'beautify the tragedies' that urbanisation creates socially, culturally and economically. The closest one might get within the UN to anything that opposes urbanisation is the 'Permanent Forum for Indigenous Issues'. The 2008 United Nations Declaration on the Rights of Indigenous Peoples has some strong wording in Article 8 and Article 10 to prevent forced removals.[14] It is important to note this document focuses on the rights of indigenous peoples as individuals within the existing occupying state of America, Australia or the like. It does not focus on First Nations or recognise nation to nation existence. It recognises the occupying state as the primary institution that should uphold the rights of the indigenous people within the territory it dominates. It certainly doesn't call for occupiers to leave the lands they are occupying, nor for indigenous nations to be recognised as the main and leading governments that occupiers need to 'sign up to' if they wish to stay on other people's lands. There is very little else noteworthy within the UN vastness that seeks in any way to challenge the processes of urbanisation and the movement of people to cities. The UN appears to uncritically see the creation of the Urban Age as 'natural' or overwhelmingly a good thing that doesn't need preventing. They are not alone it seems as #preventurbanisation isn't trending on Twitter. Not a single tweet has been sent with such a hashtag[15] but it is possible to find tweets linking to a video of UN-Habitat's director claiming, without a hint of irony, that "Good urbanisation can prevent Climate Change"[16].

It is in this context that UN-Habitat's activities exist. Briefly we will look at three: World Cities Day, Urban Thinkers Campus and World Urban Campaign. Perhaps it doesn't need stating: all these initiatives champion urbanisation and the creation of the Urban Age and relish the opportunity to manage the wished-for urbanised world. Cut from the same Urban Industry cloth, each of these programmes provides diverse insights into the scale and depth of the Urban Industry's narcissistic and rapacious promotion of urbanisation.

UN-Habitat's newest initiative – intended to become a global promotion via interaction event like World Environment Day – the first World Cities Day occurred on 31 October 2014. Established by the UN's 68th General Assembly, its aim was to "greatly promote the international community's interest in global urbanization, push forward cooperation among countries in meeting opportunities and challenges in urbanisation and contribute to sustainable urban development in towns and cities around the world."[17] It was staged as the culminating event of 'Urban October' which is billed as "one month of raising awareness, promoting participation, generating knowledge and engaging the international community towards a New Urban Agenda."[18]

Themed as 'Leading Urban Transformations', this first World Cities Day intended to "highlight the pioneering power of cities".[19] The website eulogised the 'checklist' items of every cities NGO: reducing greenhouse gases, strengthening resilience and, of course, ensuring basic services such as water and sanitation. The UN itself hosted a large roundtable event which featured sponsors who were also the speakers, including two nations notorious for government-inflicted human rights abuses: Sri Lanka and Kazakhstan. Another of the sponsors, SpartaMatrix, seemingly supplied David Hanna, one of the 'security' company's directors, as a speaker. Registered possibly in Singapore, the Philippines or Los Angeles, SpartaMatrix seems to have collapsed three years previously and its director 'Dr' Philip Wainwright, with two doctorates from two non-existent universities ('London Economics' and 'London International Law'), seems to have been in hiding since then[20]. Did the United Nations even take a quick look at the company's website, logo and particularly its Twitter and Facebook accounts which reveal a comic-book version of a 'boiler room' company? The diagrams for the 'SpartaMatrix System Overview' are particularly hilarious for "a leading global security solutions provider with a proven record of success"[21]. One of the few pages still working on their website states:

The Sparta Master Project is poised to create and reinforce Croatia's position as Gateway to Central Europe; a project of profound international interest. Additionally, Sparta's technologies will be used by other elements within the SpartaMatrix group of companies in order to foster other development projects world wide; in areas such as Central and South America, Africa, the Far East, the Middle East and other areas in Central Europe.[22]

SpartaMatrix, like the Sri Lankan and Kazakhstan 'government' representatives, shouldn't be anywhere near, let alone speaking at or sponsoring an event that could or will influence the lives of many billions of people. This is just one example from a peculiar list of sponsors. If you have some time take a look just at this one World Cities Day event and research some of the sponsors; you will likely be quite concerned. What can be done to prevent the 31 October 2015 World Cities Day from going ahead or how can it be refocused on the real causes of the movement of people to cities? How can World Cities Day tackle the Urban Industry? Can World Cities Day be a platform for those whose lives and cultures are devastated by urbanisation? How can World Cities Day prevent the processes that displace people into cities? How can World Cities Day advocate the re-booting of ancient cultures that long existed outside and without modern cities? Could World Cities Day be an annual event where reparations are paid?

The next UN-Habitat programme, Urban Thinkers Campus, puts together three words that many people want to be associated with and involved in, and with an 'all expenses paid' week in an Italian palace-turned-resort, few would turn down the 'opportunity'. This was, however, a strictly limited, invitation-only happening and overwhelmingly dominated by Europeans. Even invitees representing Kenya and other non-European nations were white and not likely citizens of the nation they are listed as representing. To be invited, it clearly states in the programme and subsequent report, you will already be in agreement with the dominant meta-narrative:

> *You are convinced that humanity is at a crossroads, undergoing a major urban shift that is transforming our world. Urbanization has become an inevitable process that presents tremendous challenges, with cities growing at unprecedented rates in many nations. If not critically re-examined, urbanization will continue to propagate negative trends. Like many researchers, professionals, and decision-makers, you believe that urbanization is an opportunity and that the potential of cities should be harnessed to lead a positive transformation.*[23]

You may end up being able to choose the colour of paint but, whatever you do, don't ask why the walls even exist in the first place! How could anyone dissent or deviate from the New Urban Agenda[24] in this context? Such an event is created to flatter the invitees and ensure the organiser's expectation of 'building consensus' for the next stage[25]. Predictably asinine conclusions came out of the self-declared 'unconference' that can be paraphrased as: The city we need is socially inclusive, well planned, a regenerative city, economically vibrant and inclusive, has a singular identity and sense of place, is a safe city, a healthy city, affordable and equitable, and managed at the metropolitan level, and so on and so on.

The four-day event included a one-day Urban Journalism Academy (UJA): "a pioneering and innovative UN-Habitat initiative to further the knowledge and understanding of international and national journalists and media professionals of the social and economic issues facing cities in the twenty-first century." If something similar to this UJA – 'The News We Need for the City'[26] – was even proposed to take place in countries like North Korea, Russia or Cuba it would result in widespread and thorough ridicule by 'the west'. As an endeavour it exposes the ambition to saturate all possible information 'outlets' with the Urban Industry 'line'. Highlighting how any questioning of the displacement of people to cities has all but disappeared from the context of academic and NGO forums, the Urban Thinkers Campus is focused on managing the consolidation of the world's rising population into increasingly dense cities and isn't in the slightest bit interested in challenging or preventing the processes that force people to live in cities.

The World Urban Campaign (WUC), which spawned the Urban Thinkers Campus, also unambiguously champions urbanisation. It states:

> *The goal is to place the urban agenda at the highest level in development policies ... to raise awareness about the positive urban change by engaging citizens in voicing issues and solutions to change their urban communities and to achieve green, productive, safe, healthy, inclusive and well-planned cities. It is meant to build catalytic and transformative alliances by engaging the civil society, the business sector, the research community and governments in a global movement of converging interests, providing a knowledge and action-oriented platform to address urban challenges.*[27]

Its 'Manifesto for Cities' published in 2012 presents some of the most abrasive, zealous, dogmatic and ideological (and clearly unfounded) statements from UN-Habitat, forging a hegemonic position on cities and urbanisation. Using bold for increased visual emphasis, the preamble claims that urbanisation is "inevitable" and is "at the heart of our civilization"; it acknowledges "the

increasing dominance of urban space" but claims it is "the single greatest development challenge and opportunity for the 21st century"; asserts, despite evidence to the contrary, that "urbanization is a positive force to be harnessed in support of social equality, cultural vitality, economic prosperity and ecological security"; and claims that cities are "the world's greatest asset for pursuing sustainable development" – and so on! It admits, we suspect unwittingly, that "the battle for a more sustainable future will be won or lost in cities".[28]
While a manifesto should have verve and conviction it is troubling, to say the least, when the statements don't come close to lining up with facts, when so many lives and cultures are under threat as a result, and when these sweeping, smothering statements have been given the rubberstamp of a so-called 'global consultation and consensus'. By way of anecdote, so metaphorically toxic is the document that the last time we tried to download it a Malware Warning came up on our computers which wouldn't let us proceed.

Once again the list of sponsors is a remarkable collection of global corporations long held in disrepute that a self-respecting UN shouldn't be doing any business with. It includes companies that are part of the Urban Industry with obvious vested interests in the concentration of humans in small definable geographies either 'to improve access to resources' or to supply services. Corporations also have the ambition to 'normalise/harmonise' cities, so the same products can be available around the world and comparisons and measurements can be readily available. Below we highlight just two of the corporations that have evident conflicts of interest. The UN should have excluded them long before even receiving an offer from them let alone involving them – an oversight or core behavioural trait of the UN?

For example, one of the sponsors is Veolia, the French global corporation "resourcing the world".[29] The corporation has jumped on the hype around cities whilst 'fanning the flames' through documents and events such as 'Lifestyle scenarios 2050' by the London School of Economics, 'Smart cities – Looking toward the future of urban life', 'Shaping the cities of tomorrow' and so on. It seems every self-respecting corporation needs an IT partner and Veolia has teamed up with IBM for a special programme called 'New Digital Urban Solutions'. Yet, among numerous other concerns, Veolia has long been heavily criticised for its involvement in building and operating infrastructure that directly links UN-declared-illegal occupation-settlements in and around Jerusalem.

GDF Suez, the French part-government-owned colonial company and one of the oldest continuously existing multinational corporations in the world, is another example of the nefarious transnational corporations that are among the World Urban Campaign's main sponsors. Numerous indigenous nations of 'the Amazon' – the very people the United Nations ought to be doing everything humanely possible to support – have been protesting against GDF Suez plans to build dams on and close to their lands. While protests are focused on the GDF Suez track record throughout the Amazon, there is particular outrage at the impacts resulting from the Jirau mega dam project near the Bolivian border, on which the indigenous nations were not consulted despite Brazilian law and UN statements requiring their consultation. Quoting Amazon Planet, Amazon Watch's recent report states: 'Companies like GDF Suez are directly responsible for the alteration of a unique and irreplaceable environment and unbearable rights violations of vulnerable indigenous populations."[30] How could the UN's World Urban Campaign consider involving this corporation? Does UN-Habitat even have a vetting and appraisal process for its sponsors and partners?

The connection between colonialism, forced urbanisation and today's exploitation is clear and can be seen in London today. GDF Suez is well known to many in London as one of its sub-companies, Cofely, which runs some of University of London's cleaning services, has acted in a way that should rule it out as a partner or sponsor of anything to do with 'cities'. Protests were held at GDF Suez London headquarters against the planned redundancy of more than 80 low-paid workers, the majority of who are forced migrants from nations in 'South America'. The company continues to refuse to acknowledge the workers' union.[31]

Such is the interest of GDF Suez in urbanisation and cities that it has set up its own urban spin tank, grandly titled the 'Urban Strategy Council', which aims to "develop ideas about the city of the future at the earliest possible stage ... with the aim of formulating an integrated and innovative vision of the city of tomorrow".[32] Their various websites sprout numerous advert-reports: the predictable 'Cities for Tomorrow' and the salt-in-wounds absurdity, 'Paving the Way for a Good City'.[33] Unfortunately one can't just laugh these endeavours off or turn the other way. Their intention and impact is deadly.

The World Urban Campaign and its manifesto show how organisations like the UN are silencing any criticality and dissent that might prevent urbanisation by making smothering statements such as "We affirm that urbanization is inevitable" – treating falsehoods as facts and proclaiming them universal truths. Here we can also see the violence of participation as the deeply flawed New Urban Agenda/ Global Urban Agenda[34] is rammed through several 'consultations' in order meet the 2016 Habitat III conference deadline, which will enable it to be possibly included in the new Sustainable Development Goals to be declared when the UN Millenium Development Goals expire in 2015.

So serious is the ambition to urbanise the absolute majority of the world's population that unfathomable resources are being 'invested' by the Urban Industry theft and impoverishment machine to make sure it happens. It is part of the process of over 500 years of devastating human, cultural and environmental crimes that can only end in catastrophe and utter dystopia.

To bring people with you

It is within this context, with these facts, we are told we should use methods to bring people with us rather than methods that some people might find uncomfortable. We have been told, often by those in the Urban Industry, to use positive examples and maintain an upbeat atmosphere to attract more people 'to our cause'. It is fair to say we have always found this approach, which does little than tickle the status quo, to be truly ridiculous – technically and given the outrageous resources amassed by the vested interests over the 500 years. Furthermore we have been told to avoid focusing on specific examples – 'to play the ball and not the player' – so as not to break 'polite society' codes of conduct. We should, apparently, join forces with anyone with a remotely similar perspective to forge another universalist 'left unity' wherever possible. But so unjust is the situation that all codes of 'decency' have already clearly long ago been trespassed.

The status quo argues revolutions and protests are only legitimate and to be respected if they are so-called peaceful and non-violent, and the only appropriate way to change 'public opinion' is to charm and convince people of your side of the argument. One is meant to slowly and steadily bring more and more people over to one's position. Adhering to these ideas, of course, means the status quo is only ever humoured and entertained. Confrontation, shock and awe methods (armed with nothing but the facts) and direct action are seen, at best, as hot-headed, impulsive and un-calculated, and at worst, 'against the law', trangressing acceptable conduct. Having never been supporters of the status quo, we shed our final polite–society skin in early 2012 before the publication of *Critical Cities* Volume 3.

We expect the precise, poignant and percipient essays in this book, which take the Urban Industry to task and problematise status–quo understandings of cities, will result in a volley of mean–spirited swipes from the establishment and the aspirational petite bourgeois commentators and academics based not on facts but on self–interest. Many people and most corporations choose to ignore the painful evidence and inconvenient truths in order to avoid acknowledging guilt, loss of status and comfort, or to attempt to shore up an academic or other career knowingly or unknowingly constructed on a scaffold of falsehoods.

This volume and others in the *Critical Cities* series were created to circulate the facts with the authority, vigour and rigour that comes from those historically and currently impacted by the ethos and processes that drive urbanisation and the centuries of terror and injustice which continue to this very day. We hope you will share these important essays with friends, family and colleagues.

1. 'Urban Age' is both the name of a number of organisations in different parts of the world as well as being a regularly used (though rarely tested or proven) phrase that suggests the world has entered a new phase of human existence. It is a new age in which the human has evolved through the Stone Age, Bronze Age and Iron Age into the Urban Age. Unlike the other ages, which are based on tools used, this 'age' is measured by the number of people living in urban areas. It became widely accepted in 2007–09 that for the first time in human history more people lived in urban areas than rural areas. It is remarkable how often this largely unquantifiable statistic is quoted as fact. So entangled is it with the idea of human evolution and progress most people don't seem to even care if it is true or not.
2. The 'Urban Industry' was coined by Naik & Oldfield in 2008 and used in *Critical Cities* Volume 1, published in 2009, in order to demonstrate the various interests that benefit from land clearances and the concentration of the human population into defined spaces. More in *Critical Cities* Volumes 1–3, with 'The Urban Industry and its Post Critical Condition' essay in *Critical Cities* Volume 2.
3. Like the Urban Age, the idea that 'urbanisation is inevitable' has also been picked up and is used with general abandon despite inaccuracies and clear political agendas. This statement can be read in articles such the one authored by Sir George Alleyne in *The Guardian* 'Urbanisation is inevitable. Public health must embrace this fact', www. http://www.theguardian.com/global-development/poverty-matters/2011/feb/03/urbanisation-health-systems (accessed 21/12/14) or the *Unleashing the Potential of Urban Growth* report

published by United Nations Population Fund in 2007, or more recently the statement in the UN's Manifesto for their World Urban Campaign launched in 2014 where they state "We affirm that urbanization is inevitable".

4. Bold and unfounded statement made by organisers in the programme for the UN's invitation-only Urban Thinkers Campus held in an Italian Palace 15–18 October 2014.
5. The multinational corporation Lafarge even has its general strap line as 'Building Better Cities' and its many different websites include documents such as 'The Happiness is in the City' along with a whole section on 'Contribute to Better Cities'. On first visiting their many websites it was difficult to ascertain what exactly Lafarge did. We wondered for a while if it was a university urban lab so similar are the headings and research reports shared on the websites.
6. *The Guardian* newspaper has a dedicated section on its website www.theguardian.com/cities. All 'stories' on this page are funded by the Rockefeller Foundation. All articles opened are interpreted with at least one advert from the foundation. *The Guardian* states, "The site is editorially independent of any sponsorship". http://www.theguardian.com/cities/2014/jan/27/cities-about-this-site. As a result one shouldn't be surprised that the Rockefeller Foundation director Judith Rodin's new book received a very handsome news report /advert on the very site itself? http://www.theguardian.com/cities/2015/jan/27/judith-rodin-warning-world-crisis-new-normal-rockefeller-foundation. Most 'stories' on the site are gossip ('New year's resolutions for architects in 2015', 'The world's best tall buildings of 2014 - in pictures', 'What is the World's Coldest City') and city guides by urbanists. There is loads of poverty porn including 'Berlin's rat baths: inside the ruined swimming palace Blub – in pictures'. The site is remarkable for its post-criticality and its open platform to communicate the aims of the Rockefeller Foundation.
7. Bloomberg.com the financial news agency continues to showcase 'The Future of Cities', which is a co-sponsored project with Shell, and Shell is running its 'Make The Future' campaign alongside it. The websites invoke the usual clichés about cities and urban life and highlight the same few 'success stories': buses in Colombia, football pitches in Brazil etc. http://www.bloomberg.com/sponsor/shell/the-future-of-cities (accessed 21/12/2014).
8. For those that aren't aware the Royal Geographic Society isn't a neutral institution. It was at the forefront of brutal European colonialisation providing a meeting place, information exchange and resource depository for the British attempts to dominate the world through its empire and corporations. Membership then and now should be an embarrassment and disgrace. Organising events here, be it a university urban lab or a global corporation, is a nod to an organisation with a long and very problematic history.
9. 'We' is used in this context to communicate Deepa Naik and Trenton Oldfield, co-ordinators of This Is Not A Gateway.
10. 'We' is used in this context to communicate a collective 'we', all those that have contributed to the This Is Not A Gateway Festivals, salons and books.
11. Well-known and regularly used Masonic symbols include the pyramid and the single 'all seeing eye'. These are thoughtfully combined in UN Habitat's logo.
12. From 'Sustainable Urbanisation, For a better Urban Future' published by United Nations Human Settlements Programme (Un-Habitat); also available online at mirror.unhabitat.org/pmss/getElectronicVersion.aspx?nr=3009&alt=1.
13. http://unhabitat.org/about-us/.
14. http://www.un.org/esa/socdev/unpfii/documents/DRIPS_en.pdf.
15. Twitter (accessed 21/12/14).

16. Introduction by UN Habitat's director Dr Joan Clos to UN Habitat's YouTube video series – Global Urban Lectures, https://www.youtube.com/watch?v=qwA1fwAdxxY (accessed 21/12/2014).
17. http://www.un.org/en/events/citiesday/background.shtml (accessed 21/12/14).
18. http://unhabitat.org/wcd/worldwide-celebration/ (accessed 21/12/14).
19. Statement by UN Secretary General 31 October 2014, http://unhabitat.org/wcd/sg-statement/.
20. Claims made by SpartaMatrix CEO on the very sparse SpartaMatrix website, http://www.spartamatrix.com/our-team.html. Neither institution exists in London or anywhere else. It is highly unlikely he has been awarded a PhD. There has been no information posted on the website in over three years. It is remarkable the UN didn't check the credentials of the organisation that sponsored and supplied a speaker for its event.
21. http://www.spartamatrix.com/history.html.
22. *ibid.*
23. Welcome statement in the programme of Urban Thinkers Campus – The City We Need, 15–18 October 2014, available for download on https://www.planning.org/international/habitat/pdf/oct14meetingprogram.pdf and unhabitat.org.
24. Many will be familiar with the New World Order. Is the UN's New Urban Agenda part of this? The New Urban Agenda is to be agreed in time for the UN Conference on Housing and Sustainable Urban Development (Habitat III) which will be held in Quito, Ecuador in 2016. http://unhabitat.org/the-new-urban-agenda-will-be-decided-in-quito/ (accessed 27/01/15).
25. One of the elements of the New World Order is homogenised and seemingly agreed 'order' though almost always reflecting the interests of the west. It is unsurprising invite-only events like Urban Thinkers Campus are pressed to 'build consensus'.
26. http://unhabitat.org/programme-urban-journalism-academy/.
27. World Urban Campaign, http://www.worldurbancampaign.org/about/ (accessed 21/12/14).
28. http://www.worldurbancampaign.org/wp-content/uploads/2013/07/Manifesto_For_Cities_with_PDF.pdf (first accessed 14/12/14, later unavailable due to Malware but available again 27/01/15).
29. http://www.veolia.com/en/resourcing-world/introduction (accessed 21/12/2014). It highlights their aim of 'Improving access to resources'.
30. 'Brazilian Indigenous Movement Denounces GDF Suez Over Amazon Dams', http://amazonwatch.org/news/2014/0428-brazilian-indigenous-movement-denounces-gdf-suez-over-amazon-dams (accessed 21/12/14).
31. http://3cosascampaign.wordpress.com/2014/05/21/press-release-occupation-of-cofely-gdf-suez-headquarters/.
32. http://www.gdfsuez.com/en/gdf-suez-imagines-the-city-of-tomorrow/urban-strategy-council/.
33. https://www.gdfsuez.com/wp-content/uploads/2013/07/Visions-ville-Paving-the-way-for-a-good-city-Mars-20131.pdf, and https://www.gdfsuez.com/wp-content/uploads/2014/05/gdfsuez_villesdedemain_en.pdf (accessed 21/12/14).
34. New Urban Agenda and Global Urban Agenda are regularly interchanged in World Global Campaign documents.

THE ROBBED WORLD & THE MAKING OF MODERN CITIES

Introduction

DEEPA NAIK & TRENTON OLDFIELD

The contributors to this chapter individually and collectively make the case, via examples from their own lives, for ending the use of terms such as 'the global south', 'the third world' and 'developing country'. It is more helpful, candid and factual, we learn, to use the term 'the Robbed World' when referring to nations with low Gross Domestic Product or low levels of industrialisation. It is also important to rename the so-called 'first world' as 'the Thieving World'. The one visual and ten verbal essays effectively show how modern cities such as London, New York, Paris, Toronto, Sydney and alike could only have been created via and with the resources, land and knowledge robbed from the majority world during the last 500 years.

Our daily lives in western/westernised cities not only derive from this historic theft but continue to depend on the large-scale, highly co-ordinated robberies of the majority world occurring this very minute. Although the methodologies of thieving have changed over time, the robberies have never stopped, and despite the so-called end of colonialism and decline of the European and American empires, the domination processes have, in fact, speeded up. The essays here provide an insight into some of the economic theorists and moral justifiers of these grand thefts and pre-meditated genocides. We learn how the vast wealth was transferred, who benefited including specific families that profited then and continue to benefit today, and how the immense scale of the stolen wealth deposited in western cities has been used to shape and enforce an unprecedented global domination.

This chapter contains material unlike that found in the overwhelming majority of urbanism books. It confronts the difficult but urgent issues that underpin the development and maintenance of modern cities. There is not a single line about pop-up shops or urban farming, nor are there photographs of declining and abandoned industrial areas, and none of the essays adds even a sentence to the 'false promises' circulating through the Urban Industry that suggest cities are good for us. The analyses in these 11 papers from around the world work with facts that demonstrate the very real processes of the wholesale transfer of wealth from the Robbed World into the creation, maintenance and subsequent domination of modern cities.

We learn how there has been a full-scale relocation of the majority world's people off their lands and into urban areas, resulting in most of the world's rapidly growing population living on an increasingly tiny percentage of the earth's land surface. This process has been underway for over five centuries but has accelerated in the last 50 years and particularly so in the last 10 years. Population centralisation will no doubt result in a human calamity of a scale unseen before; displacing people of their land has already caused cultural devastation and the deaths of hundreds of millions. The emptying of 'the interior' and the inundation of cities has been achieved either by force (including legislation) or by various inflicted poverty conditions that make cities seem better places in comparison. Land clearances, a demand of resource and financial capitalism, enable the elitist classes to gain unchallenged access to and domination over resources, including basic necessities of food and water. And the Urban/Urbanising Industry works hand in glove with global capitalism; with international finance, mining companies, food corporations, property developers; and with university 'urban labs' bursting with profoundly uncritical, self-interested, useful-idiot PhD-holders and professors who seem unable to grasp what it would mean for their family to be massacred so someone else could have a faster computer or bigger 4x4.

Slavery, theft and London 2012

The London 2012 Summer Olympic Games was the background noise to our lives in the months leading up to the 4th This Is Not A Gateway Festival from which this book's material is derived, and the opening ceremony in particular provides a germane context for this chapter. Bid, won, designed and staged by the UK's uber-privileged, the 2012 Games used an estimated £24 billion of public money, and it is fair to argue, the climax of the seven-year build up was the opening ceremony. An ostentatious muddle that took three hours and cost an estimated (though still to be independently audited) £27 million[1], its narrative was pro-urban, pro-industrialisation and overwhelmingly pro -'progress'. It centred on Danny Boyle's dramatised performance titled 'Isles of Wonder', described by its creators as a focused history of the UK. Few do propaganda as openly and tactlessly as the British elite and it certainly warmed the cockles of most if not all remembrance-poppy wearers. The benefits of empire for the ruling classes were displayed in every aspect of each act of the pantomime. There was acknowledgement that the working classes in Britain had a hard time but, dramatically and critically, it failed to speak of the devastating impact of Britain's 450+ years of imperialism on the colonised countries and peoples.

On the night any criticism seemed to die away and be replaced with proclamations of 'pride' and genuine emotion when the pageant presented Boyle's interpretation of Britain's 'industrial revolution'. Titled 'Pandemonium', this was the longest act of the opening ceremony and perhaps the support that erupted for it was because Brits today subconsciously feel like the collective survivors of that brutal period, that they have been through something truly horrific together? Or perhaps Brits know that period was integral to their expansion around the world and is why they experience such significant material and psychological comforts today? That evening the hashtag ProudOfBritain was trending on Twitter as well-known journalist Piers Morgan used it to tweet his four million followers: "We need to be an Empire again – seriously." This was re-tweeted over 1,400 times that evening alone.[2]

Many watching the opening ceremony probably chose to not know that the so-called 'industrial revolution' was not only funded by Britain's earliest colonial projects – chiefly transatlantic slavery – but that most of the ideas employed in London and other UK cities to create the revolution were taken from the rest of the world; appropriated and re-packaged as 'British'. Most of the materials used in the industrial revolution were, of course, not from within Britain or Europe. Britain and Europe were largely resource-less and socially, politically and economically in freefall. Minerals such as iron ore and bauxite existed in Europe though in very small quantities and were said to be of low quality. Europe had largely been deforested in the processes of the early industrial revolution and timber, particularly for charcoal used in smelting, was increasingly scarce so the European search for timber went global in the early 1700s. European nations raced to accumulate whatever resources they could before their neighbours did.

For Britain one of the most lucrative imperial trophies was the cotton plant and the dramatic use of the cotton loom in the ceremony caught our attention.

It seemed extraordinary that the cotton loom could be displayed with such smug satisfaction as an exemplar of British history; that it could be so blithely and blatantly stripped of its reality, which was and is the systematic theft of resources and labour, and the millions of deaths, past and recent, that are directly and indirectly linked to the garment industry.

We could have chosen to examine any other part of the Olympic ceremony with similar results. Try doing a social and political economy history of any item around you. Look into the minerals used for your laptop, for example. Or perhaps palm oil, which is found in the vast majority of processed food. Or the cheap chocolate bar you had with your cup of so very 'British' tea? Most items used every day in modern cities can reveal the wholesale and continuous transfer/misappropriation of wealth from the Robbed World to Europe and 'the west'.

Cotton

Cotton is, of course, indigenous to equatorial lands in Asia, Africa and the southern 'Americas'. It had been cultivated and used for many thousands of years, notably in India, Egypt, Mexico, Ecuador and Peru, to make fabric of outstanding quality and beauty as well as utilitarian cloth for everyday items. There was no cotton in Britain before the 1600s – although there are some references to its use for candlewicks – yet British cotton mills were a special focus in the Olympic opening ceremony, with oversized mechanised looms being used for dramatic effect. The director was right to include them. Manufactured cotton textiles were Britain's foremost export for generations, enriching the colonising classes. The opening page of the website 'Cotton Times' states:

> *Lancashire became synonymous with cotton and cotton spearheaded the Industrial Revolution, its export in huge quantities to all corners of the globe not only bankrolling an empire on which the sun never set but, at the same time, forcing the rest of the civilised world to industrialise, too.*[3]

Cotton plants and seeds were appropriated by British colonialists and planted and harvested with the enforced labour of people transported from Africa against their will and enslaved in 'America' and in the Caribbean islands on European 'owned' and run plantations. And it was not only the cotton plant but also knowledge of its cultivation and cloth production methodologies that were appropriated. Samples and recorded information on colour and block -printing techniques were taken from Mexico and Peru to Europe in 1519 by colonial occupiers Pizarro and Cortez. They also stole and traded cochineal, the insect used in the production of almost all shades of crimson, red, scarlet and pink.[4]

Cotton, the first industrialised global trade, was based on some of the most gruesome abusive practices ever undertaken by man: slavery, plant and land theft, child labour and toxic processes, and it became an important symbol in many anti-colonial struggles. In the UK itself, there were the appalling working and social conditions of the infamous 'satanic mills' documented and so vividly described in the 1844 book *The Condition of the Working Class in England* by Fredrick Engels, who himself owned and managed such cotton mills in Britain. And, as is well documented, cotton and cotton technologies were taken from India, employed in British mill towns, and then the 'British' products were forced on Indian markets at exorbitant prices, creating poverty for all but the mill owners. Today the cotton mills, factories and workhouses are located around the world to exploit cheap labour and with worse conditions than ever, as exposed in the recent collapsing buildings in Bangladesh that injured over 2,500 and killed more than 1,100 desperately poor workers[5].

Just a handful of Euro-American corporations, such as Louis Dreyfus Commodities (France/Switzerland) and Monsanto (USA/Sweden), currently dominate all stages of the £1.6 trillion global cotton and textile business – a monopoly of companies based in countries that have never had indigenous cotton. Some in 'the west' call practices like this 'innovation' and 'creativity'. In the last 15 years alone over 300,000 farmers, including cotton farmers, in India have committed suicide related to unfair debts payable to corporations. A deadly spiral is created when companies such as Monsanto actively promote seeds, fertilizers and pesticides etc., that promise high yields but rarely deliver anything, leaving the farmer in an impossible position to repay the money borrowed to buy the products. Reduced yields and the debt that must be paid forces the farmer to borrow more money to try new heavily promoted products, which only leads to greater debt.[6] It is estimated one farmer commits suicide every 30 minutes in India as a result of these entrapment methodologies[7] It is near impossible for a small farmer in rural India to undertake legal action against an immensely wealthy, faceless, global corporation such as Monsanto.

Furthermore, cotton is one of the world's 'dirtiest' crops, using the most insecticides of any single major crop. Contemporary cotton practices use 16% of the world's insecticides on 2.5% of the world's cultivated land, with dire implications for cotton farmers and workers. These insecticides are linked to massive increases in cancers, deformities in children, disabilities via byssinosis and general ill health such as rhinorrhea, loss of consciousness and general weakness, which may progress to paralysis.[8]

Clearly the modern corporatised cotton trade continues to be synonymous with unfair finance and trade processes, worker exploitation, death and poverty, i.e. with inhumanity and callous profiteering little different from its slave-plantation history. When considering buying a pair of denim jeans for just £7 it is impossible not to think of the violence and injustice perpetrated at all stages of the process to get them to the shop. Corporate domination of course also extends to the 'high street'. The UK's clothing retailers are largely monopolised by the Arcadia Group, a company founded at the 'height of empire' some 130 years ago and current owner of more than 2,500 shops in the UK alone. These include Topshop, Topman, Miss Selfridge, Burton, Evans, Dorothy Perkins, Wallis and BHS stores.[9] Violently rubbing salt in the wounds of those who have been robbed, the corporations manufacture and sell products 'inspired' by indigenous designs. Described as 'Tribal', 'Aztec', 'Native', 'Ethnic', these ancient designs, patterns and clothing styles have been appropriated and sold without licence, request or royalty. Shop windows on London's Oxford Street (and elsewhere) often have displays that entirely appropriate ancient cultures. Ceremonial objects such as dream catchers, drums and headdresses are stripped of their cultural meaning, reduced to signify an abstract 'exoticism' and exploited solely in pursuit of financial profit.

ASOS, one of the UK's largest online retail outlets, currently has over 350 products available under 'Aztec' and more than 50 under 'African prints'.[10] Of course there are many hundreds, probably thousands of items that don't even make reference to the culture they have appropriated. Under 'tribal' one can buy a suit in fabric based on African patterns for $325 by fashion designers 'Libertine Libertine' based in Copenhagen. A freelance designer who has done work for the companies mentioned above clumps people and their cultures together when referencing some of 'her' designs on her website: 'Aztec–tribal–native–navajo–geometric–native–kaleidoscopic–kitsch–colourful–bold–ikat–peruvian–triangles'[11]. This young designer, who is originally from Lithuania and currently lives in the UK, complains on her blog that a large UK textile company stole one of her designs[12]. So unjust has the world become that today a European can sue a UK company for the theft of a design that she stole from the Majority World. The violence that started with the earliest colonial thefts continues in the abuse and erasure of these ancient cultures. So, yes, cotton is an integral part of the UK's cultural narrative – both historical and contemporary[13] – but the real facts were simply erased from London's jingoistic 2012 ceremony.

So unjust are the lives of the Robbed World that when slavery was being 'phased out' it was the slave-masters rather than those enslaved who were compensated via the Palace of Westminster parliamentary act.[14] Many of Britain's already immensely wealthy families were given huge financial handouts. Prime Minister David Cameron's family was one of them. Other 'compensated' families include those of Chairman of the Arts Council England Peter Bazalegette and renowned authors Graham Green and George Orwell. The payments made to former slave-owners are estimated to have been the equivalent of over £16.5 billion today. It was 40% of the entire state budget at the time.[15]

It is reported that much of this compensation money was re-invested in the industrial/colonial revolution in industries such as the railways and the universities – often making these families even wealthier and gaining the support of academic institutions to encourage and justify ongoing colonialism. Kings College London, for example, is known to have been funded by a good number of people who were 'compensated' slave-owners and agents.[16] European universities were, and remain, key agents in the justification of colonialism and capitalism. Cambridge's Charles Darwin is the most obvious case but there is also his less known though equally problematic cousin Francis Galton, who founded UCL's 'National Eugenics' department. Today universities are dominated by business courses that (directly or indirectly) teach different varieties of a resource-exploitative, globalised economic and financial system.

Urgent study and action are needed to counteract the immense human catastrophe being propelled by the west's greed for resources, 'growth' and 'progress'.

11 new critical insights

David Bedford and Thomas Cheney's paper 'The Left: Enemies in the First Nations' Struggle for Justice?' handsomely sets the scene. It tackles one of the least critiqued but most problematic aspects of Marxism: the idea of progress, that communities/nations must evolve/pass through certain stages before being considered ready for the utopia of European-constructed communism. This proposition of evolved and evolving economies, that the majority world was uncivilised and at an early stage of economic development, allowed for and continues to encourage the occupation of other people's lands and the exploitation of their resources with the express aim of 'transitioning them' to 'technologically advanced economies' whilst 'equitably sharing' their resources with those who don't have them, i.e. western occupation would assist in the evolution of so-called primitive economies. The destruction of indigenous cultures was, and still is, seen as development and progress.

Bedford and Cheney's paper points out that Marx and Engels' ideas were embedded with the self-serving myths of western superiority, and it destroys the assumption that 'the Left' are or have been allies to indigenous peoples around the world. It shows that First Nations peoples, such as those of Turtle Island ('Canada'), are considered an obstacle to 'progress' by people on both the left and the right, and how, in their continuous resistance to genocide and ongoing occupation, indigenous people have seen Marxism for what it was: just another European methodology of undermining their cultures in order to gain access to their resources. 'The Left' – who are overwhelmingly white males from the bourgeois occupier-settler class – have continually failed First Nations peoples mainly through inaction, passive agreement and even support of exploitive endeavours that are destroying indigenous communities throughout the world.

In his paper, 'Sto:lo Territory: Unsurrendered Territory of the Sto:lo People', Sakej Ward makes it clear that non-indigenous peoples have no legal or moral legitimacy to be anywhere on Turtle Island ('Canada'). Using the Salish people's experience, he deconstructs the methodologies used by European occupiers in their attempts to legitimise the early[17] and ongoing occupation, which, for example, included reliance on the Pope's 'Doctrine of Discovery' which granted:

> *... the full and free permission to invade, search out, capture and subjugate the Saracens and pagans and any other unbelievers and enemies of Christ wherever they may be as well as their kingdoms, duchies, counties, principalities and other property and to reduce their persons to perpetual slavery.*[18]

Notably, soon after the split from Rome, the English monarchy started to issue documents very similar to the papal bulls to 'legalise' their own occupations.

Sakej discusses the lack of consent and the failure to acknowledge long-existing democratic processes of the resident peoples, such as Potlatch. We learn about the racism, brutality, hypocrisy and greed of European colonialism in the processes of creating reservations, the use of state and church boarding schools and of Dual Mandate in practices of neo-colonisation, and the urbanisation of First Nations. The Indian Relocation Act (or Public Law 959) of 1956 resulted in forced urban relocation programmes and centres. At the time only 10% of the First Nations population lived in cities. By 1980 over 52% had been moved to cities, and by 2000 over 61% of the indigenous population were understood to be living in urban areas.[19] Modern cities are death camps for most First Nations peoples due to cultural alienation, loss of community and the structural and everyday racism in institutions such as the police, in education and employment. Urbanisation fulfils the occupiers wish to see indigenous people disappeared or assimilated (westernised) as cheap labour – certainly with no legal traction over their lands and resources.

It is widely agreed between indigenous peoples that the attacks against them tend to spike in certain periods, and in response, the defiance of the First Nations also rises. In the next contribution, titled 'Why Nobody Has Ever Been Idle in Centuries of Genocide', we learn about the recently re-invigorated resistance campaign Idle No More through a conversation between Sylvia Mcadam Saysewahum, one of the campaign's co-founders, and Steve Rushton. Sylvia Saysewahum speaks in detail about the 410-page 'Bill C-45' that passed through the Canadian parliament without consultation with, or consent of, any indigenous peoples, but with the full support of both sides of the parliament.[20] It is important to note that these parliamentarians are occupiers on other people's land and, as Sakej Ward makes indisputably clear, there is no legitimacy to their parliament or their laws. However, they have the guns, the courts and the jails, and nowadays the demographics are on their side.

Bill C-45 set out to assimilate First Nations 'reservations' into the Canadian system, removing protection from all but one waterway and allowing various industries to commence exploiting the First Nations' natural resources. This includes tar sands oil extraction, which will soon take up an area the size of France and Indonesia together.[21] The impacts on First Nations are nothing less than an orderly polite genocide – undertaken by state officials and corporation workers. It is a human catastrophe that almost everyone turns away from, but now "Idle No More has exploded globally, using social media to share information as well as direct-action protests".

Shifting focus to the southern region of the continent, which is called Cemanahuac, Awqapuma Yayra Colque and Nemequene Aquiminzaque Tundama explain 'The Untold Story of the So-Called Latino: Colonial Cities Built on the Blood and Bones of our Nican Tlaca Ancestors'. Societies in Cemanahuac were once rich and sophisticated. In fact, the colonisers noted in their diaries and correspondence the absence of poverty and hunger, which were common in their own lives and history back in Europe. The paper exposes a number of the signature colonising strategies including religion and urbanisation. For example the main cathedral in Cusco was sited on the foundations of a Wiracocha Inca palace destroyed by the European invaders and built with the stones from the demolished walls and buildings of the existing city. Its construction started just six years after the Spanish invasion and took 100 years of brutalised slave labour, overseen by Spanish priests and architects, to complete. The interior Christian iconography was fashioned in gold and silver stolen from local occupier-controlled mines where millions were worked to death over a 300-year period. The cathedral was both the symbol and the co-ordinating hub of the Spanish expansion of Christianity and colonial rule, a physical and cultural invasion that has been relentless.

Biological weapons were also systematically deployed by the occupier forces. Small pox, for example, killed 95% of the local population estimated to be around 100 million people.[22] The indigenous people alive today are descendants of the 5% that survived and they are still fighting full-force assimilation and culture wars, including the occupier labels of 'Latin America' and 'Latino'. 'Latin' of course indicates belonging to southern Europe: Spain, Italy, Portugal. Alongside this is the heavily promoted idea of the 'mestizo' – that people are of mixed blood, which is, however, not an acknowledgement of the rape of indigenous women by Europeans; most European occupiers married other European occupiers, rarely if ever inter-marrying or assimilating to the local cultures. Over 90% of Cemanahuac countries remain governed by Europeans of mostly Spanish and Portuguese descent. And we learn that Simon Bolivar was no revolutionary for indigenous self-government but rather an occupier/settler who wanted a much greater piece of the 'empire pie' for himself and his slave-trading Spanish family and European friends.

The paper highlights that much of the food we eat today is in fact indigenous to Cemanahuac. In processes similar to the cotton trade, resources including corn, tomatoes, chillies, potatoes, peanuts, strawberries, pineapples, chocolate, tobacco, vanilla and much much more were appropriated from Cemanahuac without consent or any financial compensation, for the enrichment of European elites and cities such as London, New York, Amsterdam and Melbourne. Importantly, Colque and Tundama explain how the processes perpetuating these injustices can be halted and justice for the people of this continent can be reached.

One of the greatest tragedies inflicted on the people of the Robbed World is the continuing existence of the occupation and domination by alien Europeans and European institutions. Katherine Maich's paper, 'Geographies of Racism and Inequality: Peruvian Household Workers Navigate Spaces of Servitude', shows how this dominance is entrenched in a particularly potent and violent way on and through indigenous and black women's bodies.

The processes of European colonisation systematically undermined societies by breaking up long-existing social relations. Forced removals from the land, for example, severely reduced women's economic possibilities and agency. Many women were, and continue to be, forced or pulled into domestic service, mostly in cities, primarily for people of European descent who are occupying their lands. Katherine Maich quotes from Susan Socolow's book *The Women of Colonial Latin America*:

> *In the 16th and 17th centuries young Indian women were taken from their villages to work as domestics in nearby urban centres. By the late 18th century, the opportunity for domestic employment was a major factor in attracting poor rural women to the city ... and provided 'employment' for 75% of them.*[23]

Colonialism instituted not only physical but also mental and emotional violence. In the context of inflicted poverty, for example through introducing forced payment of taxes to colonial authorities, migrating to cities for paid employment undermines and restructures personal relationships. This has a profound impact on women and families, particularly if children have to be left behind. The paper draws our attention to the way colonial relations are perpetuated through the everyday practices that women are subjected to in the vulnerable and isolated environment of domestic service. We learn that the violence and hierarchy is very often embedded in the architecture of a house or apartment building, with spaces and circulation designed to enforce discrimination, such as separate entrances for live-in domestic workers. In addition, the Household Worker's Law, recently brought in to normalise domestic workers' conditions, is critically examined and inherent contradictions in colonial legislation are discussed.

Importantly, we hear the voices of the indigenous women themselves throughout this paper, and the author explores her own positionality and intervention in the lives of these women and in the broader socio-political context. Most 'urbanists' fail at the outset of their work to understand their own privileges and biases and how these impact on their research and the lives of others – an inherent structural failure right across the western-dominated Urban Industry.

From Cemanahuac we move to Africa where Jason Larkin's photographic essay, 'Tales from the City of Gold', highlights important aspects of Europe's colonial legacy. When Europeans 'discovered' the ancient goldmines in the area later known as Johannesburg, a European gold rush swiftly ensued and became one of the causes of the 'Boer War'[24]. As a result of victory in that war, the British claimed control of this vast resource-rich area and set about removing long-established African communities from their lands. The indigenous people were displaced and forced to live in the area that we now know as Soweto – far enough away so that the communities wouldn't be able to prevent or slow down access to the gold but strategically close enough to be transported on a daily basis to work in the mines. Two cities sprang up: one comprised of high earning, mostly European-migrant bosses; the other, a city of violently exploited African workers. In less than 50 years Johannesburg and Soweto were estimated to have a population of over 300,000 people. The European greed for gold not only rapidly transformed the landscape but embedded social Darwinism and racism – this separation of 'blacks' and 'whites' the early stages of what became known as 'apartheid'. A once rich, first nation was colonised, changed into an atomised, landless and impoverished workforce for the foreign occupiers of their own lands.

Johannesburg was built from, on and around the 'waste' of these mines and Larkin's powerful images show how the often-toxic remains of the mines are part of the everyday landscape of this now large and modern city. The European miners didn't feel obliged to clear the waste and post-apartheid governments have been unable to compel the companies responsible to undertake much needed environmental clean ups. The majority black population has no choice but to live amongst the toxic waste dumps – a very visible legacy of their stolen resources. Recently, with the price of gold increasing, a number of mines have become operational again, right in the middle of suburban neighbourhoods. A number of Larkin's images include a man wearing Christian priestly robes who hauntingly brings to mind Desmond Tutu's statement:

When the missionaries came to Africa they had the Bible and we had the land. They said 'Let us pray'. We closed our eyes. When we opened them we had the Bible and they had the land.

The places in Larkin's photographs provide a direct historical link between Johannesburg's rapid growth and wealth and today's vast inequalities including the effects of historic and contemporary racism. The images offer us the opportunity to reflect on what was taken, who benefited from the gold, and the legacy for the first nations. Rather than turning Johannesburg into a so-called 'Smart City', should we not instead be working to make Johannesburg a 'just city'? Should we not be considering compensation for the gold and other minerals that were stolen from the rightful owners?

There are many ancient cities throughout the continent of Africa, however, the one chosen to be the headquarters of the African Union, Addis Ababa in today's Ethiopia, is not one of them. Addis Ababa ('New Flower' in the Amharic language) is little over 100 years old. In Clara Rivas Alonso's essay 'Visualising Addis Ababa: Deconstructing Privilege-Making Narratives', we learn that the city is a product, an indirect result, of Europe's deadly 'Scramble for Africa', which sped up with the 1869 completion of the Suez Canal. It was commissioned by the recently created Emperor Menelik II to be the capital of his new empire, and its location, on the indigenous Oromo people's land, was chosen for its strategic geo-political benefits, without consultation or permission of the Oromo. Supporters argue Menelik II had no choice but to establish an empire in order to confront, compete and ultimately limit the rampaging European empires. Others argue he was the forerunner of Dual Power arrangements whereby European (now also American) powers work hand in glove with a 'native' leader, flattering and enriching the ruler's family while embedding their own corporations and maintaining their 'national interests'. It is a particularly effective methodology for limiting dissent from the wider population who can no longer mobilise around an obvious foreign occupation.

Nonetheless the Oromo peoples continue to protest the existence of Addis Ababa and resistance has recently increased due to the government's new plans to significantly expand the city, pushing further onto 'protected' Oromo lands. At the same time they are also resisting the formal and informal land grabbing by corporations from nations such as the UK, Saudi Arabia and India facilitated by the Ethiopian elite. So high are the stakes, recent reports suggest 5,000 Oromo people have been jailed and many thousands are subject to abuse including rape, torture and beatings. It is estimated more than 200 have been killed.[25]

In just over 100 years the population of 'New Flower' has grown to more than three million inhabitants, and it is expected to continue to grow as people are forced off their lands and the city's 'Unique Selling Point' as the 'diplomatic capital of Africa' increases in importance. It is no surprise that the United Nation's recently opened its third largest building – the UN Economic Commission for Africa – in the city.[26] But Addis Ababa combines this role as a shiny 'Summit City' with being home to a steady stream of forced landless peoples. Clara Rivas's paper takes us down the streets and over the bridges that were built specifically for the location of diplomatic mission residences and compounds. We learn how the preparations for the 50th anniversary of the African Union eased the way for informal settlement clearances and significant new construction. Here Clara shows us the billboards that advertise apartments and houses via globalised narratives – 'Shabby to Chic' with clichéd homogenised 'urban' images alongside – which echo the modern cities of westernised Dubai or Vancouver. Such images, Clara argues, reflect the internalisation of colonialism and show how society in Addis is changing. Hierarchies of urban space are being cemented and elevated into the sky, and therefore likely fixed for generations.

Concurrently Ethiopia is being deeply neo-colonised for control of its very fertile lands. An area the size of many European nations has been land grabbed – leased or bought from the government for international corporations to grow and harvest crops for export. This process has been encouraged by the government.[27] The aim, according to government ministers including the current Minister for Agriculture Wondirad Mandefro, is to industrialise the nation through the urbanisation of its population and to provide significant incentives for foreign investment in large-scale agriculture in the rest of the country.[28] In a recent interview he said Ethiopians "have to abandon their previous way of life".[29] The idea is that concentrating the population in urban areas will encourage citizens to move away from 'subsistence farming' and towards an 'innovation economy'. Urbanisation will 'free up' the majority of the land for natural resource exploitation as well as generate foreign exchange as a result of foreign-lead farming operations. This approach echoes early 20th-century Russian policies that considered farmers ignorant un-evolved peasants holding back the creation of an advanced utopia. It seems the idea of western -style industrial 'progress' has taken hold of the imaginations of Ethiopian elites and full-scale tragedy for the Oromo and other indigenous peoples is on the horizon.

In India, tragedy has already befallen the Dhangar, Koli, Katkar, Thakar and Marathas peoples in central Maharashtra state. These first nations were removed or persuaded to sell their lands so the private city of Lavasa could be built by a group of national and global corporations. At one time this group included the Hilton Hotels and the University of Oxford. The latter, while it denies it, was shamed into withdrawing its involvement with one of India's most controversial and unjust projects.[30]

This private city could not have happened without the removal of the Adivasi, the indigenous 'protected' peoples. It is being built upon their very land. However, such is the potency and pollution of the caste system, along with the media's overwhelming support for the narrative of western-style modernity, that the campaign to build Lavasa has long portrayed the scheduled tribes and 'other backward castes' as useless and helpless. Nonetheless their apparent 'uselessness' hasn't stopped Lavasa and its supporters from suggesting the private city in and of itself could 'bring these people successfully into the modern world'.[31]

The 'collateral damage' inflicted on these first nations is explained away either with that special kind of nonchalant indifference or with the kind of detailed and relentless pursuit we see in Madhu Purnima Kishwar's 14-page, person-by-person assault published on the charity Manushi's website[32]. The ability to blatantly disregard the people and cultures seems to revolve around the idea the Adivasi are ignorant, damaging the environment, cash poor, outside the system and generally just very dirty; an eyesore for 'modern' India. Commentators and academics argue, without irony, that these families certainly shouldn't be able to criticise, let alone prevent or slow down, such a modernising project as Lavasa. Madhu Purnima Kishwar suggests the full force of the law should be brought against any such people in order to compensate the corporations who might lose money and slow India's 'development'. The predominant narrative is that those who have been robbed, more than once, of their lands and who are being pressed into abandoning their culture should actually be compensating the development corporations.

This is the background to Persis Taraporevala's essay 'Creating Subjects: Citizenship in a Private City', which examines the establishment of contemporary private cities, the formation of citizenship in them, and how their governance structures create a process of depoliticisation within highly political development projects and geographies separated out from the rest of the nation. There is just one entrance and exit to Lavasa. Once one is granted access through its enormous gateway it soon becomes obvious how separate and alien Lavasa is. The master plan was done by HOK architects, the USA's largest architect-engineering firm[33], and is in fact not modelled on a city at all but on Portofino in southern Italy, a summer holiday resort town for Europe's rich[34]. The 'City Manager' or head of governance is an American who had not worked in India previously[35] and many of the institutions that have signed up to have campuses or businesses in Lavasa are Euro-American.[36] Films promoting the city on Lavasa's website and YouTube comprise images of European resort towns and American college campuses.[37] The official 'Making of the City Lavasa' promotional film opens with a poem by Lord Byron, a British imperialist, and closes with a poem by Maurice Genevoix, an avid supporter of French colonialism.[38] Rutgers University, one of the nine colonial universities of America[39] has been chosen to educate and assess Lavasa's future lecturers. Is it fair to say that Lavasa comprises all the components of a western globalised dystopia?

One of the main marketing messages, repeated without irony, is that Lavasa is India's first post-independence hill station. European colonialists established 'hill stations' to house them when they wished to retreat from the 'too hot' weather or escape "from the noxious odours of native habitation"[40]. Hill stations also doubled as military garrisons and hideouts for colonialists should they come 'under attack'. Another of Lavasa's deeply problematic marketing tropes is its appropriation of indigenous people's narratives of nature through phrases such as: 'be at one with nature', 'experience nature at every shade', 'refuge in the serenity of nature', 'give in to nature'.[41] In contrast, in reality, legal proceedings have been instituted against the company for environmental degradation, particularly land clearances and lack of a thorough Environmental Impact Assessment[42]. Lavasa said, in 2011, it would set up an environmental restoration fund, however, to date, there is no evidence of this fund's existence.[43]

Euro-Americans such as Christel De Haan have been invited to deliver sections of Lavasa's Corporate Social Responsibility (CSR) mandate. By law the company is obliged to spend 5% of the total project cost on CSR activities - however this is ring fenced for a required Environmental Restoration Fund. De Haan has established a school, named after herself where 170 students are currently "receiving a mainstream education" or what we know as western education. It is suggested 700 places will become available.[44] The school hopes its graduates will be able to work in Lavasa itself. Other CSR activities are re-educating the previous inhabitants to work in the hotels, on the construction sites and making furniture, which will be sold in the new shops - all on the land they had lived on without outside intervention for generations. This is the life of the robbed, the world over.

All geographies that seek to benefit from globalisation or wish to see themselves as 'global' rather than 'local' attempt to stage 'global' cultural events. This year Lavasa is playing host to WorldFest, which its promoters say is "an arts festival that attempts to bring the world together in one place" and "takes Globalisation to new levels".[45] Another mechanism is globalisation's close friend TED and TEDx talks. Lavasa plans to host its own Smart Cities TEDx event next year and is currently running a submission process where an applicant "has the opportunity to showcase your idea of a Smart City on a global platform"[46].

The first major period of globalisation is the focus of the next paper, which offers a guided walk through the streets of central London. University College of London's Legacies of British Slave-ownership project researchers Katie Donnington and Nicolas Draper have developed a route that demonstrates how slavery was a key agent in the building of this modern metropolis and why it continues to prosper today. As the data is so vast, Donnington and Draper have selected aspects of the everyday life of one individual, George

Hibbert MP, to highlight how ordinary and unremarked slavery was in the UK for over 250 years. Hibbert was a staunch advocate for and one of earliest profiteers of slavery. Much of his wealth and influence came from plantations in the Caribbean. Descendants today remain in finance, property and fine art, for example, the west end gallery Hazlitt Holland–Hibbert which represents darlings of 'the left', artists Rachel Whiteread, Grayson Perry and Gilbert & George along with well–known establishment artists Lucian Freud, Henry Moore and Order of the Companions of Honour David Hockney.

It is difficult to underestimate just how much of London and the UK's extraordinary wealth is a result of the combination of enslaving people and purposefully setting out to colonise significant populations of the world. There is a strange state of mind among most British people where they know this is true and reference it with some sort of pride and sense of achievement in books and particularly in TV 'documentaries' presented by establishment figures. However, if someone else brings these issues up, particularly someone whose family has suffered from colonialism and enslavement, it often sends Brits into a fury of denial and quite often into volleys of insults and nonsensical comparisons. Accompanying this is an industry of complication and obfuscation. Among the regularly propagated ideas are the notions that the transnational corporations and the British Empire all happened haphazardly and that everyone benefited, both coloniser and colonised; that colonialism is a two–way street, all very dynamic with loads of 'feedback' and so on. Let there be no mistake, empire and European colonialism was systematic, calculated, co–ordinated and purposeful. It was an extension of centuries of Europeans trying to subjugate other Europeans and control resources. Colonialism and the waves of globalisation have only ever benefited 'the west', with some crumbs given to corrupted local elite colonial collaborators. A whole nation can be robbed with the support of just a few local collaborators in pursuit of 'whiteness' and self–enrichment.

It is important to understand the last 500 years of European colonialism (ongoing) is quite unlike anything that came before it. It is puerile, ignorant and probably self–serving to suggest 'humans have always been like this, done this to each other'. This statement clearly cannot be evidenced outside Europe and is an attempt to normalise this very abnormal behaviour. European colonialism is defined by being the first multi–continent colonialism. 'Race' and specifically whiteness and white supremacy were invented in order to justify colonial actions. The false notion of white supremacy and consequently of 'lesser races', the idea of 'the civilised' and 'the uncivilised', was the 'reason' given for the systematic and pre-meditated slavery and mass genocide of tens of millions of people around the world; murder on a truly colossal scale. These genocides were and continue to be committed purely in pursuit of other people's resources. The stolen resources have made and continue to make London and the UK (and other European colonising nations) unjustly wealthy – a wealth that has been and is currently invested in subsequent European resource grabs.

Europeans, particularly the British, also undertook a demographics war as government policy; high birth rates and mass migration to the 'colonies' were encouraged and funded. Today 480 million people of European descent live in every nation on earth.[47] There are almost as many Europeans living outside Europe as in Europe and Europeans still occupy Australia, Canada, America, South America, New Zealand, French Polynesia, many islands in the Caribbean, central and eastern Russia and so on. Today the US, France and Britain have military bases in almost every country on earth. Many indigenous languages have been degraded or even died out as English was inculcated as the 'global' language. Nothing in history compares with the devastation wrought on the majority world by European colonisation. The genocide, cultural and environmental destruction and robbery are real despite the scale seemingly being too vast to comprehend. So outrageous are the injustices sometimes they just don't seem possible. For example, at the time of the parliamentary 'abolition of slavery' George Hibbert was one of those compensated for his losses resulting from the formal cessation of the transatlantic enslavement industry. The people enslaved received absolutely no compensation then and none to this day. There is no possibility to make a mistake about this; there is no grey area, no complexity to it.

In the next paper Awqupuma Yayra Colque highlights still more injustices embedded in the modern metropolis for those from the Robbed World should they live in cities such as London, New York, San Diego, Madrid, Melbourne etc. Her essay 'Why Are Our People Cleaners?' critically examines the disproportionate number of people from the Robbed World found in the least respected, most vulnerable and most exploited jobs in western cities. How did a people who thousands of years ago built cities, which western architects and planners try to ape today, become the cleaners of the modern metropolis? Awqupuma focuses on the people from her own lands showing how the processes of hundreds of years colonisation still continue and how the poverty and violence it has forced on her once proudly independent people has forced them to flee to unexpected and undesired places. We learn how these processes have chipped away at self–esteem and how the continuation of white supremacy and institutional racism pushes people, often with professional qualifications, towards jobs like cleaning where they become invisible and irrelevant in the modern western city.

The paper precisely explains that people have come to western cities as they have no choice but to follow the wealth that was taken from their lands or to flee the violence that has resulted from colonialism. Given European politicians' and their mainstream media friends' current malicious and disingenuous obsession with 'immigration', a counter offensive is called for, probably using guerrilla direct action that relentlessly communicates 'We Are Here Because You Are Still There'. This statement is the absolute truth of the matter. Many people have made it clear for generations that until Britain and other European colonial nations return the resources stolen or pay reparations and make restitutions and establish systems that pay for the use of the flora and fauna, there is no moral or legal way for Europe to even attempt to close its borders. The loot, all that was robbed, is jamming the doors open. If the people of Europe want to close the door all they need to do is return everything they have stolen.

Currently most migrant organisations and charities try, largely in vain, to argue that migrants contribute to their 'host' society financially, culturally etc. These are always defensive campaigns, apologetic and arguing for acceptance. As Awqupuma outlines, there is no logical reason to ask to be accepted and certainly no logic for wishing to assimilate into a culture that has caused your pain and suffering. The 'migrants contribute' argument can never be useful as the 'contribute' goal posts, the way 'contributing' is measured and calculated, and the cultural narrative can and will be changed when it suits those in power. Regardless of moving goal posts, it places people of the Robbed World on the back foot. It is hard to believe a migrant organisation could have come up with such a campaign.[48] Despite the hundreds of millions spent on films, TV shows, books and organisations that attempt to complicate and look for subtlety in colonialism, it is a fact that the majority world was robbed and continues to be robbed of its riches and its cultures undermined and destroyed. As Awqupuma argues, the focus should be on these facts. If migrant organisations sincerely wish to change the social conditions of migrants in a 'host' country and, more importantly, the conditions of their home nations, campaigns would do well to focus on the simple but powerful idea of 'We Are Here Because You Are Still There'.

As we learn in the final essay in The Robbed World chapter, so anxious is 'the west' about its guilt, so anxious is it about justice being sought for its 500 years of crimes against humanity, that the Thieving World's governments are now making it a crime to care. Caring is being criminalised. If you live in the Thieving World, so threatening is it to care that you can be 'stripped' of your citizenship and deported; whole communities are being criminalised, treated as suspects. Through the processes of indefinable securitisation policies, laws and propaganda, absolutely any social or political activity can be considered as problematic and thus a threat to national security. The rise of the police state and the criminalisation of caring is a threat to us now but the greatest threat is to our future generations as every day harsher policies are launched and given royal assent.

Les Levidow and Saleh Mamon's paper 'UK Securitisation Targeting "Suspect Communities"' is a detailed, highly referenced study of the processes of securitisation from post World War II until today. We learn about the over–exaggeration of the US and UK's idea of vulnerability and how the idea of 'national security' evolved and began to take precedence over 'human security'. The paper looks in detail at the general and relentless pressure on Muslims in the UK and highlights three specific UK communities – Kurds, Tamils and Somalis – that are currently being harassed and intimidated by British government institutions.

Levidow and Mamon point out that cities are a focus for securitisation policies and practices as they usually house the main NGO, diplomatic and government institutions, regularly hold high–profile events such as the Olympics that garner worldwide press coverage, and contain diaspora communities which the elite fear the most. Major cities often have more in common with other major cities than they do with the country they are in; they are part of a globalised and interlinked economy and military network and, as a result, any perceived vulnerability is a threat to the global elite structure. Furthermore cities are limited and defined geographies (increasingly so) thus relatively easy to contain, to surveil, to defend. The high-speed urbanisation of the world's population is relevant in this context, with most of us now living in urban areas on just 2-3% of the earth's surface with surveillance and movement increasingly managed - particularly with the advent of 'Smart Cities'.

The Robbed World is a vast chapter. These 11 significant papers critically examine the processes involved in building the west's modern cities and maintaining their dominance today. They contain facts - even if these aren't widely admitted, shown in the opening ceremony of the Olympic Games or taught in most universities - and they contribute to an honest and truthful redefining of the 'third world' / 'global south'/ 'underdeveloped countries' as the Robbed World.

1. http://www.theguardian.com/sport/2012/jul/27/olympic-opening-ceremony.
2. https://twitter.com/piersmorgan/status/228957895851646976.
3. Cottontimes.co.uk (accessed 15/12/14).
4. Elena Phipps, *Cochineal Red: The Art History of a Color* (New York: Metropolitan Museum of Art & Yale University Press, 2010).
5. http://www.labourbehindthelabel.org/news/item/1140-bangladesh-building-collapse-kills-over-80-workers-primark-and-mango-labels-found.
6. http://rt.com/news/206787-monsanto-india-farmers-suicides/.
7. 'Every Thirty Minutes: Farmer Suicides, Human Rights, and Agrarian Crisis in India', a 54-page report from NYU School of Law's Center for Human Rights and Global Justice (CHRGJ) examining human rights concerns surrounding farmer suicides in India, 2011, http://www.chrgj.org/publications/docs/every30min.pdf.
8. Environmental Justice Foundation, *Deadly Chemicals in Cotton Report* (London: Environmental Justice Foundation, 2007), http://ejfoundation.org/report/deadly-chemicals-cotton.
9. www.arcadiagroup.co.uk/ (accessed 14/12/14).
10. www.asos.com (accessed 14/12/14).
11. http://vasare.co.uk/my-portfolio/my-work-2/aztec-tribal-native-navajo-geometric-native-kaleidoscopic-textile-fashion-print-trend-style-summer-2015-2016-urban-outfitters-topshop-freelance-designer-portfolio-kitch-colourful-bold-ikat-peruvian-tr/.
12. http://vasare.co.uk/2014/09/30/my-artwork-stolen-by-asos-com-and-used-on-a-bikini/ (accessed 14/12/14).
13. *Empire of Cotton: A New History of Global Capitalism* by Sven Beckert, published by Allen Lane, was realised as we were writing this introduction. From the abstract it looks like it could provide much greater detail than is possible to do here. Written by a Harvard professor, we reserve judgement for now on its politics. It is highly likely a eulogy to western 'innovation', 'aspiration' and capitalism.
14. Slave Compensation Act 1837; See Catherine Hall, Keith McClelland, Nick Draper, Kate Donington and Rachel Lang, *Legacies of British Slave-Ownership: Colonial Slavery and the Formation of Victorian Britain* (Cambridge: Cambridge University Press 2014).
15. 'Britain's colonial shame: Slave -owners given huge payouts after abolition', http://www.

independent.co.uk/news/uk/home-news/britains-colonial-shame-slaveowners-given-huge-payouts-after-abolition-8508358.html (accessed 14/12/14).

16. Rachel Lang, 'Cultural Legacies 1: Philanthropy and Institutions', in Catherine Hall *et al.*, *op.cit.*
17. "… his sons or their heirs and deputies may conquer, occupy and possess whatsoever such towns, castles, cities and islands by them thus discovered that they may be able to conquer, occupy and possess, as our vassals and governors lieutenants and deputies therein, acquiring for us the dominion, title and jurisdiction of the same towns, castles, cities, islands and mainlands discovered; in such a way nevertheless that of all the fruits, profits, emoluments, commodities, gains and revenues accruing from this voyage, the said John and sons and their heirs and deputies shall be bounden and under obligation for every their voyage, as often as they shall arrive at our port of Bristol …", 'First Letters Patent granted by Henry VII to John Cabot , 5 March 1496', in H.B. Biggar (ed.), *The Precursors of Jacques Cartier, 1497–1534* (Ottawa, 1911), pp. 8–10. Latin text first printed by Hakluyt in 1582. Manuscript: National Archives PRO, Treaty Roll 178, membr. 8, http://www.bris.ac.uk/Depts/History/Maritime/Sources/1496cabotpatent.htm.
18. Robert Hill (ed.), *Marcus Garvey and Universal Negro Improvement Association Papers, Vol.7, November 1927 – August 1940* (Berkeley and Los Angeles: University of California Press, 1990). Diana Hayes, 'Reflections on Slavery', in Charles E. Curran (ed.), *Change in Official Catholic Moral Teaching*, Readings in Moral Theology no. 13 (New York/Mahwah: Paulist Press, 2003).
19. Roxanne Dunbar-Ortiz, *An Indigenous Peoples' History of the United States* (Boston, MA: Beacon Press, 2014).
20. http://openparliament.ca/bills/41-1/C-45/?page=6.
21. Joshua Kahn Russell, Naomi Klein, Stephen D'Arcy, Toban Black and Tony Weis, *A Line In The Tar Sands: Struggles for Environmental Justice* (Oakland, CA: PM Press, 2014).
22. Roxanne Dunbar-Ortiz, *op.cit.*
23. Susan Migden Socolow, *The Women of Colonial Latin America* (Cambridge: Cambridge University Press, 2000); a second edition is to be launched in February 2015.
24. Bill Nasson, *The Boer War: The Struggle for South Africa* (Stroud: The History Press, 2011).
25. *'Because I am Oromo' – Sweeping repression in the Oromia region of Ethiopia* (London: Amnesty International, 2014), http://www.amnesty.org/en/library/asset/AFR25/006/2014/en/539616af-0dc6-43dd-8a4f-34e77ffb461c/afr250062014en.pdf.
26. http://www.un.org/apps/news/story.asp?NewsID=49184#.VNC_KGTkfoE.
27. Lorenzo Cotula, *The Great African Land Grab? Agricultural Investments and the Global Food System* (London: Zed Books, 2013).
28. http://www.worldfolio.co.uk/region/africa/ethiopia/n-1280-committing-the-private-sector-to-sustainable-agriculture-led-industrialisation.
29. http://www.journeyman.tv/62390/short-films/land-grab.html.
30. http://www.cherwell.org/news/2010/02/13/university-pulls-out-of-lavasa-project.
31. http://www.sunday-guardian.com/investigation/jairam-ssis-being-environment-terrorist-with-lavasa-an-ideal-green-city.
32. 'Medha Patkar's Baseless Targeting of Model Hill City, Lavasa (Part One)', http://www.manushi.in/articles.php?articleId=1495&ptype=&pgno=1#.VNDQrWTkfoE.
33. http://www.hok.com/about/sustainability/lavasa-hill-station-master-plan/ (accessed 14/12/14).
34. http://www.lavasa.com/high/apartments.aspx (accessed 14/12/14).
35. http://www.weforum.org/global-agenda-councils/scot-wrighton; and http://mumbai.ctbuh.org/scott-wrighton.html (accessed 14/12/14).

36. Education institutes include Ecole Hôtelière de Lausanne, Redgrave Rowing Academy, Rutgers University, http://www.lavasa.com/learn/learn-home.aspx (accessed 14/12/14).
37. 'Lavasa: India's First Planned Hill City', https://www.youtube.com/watch?v=lSGlZxe9NSA (accessed 14/12/14).
38. 'Making of the City Lavasa', https://www.youtube.com/watch?v=kee7cz4NEDg (accessed 14/12/14).
39. http://www.rutgers.edu/about/history.
40. Ambe Njoh, *Planning Power: Town Planning and Social Control in Colonial Africa*, (Abingdon: Taylor & Francis/UCL Press, 2006). See discussions in the subsection 'Colonial public health policies with spatial dimensions'.
41. 'Tourism Lavasa AV', https://www.youtube.com/watch?v=xQy399hQSWc.
42. 'Lavasa: The Controversial Lake City Project', https://environmentallysound.wordpress.com/lavasa/93-2/.
43. All Corporate Social Responsibility information is directed to Christel House with nothing listed for environmental projects. It is unclear if Lavasa Company contributes to Christel House or not aside from a donation in 2010. This report dated 25 October 2011 from the Ministry of Environment, Forests and Climate Change (MoEFCC) outlines the requirements expected of Lavasa as a penalty for their environmental degradation, http://envfor.nic.in/sites/default/files/Report_profKTRavindran.pdf (accessed 27/01/15).
44. http://www.hccindia.com/hcc_admin/data_content/fourpillarsofcsr_files/Education_-_Christle_House.pdf.
45. http://mumbainewsnetwork.blogspot.co.uk/2014/12/worldfest-2014-at-lavasa-city-17th-to.html (accessed 14/12/14).
46. http://www.smartcityideas.com/ (accessed 14/12/14).
47. http://en.wikipedia.org/wiki/European_diaspora.
48. International Organization for Migration NGO based in Geneva, Switzerland, is the organisation behind 'Migrants Contribute'. The organisation evolved out of the ruins of WWII and was focused on the movement of people within Europe. The organisation owns the domain http://www.migrantscontribute.com/.

The Left: Enemies in the First Nations' Struggle for Justice?

DAVID BEDFORD & THOMAS CHENEY

This paper interrogates the usefulness and appropriateness of Left politics as the principal form that the struggle for justice by First Nations now takes on Turtle Island (known to the European settler society as North America). We argue that First Nations have largely rejected this form of resistance politics. The Left has adopted, uncritically, many key elements of the very capitalist ideology against which the First Nations have contested over the past 150 years. Importantly, these elements – the inevitability of progress defined as the constant increase in the technological transformation of nature in the processes of production, and the desirability of ever-increasing abundance defined as consumption – are inconsistent with the continued survival of First Nations' traditional ways of life. In fact, the Left is not merely indifferent to, but actively opposed to, this survival, as they assert (as does capital and the state) that such a continued existence is an obstacle to 'progress'. However, we conclude by arguing that this antagonism is not necessary. It is rooted in a particular reading of Marx, which is neither the only possible reading, nor, we argue, the proper one. This leaves us with a series of questions: What is the context and character of the struggle of First Nations presently? What are its legal and political parameters? Can the Left – dominated by members of the settler society and hitherto an opponent of the strivings of First Nations to preserve their traditions – become an ally?

Idle No More: the resistance continues

A recent and important example of the First Nations' unbroken resistance to the continuing colonisation of Turtle Island began on 12 November 2012 when four women – Nina Wilson, Sheelah McLean, Sylvia McAdam and Jessica Gordon – from what the settler society refers to as the Canadian province of Saskatchewan organised a 'teach-in' in Saskatoon to raise awareness of the urgent threats to the environment, and of an escalation of the attempts, posed by the recently enacted Bill C-45, to undermine the First Nations' democratic governance. This omnibus bill contained, in addition to changes to the Income Tax Act, various other unrelated items. Among these were changes to the Navigable Waters Protection Act and to the Indian Act.[1] The changes to the former Act significantly reduced the federal government's role in the environmental assessment process. The Canadian Constitution grants jurisdiction over the protection of the environment to both the federal and provincial governments. As some provincial governments are very reliant on resource extraction, the stepping back of the federal government from protecting waterways was seen as very troubling.

The alteration of the already problematic Indian Act was perhaps even more worrisome. Previously, sections 38–41 of the Indian Act had mandated that if a band was to lease reserve lands a vote in favour by the majority of the band was needed. Business and government, which wanted to have access to reserve lands for resource extraction and the building of oil and gas pipelines, argued that the requirement that a majority of the band electors must agree to such leasing was both too slow a process and one unlikely to yield a 'yes' vote. Omnibus Bill C-45 amended the Indian Act so that only a majority present at the time and place that the vote was held was needed. So, for example, if 20 people turned out for the vote on whether or not to lease land for an oil pipeline, only 11 'yes' votes would determine the outcome for a reserve with hundreds or thousands of eligible voters. When communities have been made as poor and desperate as the First Nations are in Canada[2], finding a few who will trade their lands for money or power is an easy task for the state. The settler Canadian state has long experience and great expertise in this form of subversion.

The Idle No More movement has tried to draw attention to the threat to both the environment and the integrity of First Nations posed by the policies of the Harper government. Capitalising on the opportunity and publicity afforded by the movement, Theresa Spence, the Chief of the Northern Ontario band of Attawapiskat, began an extended hunger strike to protest the especially terrible housing, health and economic conditions on her reserve. Attawapiskat is, in many ways, a test case for the economic development policies of the Canadian state and the behaviour of capital in Canada. For the past eight years the Victor Diamond Mine has operated on traditional lands of the Attawapiskat First Nation. The local environment has been severely affected and the promise of 'progress' – jobs and economic development – has become a nightmare of drug and alcohol abuse, social destruction, cultural loss and intolerable living conditions. 'Progress' and 'development' have brought nothing but suffering and deprivation. Systems of roads now crisscross what had been untouched forest. Huge stretches of land are now open pits. Tailing ponds and poisonous effluent are dispersed across their hunting and trapping territories. In addition, the undertaking to provide jobs and improved living standards has failed to materialise, as is all too often the case. Instead, a few have menial jobs, most are left unemployed, the traditional economy which had always sustained them is in tatters, the ecosystem is poisoned, and the culture which has fed their souls is also sickened by the invasion of economic activities, social relations and drugs and alcohol from a colonising, racist and alien society. And this pattern has been repeated across the face of Turtle Island. The Innu from northern Labrador are equally victims of the 'progress' brought, in their case, by Vale nickel mine. In all such cases the promise of progress has meant the destruction of traditional ways of life and the resources that the land has always provided to sustain the people. Not only has the promise of alleviating poverty not been fulfilled, but the attendant cultural destruction has left many spiritually adrift.[3] They are demonised in the media and criminalised for 'crimes' of poverty.

It is examples such as these that have led many First Nations communities to try to find an alternative to the false promise of progress and economic development. As a result, many First Nations continue to stand against such development even as they are alternatively threatened and bribed by the Canadian state and by mining, oil sands and pipeline corporations. Most notably, many have rejected the Enbridge Northern Gateway Pipelines Project for which the current Conservative government of Stephen Harper has been pushing so hard. This pipeline would carry heavy oil from the Alberta oil sands to ports in British Columbia across ecologically sensitive parts of First Nations' lands. Communities that have held referenda have consistently and steadfastly resisted this 'progress'. It was to circumvent the democratic process on reserves that led Harper to pass the Omnibus Bill C–45 to require only a majority of electors who voted rather than a majority of the community as a whole. They hoped to be able to use the new regulations to find members of the affected First Nations who would agree to the pipeline. The sinister and twisted political logic was clearly, if unintentionally, revealed by Prime Minister Harper's long-time senior adviser, Tom Flanagan, who wrote in *The Globe and Mail*: "Consultation has become a shibboleth of our times. It is, indeed, an essential part of democracy, but it can also become a constraint on freedom. Prolonged consultation may give some people a veto to prevent other people from exercising their own rights."[4]

Aboriginal and treaty rights

Such attacks on the democratic process were deemed necessary by the Harper government because, in a number of cases, the Canadian Supreme Court had determined that consultation with First Nations and their approval were required. The Delgamuukw case was particularly instructive.

Originating as a land-claim case in British Columbia, the Delgamuukw decision became a landmark ruling in Canadian First Nations' land rights. In 1987 the Gitxsan and Wet'suwet'en hereditary chiefs brought a case to the British Columbia Supreme Court in an effort to halt resource extraction on their traditional territory – a 57,000 square kilometre (22,000 square mile) area of land located in the west-central part of the province. The litigants used a combination of legal techniques, including appeals to their own traditional expressions of land ownership as well as to the legal institutions of the settler culture. The latter centred on the argument that the Royal Proclamation of 1763 – which had recently been incorporated into the Constitution Act 1982 – remained essentially in effect and upheld the principle that indigenous land title be respected and that territory could only be ceded by consent.[5] Importantly, the Gitxsan and Wet'suwet'en had never signed any treaties with the British colonial authorities or the government of British Columbia, and had therefore not alienated any of their traditional land.

The Gitxsan and Wet'suwet'en anticipated the first ruling, in 1991, with cautious optimism. In 1990 the Supreme Court of Canada had handed down the Sioui and Sparrow decisions, both favourable to aboriginal land rights. Despite such optimism, Chief Justice Allan McEachern's decision was a terrible disappointment. He ruled that the Royal Proclamation simply did not apply to the province of British Columbia and that aboriginal title existed at the pleasure of the crown.[6] Adding insult to injury, McEachern chose essentially to ignore the oral evidence presented by the hereditary chiefs, dismissing it as unscientific. The indigenous plaintiffs pushed the case through the British Columbia Court of Appeal and eventually to the Supreme Court of Canada. In 1997 the Gitxsan and Wet'suwet'en were vindicated. Supreme Court Chief Justice Antonio Lamer ruled that aboriginal title does indeed exist and that it includes exclusive rights to land and resources.[7] The ruling set down criteria, based on prior occupation, for establishing indigenous land rights. Furthermore, it included the important stipulation that while land use is not restricted to pre-contact forms, it must be sustainable.[8] Importantly, the Lamer decision did reserve for the crown the right to infringe upon aboriginal title if such an action were decided to be necessary. In such a case, however, the indigenous groups involved would have to be consulted and their interests given priority. If dispossessed of their land, they are to be properly recompensed.[9] Lamer's ruling affirmed what is known as 'duty to consult', a layer of protection that was put in jeopardy by the Harper regime's Bill C–45.

While the Lamer decision did represent an important advance in terms of its legal precedent, the discourse surrounding the case, both inside and outside the courtroom, is indicative of deep and potentially irreconcilable cultural differences. The Gitxsan and Wet'suwet'en insistence on using traditional forms to convey their claims to territory, and McEachern's racist and paternalistic rejection of their oral histories, represent only the surface of the divergent worldviews held by the indigenous and settler societies. Not only do indigenous societies represent their property rights in different ways, these rights correspond to a completely different understanding of the land, the plants and animals that live on it, and the place of humans within the ecology.[10]

Justifying dispossession

McEachern made explicit use of the Lockean logic of dispossession in his ruling. Referencing Hobbes as well, he argued that the Gitxsan and

Wet'suwet'en did not live in political society and therefore their consent was not required for their dispossession.[11] Underlying this mode of thought is the idea that the most efficient and instrumental use of resources is the genuine basis of property rights. For McEachern, the Wet'suwet'en and Gitxsan were not extracting the maximum possible quantity of value from their land.[12] This point of view characterises the settler society's approach to ecology. In short, nature is a thing to be mastered and exploited for the greatest possible human profit. McEachern's decision is not alone in adopting this logic. Many popular commentaries on the Delgamuukw episode described the Gitxsan and Wet'suwet'en territory as vacant, empty and lying in waste. Using analysis that could have been taken directly from Locke's *Second Treatise of Government*, several commentators lamented the 'duty to consult' established by the Lamer ruling and argued in favour of systems of private property rights, which in their view can produce the greatest possible economic value. The discourse around the Delgamuukw case is, in broad terms, indicative of the modern, capitalistic view of nature and its resources. In this view there is a strict ontological separation between humans and nature. Nature itself is understood as devoid of inherent value; value being incorporated only though human labour power.

The Delgamuukw case is also representative of a distinctly non-modern approach to humans and ecology. When making their claim to the land, the Gitxsan and Wet'suwet'en stressed that in their worldview humans are dynamically integrated into the ecology. Rather than separate or different from the ecological world, they see themselves as ontologically continuous with the rest of nature. This fosters a sense of deep respect for nature in all its specificity and complexity. The environment is not simply a blank slate waiting to be transformed by human labour. Instead, every specific in the ecological system is unique and worthy of moral value on its own terms. Of course, indigenous groups express this view in different ways. For example, in the Wet'suwet'en cosmology, the material world is bounded by transcendent entities that dictate communal property rights and reasonable use of natural resources.[13] The Gitxsan use crest poles and totem poles to represent their relationship with spiritual entities and the continuity of their society with the land itself.[14] The Iroquoian Great Law of Peace describes ways in which humans can give thanks to nature for providing sustenance and denies humans a privileged status within the ecology.[15]

Despite the constitutional recognition of treaties and aboriginal rights by the courts, the broad swath of Canadian history has been the sordid tale of the dispossession of First Nations and the attempted eradication by the Canadian state of all that is 'aboriginal'. The peoples of Turtle Island have had their lands and their access to resources gradually stolen and blocked, so that now all that is left are small parcels of reserve land and highly controlled access to nature. This dispossession is well documented, and even celebrated. The 'opening up of the west', 'the founding of Canada', 'the spread of civilisation' are commemorated publicly and taught in Canadian schools. The hidden subtext to these 'accomplishments' is the loss suffered by the First Nations. In addition, successive governments have tried to bleach out what they see as the stain of aboriginalness. Even if First Nations people survive, their cultures and traditional ways of life are being erased as obstacles to the project of modernisation, development, technological domination and capital accumulation. When peoples and land and resources remain 'aboriginal' – that is, retain their traditional form and way of being – they are not available to be used for profit. Fishing aboriginally, for example, feeds people; it does not generate surplus value. Hence, when the Supreme Court granted this right to Mi'kamq and Maliseet people in the 1999 Marshall case, the government response was swift and brutal. A combination of threats, violence and bribes led to the surrender of this historic right by all the First Nations communities in eastern Canada.

The tragedy of 'progress'

The reason for the dispossession of the First Nations' traditional lands and the extermination of their traditional economies has been to remove them as obstacles to the accumulation of capital. The ideological justification for this theft and cultural genocide is that failing to do so would impede progress. Canadian popular culture, mainstream and even Left–leaning progressive histories celebrate the 'nation–building' construction of railways, highways and now oil and gas pipelines, the technological marvels of hydro–electric projects that flood millions of acres and dam great rivers, the resource extraction that fuels the insatiable need to consume, to dominate, to reshape nature.

Ironically, the Left is as committed to Canadian national chauvinism, to the technological mastery of nature, to western 'civilisation', as is the corporate establishment. Their opposition to capitalism is centred on its effects on the working class of the settler society, not on the continuing dispossession of First Nations. Neither the Left nor the Right support the right of First Nations to their traditional lands and culture or their desire to live with and around nature, not re-making it, god-like, in man's image. The right of the settler society to be here on Turtle Island at all is not questioned.

Does this mean that there is no hope that a non-modern form of life may survive? Certainly the state and corporate interests will never rest until all that is aboriginal on Turtle Island is gone. They may preserve a Disney version of traditional life, with chiefs dressed up to look like a caricature of First Nations peoples – all fringes, beads and headdresses – to be carted out to show off a bit of local flavour when foreign celebrities like the queen of England or her grandchildren arrive. At times, there may be an endeavour to put on traditional ceremonies in a macabre equivalent of a black mass. But a living, real, independent traditional culture with its base in material relations will never be tolerated by current corporate-led interests.

Allies?

This leaves the Left, especially organised labour, as the only possible ally. The accumulation imperative of capitalist economies means that the drive is to eliminate anything that stands in the way of profit, and that the claims by First Nations to land and to the right to live in ways consistent with their traditions are obstacles to corporate profit-making. First Nations, like all groups that try to resist the state, need allies. Although labour, often guided by purportedly Left-wing political parties, has not been an ally in a common struggle to defend the environment, rights and traditional ways of life, they are the only ones who can possibly be won over to the struggle.

To see how such an alliance of interests and such a common understanding of an alternative to progress is at least possible we must examine the ideas of Marx. Ironically, while we argue that the basis for the possible support by the Left, and by labour, for the First Nations' desire to live traditionally is to be found in Marx, so too is the basis for the Left's embrace of the ideology of progress and the denigration of aboriginality as backward and reactionary. An important school of Marxism, dominant in the late 19th century and associated with the thinkers of the Second International, interpreted Marx as a theorist of historical 'progress'. Such political leaders and Marxist scholars as, most importantly, Karl Kautsky, and others known collectively as 'orthodox Marxists', argued quite deterministically that history moved inexorably through definite stages, with capitalism following feudalism and being, in turn, replaced by socialism. According to this view, socialism will emerge necessarily from capitalism, and doing so requires the abundance (understood, in terms immanent to the logic of capitalism, as such a quantity of commodities available to everyone that they lose their value in exchange) brought about by the intensification of industrial technology found in capitalist societies as they mature. As a consequence, through much of the 20th century Marxism sought to propel the ripening of the conditions for socialism by supporting the ever-increasing exploitation of nature and ignoring the effects that this increasing production had on the environment and peoples whose cultures stood outside the capitalism–socialism trajectory. There was such confidence that a socialism based on abundance (which would, in turn, be based on intensified technologies of production) would liberate humanity,[16] that anything that stood in the way of this abundance was condemned as reactionary. One of the authors of this paper has, for example, written on the topic previously and his work has been criticised by a number of Leftist commentators as failing to see that the social and economic forms of traditional life have been supplanted by more 'advanced' forms and that valuing traditional forms of life in any way is a disservice to progress and thus reactionary.[17]

Apart from its obvious disrespect for First Nations peoples and cultures, this critique suffers from two main problems. Firstly, it assumes that one part of the trajectory of western history (i.e. from 1500 to the present) is the whole and only possible way that human social life could unfold, when the evidence is that this is manifestly untrue. Secondly, 'progress' and 'advanced' are being used here in culturally and economically specific and, indeed, chauvinistic, ways. If we hold all other meanings and values constant, 'progress' in a capitalist economy means increased productivity. Increasing the capacity to extract value and remake nature for our purposes is regress not progress, especially as it reduces the capacity of other peoples to live as they wish.

Fetishising abundance, and the technological mastery that underlies it, was never central to Marx's thought, despite the key role it has played in his followers' work. It was not central because, as Marx argued, poverty is not a problem of lack of abundance but rather one of ownership and distribution. There are poor people because there are rich people; there are the property-less because there are the propertied. The developing world is not poor because it lacks 'stuff'. They are poor because we are rich. This is not a problem to be solved by building more factories or cutting down more rainforests. Rather, for Marx, the problem of capitalism – for which socialism was to be the solution– was the problem of alienation. The proletariat is estranged from their work life, from the products they produce, and from their life-world. They are so because they do not control production. To overcome alienation requires that the whole capitalist system of ownership, production, state control, repressive ideologies, wealth distribution and so on, be overturned.

The what/when/where/how/why of production must be removed from corporate control and left to the peoples of the different nations to decide. The lack of control at the site of production occurs because the mass of people who labour work for someone else. The owners determine the nature of the work itself. Only if those who labour own the productive forces of society can they control democratically the work process. Democracy in this sense is equivalent to unalienated work, and overcoming alienation means democracy at the site of production. Worker-owned co-operatives are, for example, a very small step in this direction. Here the interests of workers and First Nations intersect. Traditional economies and land use were based on unalienated labouring where each individual worked directly with nature and decided for themselves, or democratically as a group, how and what to produce. In fact, the form of work in First Nations communities inspired Marx in imagining how work and life could be, if freed from the exploitation and soul-destroying character of work in modern society.[18]

Conclusion

To create the western idea of super-abundance requires the destruction of the planet and the obliteration of all peoples, cultures, traditions, ideas etc., that stand in the way of 'progress'. Historically, under capitalism, the goal of 'abundance' has been a cover for the fact of capital accumulation. For indigenous peoples, the current quest for 'abundance' and increasing capital accumulation, results in, and will continue to cause, the destruction of their cultures, economies and lives.

Many on the Left, who are highly critical of any defence of traditional forms of life, argue that returning to such ways of living together and with the earth cannot overcome capitalism, will not lead to socialism, and stand in the way of progress. They see such social forms as, in a word, 'reactionary'. However, they have profoundly missed the point. We 'moderns'[19], who struggle in solidarity to help defend the interests of traditional peoples, do not do so to help the world move forward. We do so because it is right and proper to help individuals and communities live as they wish, and because in their life we see the possibility – so often hidden from us as we remain enmeshed in the norms of capitalist society – that an unalienated life, where properly human relations exist between peoples, and with the earth, can still be lived. The capitalist logic of unlimited accumulation still bears down on all of society, especially First Nations whose survival as peoples requires that this logic be problematised and undermined. The struggle continues.

First Nations protesters have stopped the process of fracking for natural gas in New Brunswick, at least temporarily. First Nations in British Columbia continue to resist all attempts to threaten or bribe them into giving up their sacred duty to the land, thus preventing the Northern Gateway Pipeline from being built. At this moment the Idle No More movement is attempting to block the proposed First Nations' Education Act that is being put forward by the Harper government. They interrupted the official announcement, arguing that the proposed Act interferes with the right of First Nations communities to educate their own children. These efforts continue to inspire resistance.

1. The Indian Act was passed in 1876. It has served since then as the principal legal mechanism for the governing of those First Nations' persons legally designated as "Indians". The Act fundamentally transformed life for those so designated, stripping them of the right to vote in Canadian elections, imposing foreign political and social institutions upon their communities, dividing up nations and territories into small local bands and reserves, and outlawing traditional spiritual practices. The Navigable Waters Act was originally passed to enforce environmental restrictions on projects that affected waterways.
2. First Nations have worse determinants of health and social wellbeing. Their life expectancy is lower, infant mortality is higher, morbidity rates are higher, unemployment is higher, incomes lower, the level of educational attainment is lower, and so on. The causes of these are many: racism, social isolation, the legacy of stolen lands, and perhaps most importantly, the almost 100 years of forcing First Nations' children to attend Residential Schools where they were taken from their homes, indoctrinated against their own cultural identity, and all too frequently abused.
3. The European invasion of Turtle Island was unprecedented in the scale of the devastation

it effected. The population declined, according to varying estimates, by 50–90%, either from direct killing, starvation or disease. The vast majority of their lands were stolen, their traditional economies undermined, their spirituality belittled and transformed. This process of dispossession and cultural destruction continues as the resource extraction projects replicate the devastation that marked early contact.

4. Tom Flanagan, 'Bill C-45 simply makes it easier for First Nations to lease land', *The Globe and Mail*, 29 December 2012.
5. Gisday Wa and Delgam Uukw, *The Spirit in the Land: The Opening Statement of the Gitxsan and Wet'suwet'en Hereditary Chiefs in the Supreme Court of British Columbia, May 11, 1987* (Gabriola, BC: Reflections, 1987) p. 71.
6. Thomas Cheney, 'Property, Human Ecology and Delgamuukw', thesis, University of Victoria, 2011, p. 55.
7. Cheney, *ibid.*, p. 59.
8. Delgamuukw v. British Columbia, S.C.R. 3. 1010 (1997) para 166.
9. Antonia Mills, 'Introduction', in Antonia Mills (ed.), *'Hang On To These Words': Johnny David's Delgamuukw Evidence* (Toronto: University of Toronto Press, 2005) p. 13.
10. The reliance upon treaties, which were contingent historical events, as the basis of the relationship between the peoples original to this land and the state of the settler society is also problematic. First of all, as historical documents, treaties are open to various interpretations. That the courts gave a fairly wide interpretation in the Delgamuukw case to aboriginal treaty rights was contingent on the specific attitudes of the justices who heard the case. It could have been otherwise, as it often is. Secondly, even if reasonably clear as to meaning, treaties often registered the outcome of a highly unequal relationship. For example, the Numbered treaties by which the First Nations west of Ontario "surrendered" their lands and sovereignty were forced upon them under extremely dire circumstances. Finally, the Canadian state defends, with force when necessary, its claim to be the sole interpreter of the meaning of the treaties. It is clearly a violation of natural justice that one party to a dispute claims exclusive right to decide the outcome. Yet this is the case with the treaties between First Nations and the Canadian state.
11. Cheney, *op.cit.*, p. 745; Allan McEachern, Chief Justice, Delgamuukw v. The Queen: Reasons for Judgement, British Columbia Supreme Court, 1991, p. 13.
12. McEachern, *ibid.*, pp. 1–12.
13. Mills, *op.cit.*, pp. 141–57.
14. Gisday Wa and Delgam Uukw, *op.cit.*, p. 26.
15. David Bedford and Thom Workman, 'The Great Law of Peace: Alternative Inter-Nation(al) Practices and the Iroquoian Confederacy', *Alternatives*, 22, 1997, pp. 89–96.
16. Of course, such a term as 'abundance' is culturally relative. John Locke thought First Nations poor, yet they did not experience deprivation. Nature always provided their needs. Systematic hunger and poverty only appeared with the arrival of the Europeans. 'Modern' societies that have 'progress', on the other hand, are drowning in 'stuff', and yet constantly demand more, putting nature to the rack to force it to yield ever-increasing resources, beyond even what it can give. And yet these 'modern' and 'advanced' societies still have poverty in the midst of their productive capacity. Both capitalism and the Left see abundance in the sense of consumption both as limitless and as the end goal of human being, so empty is the spirituality at the core of the 'modern' world and its addiction to 'progress'.
17. See, for example, the comments section on the Left-inspired website Northstar where an

article on the topic of the Left and the First Nations' struggle was reprinted. Even factoring for the inflamed rhetoric of the internet, the overwhelming response was that any support for traditional life as a way forward for First Nations was reactionary.

18. Lawrence Krader, *The Ethnological Notebooks of Karl Marx* (Assen: Van Gorcum, 1974). The *Ethnological Notebooks* are a valuable source on Marx's views on life in traditional societies. Like Rousseau, Marx was impressed by the autonomy of the individual.

19. Both authors wish to acknowledge that they, like all of the settler society, reside on land stolen from the First Nations of Turtle Island.

Sto:lo Territory: Unsurrendered Territory of the Sto:lo People

Indigenous Nationhood

SAKEJ WARD

To begin we have to look at a few political principles[1] – just so we can understand how to consider the idea of legitimacy and sovereignty. The first concept is very simple: the principle of equality. We are all equals. We are born equals, which means I cannot legitimately tell you what to do. I cannot force you to do something that you don't want to do. I can't impose my will. That is a condition of force that we accept is not legitimate between equals. What we need to do is to persuade the other person in order to get their permission to do something. When we talk in a political sense what we're saying is, 'if we're going to have leadership speaking for us, they need to persuade us'. Leadership needs to convince us and get our permission to speak on our behalf or make decisions on our behalf. Now this includes the government. And when we say the word 'permission' in the political sense, we're giving 'consent'. The idea of consent will be raised several times in this discussion.

The next principle is political legitimacy. Legitimacy is the idea of what is rightful. Political legitimacy is a question about the right to govern or the right to rule. When you apply this to a nation or to a government, what you're saying is, do they have the consent of the people to rule or govern them? That is critical to understanding the political legitimacy of any government – it is the consent of the governed (otherwise they're just imposing their will on the people).

The next concept is sovereignty. This is a huge discussion that could go on forever, but a generally accepted definition for sovereignty is the absolute power of a nation. In a western democracy that exercises the 'rule of law', it's a little bit different. They would say it is the absolute 'legal' power of a nation. Why do we insert that word 'legal'? If you're going to have a 'rule of law' (the principle that all people, institutions and even the state itself are subject to and accountable to a fairly applied and enforced law), then the laws and legal framework governing a nation become important. It is no longer the 'rule of man' (the idea of a monarchy or king that dictates to the people), but supposedly it is a nation that is run by laws. The sovereignty of a western democracy is contingent upon this idea of having the absolute legal power to run the nation.

If we understand those things, we can move on and start to apply this to 'Canada' and ask ourselves a few of these questions. Most importantly, how legitimate is 'Canada's' claim to sovereignty over indigenous peoples or indigenous nations? Based on that we can ask, does 'Canada' have the right to make law or enforce law in native nations? In order to consider these two questions, we first must have a small history lesson. Most people are probably familiar with this, but I think it's important to reflect on the past and to see how it fits in with this rationale within this critique. We have to go back and look at the Italian colonialist Christopher Columbus, who was commissioned by the expansionist Spanish crown. The moment Columbus set foot in Tiano homelands[2] he immediately did something that most nations consider an act of war – he planted a flag and declared absolute power over that nation. He declared absolute power on behalf of Spain and God and said 'this land now belongs to Spain'. How was Columbus operating? What type of rationale was he using to do this? His declaration comes from an older principle in Roman law called "the doctrine of discovery". This doctrine was used when European nations were out 'exploring' and they would find uninhabited lands (such as a deserted island), which they could then claim on behalf of their nation. Key to this was the concept of *terra nullius* or uninhabited land. Obviously the so-called 'Americas' were not uninhabited and certainly weren't in 1492 – so how was Columbus able to make such a claim to the land?

At the fall of Rome, the Church, in particular the Vatican, adopted "the doctrine of discovery". The Vatican created laws governing many European nations, the reason being the kings of Europe were Christian and they belonged to the hierarchy of Rome and referred to the authority of the pope in the governance of their nations. The Church became a voice of international law whereby the pope or the Vatican would construct new laws through something called 'papal bulls'. In 1452 a papal bull called *Dum diversas* said, "We grant you", this is the kings of Spain and Portugal, "by the present documents by our Apostolic Authority full and free permission to invade, search out, capture and subjugate the Saracens and pagans and any other unbelievers and enemies of Christ wherever they may be, as well as their kingdoms, duchies, counties, principalities and other property and to reduce their persons to perpetual slavery."[3] So, take their land, subjugate them and make them slaves. This was picked up again in 1455 in the papal bull *Romanus pontifex*, echoed in almost exactly the same words:

> *... to invade, search out, capture, vanquish, and subdue all Saracens and pagans whatsoever, and other enemies of Christ wheresoever placed, and the kingdoms, dukedoms, principalities, dominions, possessions, and all movable and immovable goods whatsoever held and possessed by them and to reduce their persons to perpetual slavery, and to apply and appropriate to himself and his successors the kingdoms, dukedoms, counties, principalities, dominions, possessions, and goods, and to convert them to his and their use and profit.*

In 1455 that logic was the general application of international law and it was therefore the rationale that Columbus was operating with. When he showed up on the shores of the Tiano homeland in 1492, the papal bulls were his justification for inserting his flag on their lands and claiming it for European crowns. But there is a problem. The Roman law said "uninhabited lands" and Columbus encountered land that was home to more than one million people. Therefore, in order to claim the lands for Europe, the Church had to disregard the idea of *terra nullius* (uninhabited) and change it in the papal bull to "un–Christian". In this way, by redefining what it meant to be human, the occupiers were able to justify their theft of lands on far–off shores. If a person was not a Christian he couldn't claim sovereignty and he couldn't own property. It gave the occupiers the right to go and seize the sovereignty or impose the sovereignty of a European kingdom on indigenous territory. Doesn't sound like consent to me.

In 1493, after Columbus returned to Europe, the Vatican issued the *Inter caetera* papal bull, which gave Spain and Portugal the whole 'new world' to divide between them. They are given these entire lands. They don't even have a clue nor care who lives there, they just claim it all. Again there is the idea of no consent – indigenous peoples never gave consent to this.

Let's move forward now. I'm going to use the example of the west coast, particularly Salish territories[4]. I'm going to go from broad picture to narrow picture a few times so you can see that this happens to indigenous peoples everywhere. In 1778 Captain James Cook lands and gives 'effect' – what I mean by 'effect' is that he actually puts boots on the ground for British claims to sovereignty. Now, the British were a little bit different. They didn't agree with the Church or the Vatican because the Vatican gave the 'new world' to Spain and Portugal. England said 'we don't agree with that, we're going to issue our own royal charters', which are, in effect, just like papal bulls. Matter of fact the wording on them is almost exactly the same as *Romanus pontifex*: to subdue, to occupy, to take away property and force people into slavery. It is almost exactly the same wording. So, when you had John Cabot come to Newfoundland in 1497 that's when the English started to claim some of the property. You had Francis Drake who also did the same thing on behalf of the English. So they were claiming the 'new world', right across, all the way to the west coast. So when you have Captain James Cook out here, he is putting boots on the ground and going to this idea of occupation, he is putting their 'claim' into effect. Now, there is a problem. Spain was given this land by the Church, so what they're starting to see is there might be a potential conflict between Spain and England over the Pacific North West. That gets resolved at the Nootka Convention in the 1790s. Spain and England sit down and decide whose sovereignty is going to rule over indigenous lands. Obviously the Salish people were not consulted. There was no negotiation, no sense of compromise or even a declaration or notification. It was an imposition of sovereignty. The British come out the winners in these negotiations and they get to claim the west coast.

What I want to do is flash forward, from 1790 to 1858 when, as soon as we see it taking on more local politics, it becomes a problem. James Douglas, an employee of the Hudson Bay Company, later becomes governor who operates out of 'Victoria', which at the time was a colony. This doesn't mean it was a political economy that extended into mainland 'British Columbia (BC)'; it was only that particular area of 'Victoria'. He has a problem: gold. Gold is found in the lower Fraser Valley. It causes a gold rush. The gold miners that were in the California gold rush come running up, tens of thousands of them. Douglas doesn't know how to handle this because he only has a few thousand British people. His worry is that the Americans are going to make a claim to the land that will be in contravention of British sovereignty. Also, he wants that gold too. His solution is to unilaterally declare mainland 'BC' a 'Crown colony'. Again, there was no consultation, no negotiation, no discussion, and no consent means no legitimacy. Indigenous people did not give consent to this so there is no legitimacy. So, Douglas makes these claims and then what we see is a rapid succession of claiming 'BC' as a colony. By 1871 'BC' as we know it, becomes an entire colony and joins Canada in the confederation, and that is how we come to this idea of the Canadian nation having sovereignty over the territories in 'BC'.

Now, what is key and critical in this is the idea of consent of the governed. In each instance, all the way from the doctrine of discovery to the papal bulls to the royal charters, we do not see any attempt on behalf of the European states to try to discuss sovereignty with indigenous peoples. We just see an imposition of sovereignty, and that, as we said earlier, is illegitimate.

Now, why would a European nation do this? Why would a European kingdom want to do this? Colonisation. That is, the idea of going into another country, settling it with the intent of accessing and exploiting its resources. Key word here is 'exploiting'. They're not there by invitation. They're not there as guests. Colonisation ... now I am going to read off Cecil Rhodes' explanation. Cecil Rhodes was a British colonial official who was actually handling Africa, specifically what was known as 'Rhodesia' (now Zambia and Zimbabwe). He explained it as: "We", as in the British Empire, "must find new lands from which we can easily obtain raw materials and at the same time exploit the cheap slave labour that is available from the natives of the colonies." As I said, he was speaking about Africa but this gets adopted as a principle and it's actually in practice at the time. That's what colonisation is and any other nation views that as a state of war. When a nation comes into your country, your nation, and declares your land and resources theirs, and tries to subjugate your people to their political authority, those are acts of war.

So you have to understand what this relationship is like, because it hasn't ceased, it hasn't ended.

If we look at the effects of colonisation on our people ... let's look at the land first and then we can talk about politically subjecting our people. For the land, I'll use the west coast as an example. 1858, you have the secretary of state of the colonies, Edward Linton, gives a directive to Douglas. He says "indians" are nomadic people and that is a problem for colonial settlement; we need to put them in permanent settlements for three reasons: (1) to protect the colonial settlers claims to the land (basically to facilitate the theft), (2) to protect the colonial settlers from the natives (to minimise interaction put them in one spot, away from where the rich resources are, then you can keep them from interacting and there will be less conflict with the settlers), and (3) to put them in a place where they can be controlled, shaped and remoulded to be compatible to colonial development interests (assimilation; assimilate us into the idea that we have to be colonised).

Douglas responds by thinking about the reserve system. He recognises that he doesn't have enough money to enter into a treaty, and he doesn't have the money he needs to try to get indigenous people to give consent to be on reserves. He also recognises that he doesn't have enough money to enter into the same model that the US is using (the American reservation system is a system of economic dependency). He doesn't have that kind of money to support the indigenous people if they are going to be a burden on colonisation of that area. He chooses the agri-reserve system, and he wants the indigenous people to be self-reliant so they aren't a burden on colonial taxes. So he awards ten acres per family, and he says, 'there is where you can move to and you can be self-reliant'. A lot of indigenous people are not going to agree to that. So in 1858 he has a solution in mind but he can't exactly put it together. By 1862 he has the solution. There is a gentleman by the name of Tom Swanky who really addresses this, and it's basically what we would today refer to as ethnic cleansing. There is a suspicious outbreak of smallpox in 'Victoria'. The Eskimo people suddenly have smallpox, and the response is to send gunboats over and fire on them, knowing that they are going to go to different villages and different communities spreading the smallpox. That began the 1862 smallpox epidemic, where close to 100,000 native people died. Ethnic cleansing that makes way for colonial settlement, that allows Douglas now to impose the 10-acre reserve, because the indigenous people are in a weakened disempowered state.

After 1862 we start to see this reserve system coming into effect. By 1864 you have Lieutenant Governor Joseph Trutch who doesn't even believe that 10 acres is good. He thinks it's too much and calls it an insult to the colonial man. He says 'one acre'. He strategically and deliberately adopts the American reservation model of economic dependency because he knows that political subjugation is cheap. If you want to control the indigenous people, you want to make them dependent on the state. So, by giving the family one acre and knowing that is not enough to sustain that family, it makes them economically dependent. So, for those of you that know about the Canadian taxpayers' association constantly complaining about indigenous people's burden on the taxpayer, you can tell them they have Joseph Trutch to thank for that. That was a deliberate move for economic dependency. Where does that leave us? What is the reality behind that? The fact that 99.75% of 'Canada' is for 'Canadians' and .25% is reserve based on that system. That is where we're at.

If we look at the way the land was handled, we must now look at the way the people were handled. When we talk about this idea of political subjugation ... I am going to ask you, for a moment, to put yourselves in the shoes of a colonial governor, and your mandate, your purpose, is to extract the resources from the colony you just took over, but doing it in such a way that you don't cause a revolt by the indigenous people. Matter of fact, if you're smart about it, you might even get them to participate in it, to help you out. This is what is referred to as the 'politics of occupation'. The first thing that has to happen is that you need to usurp the legitimate traditional power and authority of that government. Usurp, that means to seize or hold by force, without consent. Was this important to Canada? It was. Five pieces of legislation they had passed in a short period of time to ensure traditional government had its power and authority usurped and replaced with what we would today call a 'puppet regime'. I'll just quickly read off some of the legislation. The 1868 Act for the Gradual Assimilation of Indian People that includes the introduction of the band council system; 1869 the Gradual Enfranchisement Act that again brings up the band council; 1876 the Indian Act where the band council's powers start to get really fleshed out; 1879 the Department of Indian Affairs, granting the powers for the Superintendent General to impose the band council system (remember, as we said before, imposition by force is wrong). And finally, the 1884 Anti–Potlatch and Anti–Sundance Laws. Why is that so important? The potlatch is critical to traditional governance. This would be like removing the election system from western democracy. It is a critical component of how governance is done. So by attacking the potlatch, you're attacking the way governance is done. You're pulling the rug out from underneath it.

We understand now that traditional government had to be removed in a colonial setting, that power and authority for a traditional government went over traditional territory, a very large tract of land. By removing those leaders by force in most cases, you're changing the authority and the power structure. Now you have band chief and council set in place and they only have authority over the reserve and, as we said, that's a very tiny miniscule portion of land versus what traditional territory really was.

Do we have this same system today? Is this a modern concept, something that's still the reality for us? It is, but in a newer way. What we experience now is 'neo-colonisation'. What that means is that one nation enters another nation and forcibly overthrows the government of that nation and replaces it with a government that is in the interest of the coloniser. When we discuss usurping and imposing the band council, that all seems to fit the bill. It's a form of direct rule, where the coloniser is the face of that political authority. We all know the Indian Agent is the face of Canadian authority on our reserves. But that is not a very effective way of colonising people. It causes a lot of turmoil. It causes a lot of feelings of rebellion and revolt because you can see the coloniser. Neo-colonisation was best described by Frederick Lugard, who was the High Commissioner for Northern Nigeria from 1899 to 1906. He wrote a book, *The Dual Mandate in British Tropical Africa*, and he said 'here is how we have to do colonisation now': the white man is different than the Africans and the African person can see it. And because they can see it, there is more trouble in the colonies. What we need to do is find some African people who are willing to be loyal to the colonisers and make them middle managers. The African people will see that face in power and it will feel familiar. That person speaks their language, looks like them, has the same culture, has the same rituals and it is something that you tend not to revolt against. You would be revolting against one of your own. So this concept of neo-colonisation is about putting the colonised in the position to help the coloniser; they're doing the job for them. And, that is what we see with the Indian Act band council system. It's doing the job of colonising by providing access to natural resources in the way of agreements and memorandums, even in the way of a treaty. It's providing access to the coloniser by de–legitimising our own concepts. I won't say sovereignty because I know it's a touchy word, but I'm challenging their sovereignty and saying they don't have the sovereignty to do this.

What I want to impress upon you is this: if we're going to think about indigenous nationhood, number one, we have to challenge the concept of the legitimacy of 'Canadian' sovereignty. Then, when we arrive at the fact that that legitimacy is not valid, they don't have a legitimate claim to sovereignty, then we need to challenge colonial law. I would urge you to think about this. Canada does not have the right to make or impose any colonial law on indigenous territory. Not a single law. We have now a lot of people discussing the idea of 'let's oppose bill C–45' or 'let's oppose the Indian Act'. I am not talking about a single law or a single set of laws. I am talking about the entire system, it is not legitimate and it needs to be challenged, because it is that very system that attacks the traditional government and takes it down, one displaces the other. We are going to have to think about rebuilding our nations by rebuilding our families, our communities, reclaiming our language, our history and our heritage. Then we can start to think about what our nations are going to become. When I say this, I say 'do it against the consent of the coloniser'. We do not need their permission or their consent when we try to rebuild our own nation. I urge you to rise up and to take on that mentality and those actions.

1. These political principles are based on the common definitions influenced by social contract theorists Thomas Hobbes, John Locke and Jean–Jacques Rousseau.
2. Lands now known as 'Puerto Rico'.
3. Please see http://www.papalencyclicals.net/all.htm for references to papal bulls.
4. Salish territories are the lands encompassing what is now called northwest 'Washington state, US' to 'Montana state' and north to lower 'British Columbia, Canada' into the interior of the province.

Why Nobody Has Ever Been Idle in Centuries of Genocide

SYLVIA MCADAM SAYSEWAHUM
IN CONVERSATION[1] WITH STEVE RUSHTON

SR: Could you please introduce yourself?

SMS: My name is Sylvia McAdam Saysewahum. I am from the Whitefish Lake Reserve Lands, number 118 in the Treaty 6 Territory in what is now called Saskatchewan, Canada. Our people have called this land "Turtle Island" and we call ourselves the Nehiyawak.

SR: And, just to place that on a map for people who might not know where exactly it is geographically in Canada?

SMS: It's right in the middle of so-called Canada, between Alberta and Manitoba, by a city called Prince Albert.

SR: Today you have given a talk about Idle No More to a packed hall here in London, to people from around the world. You spoke about how you and three others came to found Idle No More. Could you explain how Idle No More came into being?

SMS: Idle No More indigenous resistance has been underway for over 400 years. This recent version began with four women – three are indigenous and one is a white lady, who has become a very good friend of mine. The founders of Idle No More first came together because of omnibus Bill C-45[2] that was going through the Canadian parliament unilaterally, without the consent or informed prior consultation with indigenous people as well as Canadian citizens. Bill C–45 is essentially another wide-ranging attempt by the Canadian government and British crown to extinguish our rights, our practices and our culture. Since Europeans arrived there has been a planned genocide of us in an attempt to accumulate our lands. At different times there is a peak of activity. This unfortunately is one of those times.

Let me tell you about one specific experience I had as child. Every reserve in Canada has an 'Indian Agent' and this person would implement many policies on behalf of the white settler governments, but let me tell you about one specific policy called the Sugar Beet Policy. This policy would force indigenous children – a lot of them located in the Saskatchewan area – to work on the sugar beet fields of Alberta. I was sent to work there, with my family – my mum and dad, my siblings. Year on year we would miss months of school because we were working in these fields.

SR: What age was this from?

SMS: Every child I knew growing up in my region, we would start working from about six years old. We would work very long hours, from about eight (wake up at six-ish) in the morning to about ten at night. We did this all summer. It would begin in May and end in late August. I hated those long monotonous days. Row after row of sugar beets, day after day. When we would first arrive in May, we all knew what to expect in terms of blisters on hands and feet. I remember the first month was always the most difficult because that's when we would develop blisters from carrying the garden hoe and walking all day. I remember as I got older, I would hear my younger brothers cry during the night because their blisters would break open or their legs and feet would be in pain. I hate those memories. We were made to live in shelters that had no electricity or plumbing, shelters that should have long ago been condemned and dismantled. I remember some of the 'bosses' would follow us up and down the rows of sugar beets demanding we do the weeding better. It was horrible.

It was the experience of these types of injustices that forced me to have a voice against Bill C–45. I recognised the injustice of the bill, which is moving towards the extermination and extinction of indigenous people.

SR: This is an omnibus bill put forward by the Conservative Harper government. When did they introduce this?

SMS: They introduced omnibus Bill C–45 in the beginning of October 2012 and it went through parliament very quickly – especially for a massive document. When it first started, it was 450 pages, but certain pages were removed. By the time it was passed into law, it was 400 pages. It is now law in Canada. We targeted a number of sections, one of them being the Navigable Waters Protection Act, which would remove state protection of all bodies of water and waterways for the benefit of corporations in the nuclear, oil and gas industries.[3] They would literally have free access to our water, meaning the expansion of tar sands without any environmental regulation. In places where environmental regulations are in place, the threshold would be lowered.

SR: Before this, were all these natural resources protected by Canadian law?

SMS: Yes, they were 100% protected. Today, now that the bill has passed, less than 1% is protected. It's important to note that before the Canadian government colonised us our natural environment was never under threat.

SR: It sounds absolutely ridiculous ... why would the government put this through? Can you talk a bit more about those currently in power?

SMS: The Conservative government of Stephen Harper has a very clear agenda. They wish to extract the natural resources from indigenous lands for private profit. It has been reported they have identified over $600 billion of natural resources they wish to make available to corporations to exploit. These are non–renewable resources – our lands and waters will be damaged beyond repair. The water will, without a doubt, be undrinkable for the generations to come. We are being forced into leaving a legacy of damaged and contaminated lands and waters for our children and their children.

This is a continuation of colonial policies. When the Europeans first came to Turtle Island their agenda was to exploit our land for the benefit of their people and their countries. They also established corporations to do this – Hudson Bay Company, one of the oldest commercial trading companies in the world, was used as a mechanism of the crown to map our lands, to trade smallpox infested blankets and so on. They also didn't consult, or falsely consulted, the indigenous peoples.

SR: The urgency of this is quite incredible – both how the policies were pushed through and the response and growth of the Idle No More resistance. Four months ago Bill C–45 was introduced. I understand the melting of the snow in December was also a trigger or signal for the rush to respond?

SMS: During the winter season in Canada the weather is bitterly cold and can reach around minus 45°C. In the spring – March and April – the snow begins to thaw and that is when we believe the corporations will begin to move into the lands of indigenous peoples. Bill C–45 has removed all protection from our lands and we know the corporations are simply waiting for the snow to melt before they occupy our territories. There is a short window of time and we need to move quickly to prevent Bill C–45 from being implemented this spring.

SR: Can you speak about the scale of the tar sands extraction?

SMS: So far, tar sands have grown to the size of France and Indonesia together. That's the scope of the irreparable damage to the land and the water to date. There are all kinds of new and bizarre cancers that are a direct result of the chemicals being used affecting humans who live in the area – both indigenous and non–indigenous peoples. The water is undrinkable. Indigenous peoples are no longer able to hunt on their lands because the animals have these strange new cancers; even the fish are covered in tumours and birds are no longer returning. The damage is quite devastating and far reaching.

SR: The photographs of the damaged lands and waters are absolutely horrific. It is very important for indigenous peoples to be able to live, hunt and fish on their lands.

SMS: There is a high level of poverty in our communities because of colonisation and ongoing racism. We were once what you would call 'rich' – plenty of food and resources, great family life. When a government or a crown dispossess people of their lands and resources and forces them into smaller and smaller reservations, it creates a system of dependency as a result of the poverty then experienced. There is a myth and a lie perpetuated by the Canadian state that they have title to our lands and resources, and therefore can do as they will with them. We have ongoing missing and murdered indigenous women and Canada refuses to do an inquiry. There are high rates of indigenous children in the foster care systems; who are dying in these systems. Within the last two decades 500 children have died while in care in Saskatchewan alone.

As we don't get the jobs that are made available to 'Canadians', we rely on the lands to feed us. Furthermore our relationship to the land, to hunting and fishing, is an integral part of our identity; to our ceremonies, to our traditional foods, to our medicines that are from our lands and that we need for our health. Most indigenous peoples are lactose intolerant, including me. I can't eat food that Europeans have adjusted to; I am reliant on indigenous foods and medicines. This is fundamental to our wellbeing; it is what sustains us in our day-to-day living. If these things become damaged, my health and the health of indigenous peoples become compromised on so many levels.

SR: To bring it back to Idle No More, the omnibus bill was passed in December and in an incredibly short period of time a movement has grown. Could you speak more about how you were able to build this network of resistance?

SMS: It first began when someone tagged me on Facebook in a post related to Bill C-45. I didn't understand the massive document so I took out my *Black's Law Dictionary* and tried to go through it. Keep in mind I have a law degree, and even still, I had a difficult time understanding the language. When I read it more closely, it was clear to me that there were far reaching implications for indigenous peoples. I started to talk to Nina Was'te about it and she started to talk to Jessica

Gordon – we didn't know each other at that time but we were like-minded on Facebook.

A week before that, I met Sheelah McLean for the first time at a rally against the new refugee and immigration legislation which was very racist. The new legislation would cut health benefits to refugee claimants. The claim behind these cuts was that it would save Ottawa $100 million over five years and discourage 'unfounded' refugees from coming to Canada to seek medical care. This new law is controversial because it excludes refugees from accessing medical care readily available to everyone else.

I pulled Sheelah into the Facebook chat about Bill C-45. We decided we weren't going to be silent about this bill despite the government hoping we would be idle about it. We're all educators so we decided to hold a teach-in with all our friends, family and community. We had no money – and there is no money – this is all a volunteer effort, on our own time and self-funded.

Idle No More has grown from there – with people answering our call to protect the lands, water and indigenous sovereignty. Now that Bill C-45 has gone through and is law, the only things standing in the way of the Conservative Harper government are the original treaties signed with the crown and our indigenous sovereignty. These are the only things left to protect our lands and water right now. Let me make it clear, however, that I understand these treaties were very often signed under duress and in most cases never honoured by the Europeans, who were never actually meant to stay. They were just meant to have some land to trade with us from. Nonetheless we will try and use whatever is available to us.

SR: Where was the original teach-in held?

SMS: The space was donated to us – a small community hall.

SR: Were there a lot of people there?

SMS: There were about 150 people at the first teach-in.

SR: That's quite a lot to begin with.

SMS: Yes, it was good. People were so generous and donated organic cookies. We rely on donations especially with venues to meet and to gather, and that's the way it still is, nothing has changed.

The first meeting was a very interesting gathering of non-indigenous and indigenous peoples of all ages. It was an amazing mix of Europeans and indigenous peoples, all coming together. Our speakers were incredible and inspiring. We had an environmentalist speak about the possible impacts of Bill C-45, then we had a parliamentarian David Forbes speak about the ridiculousness of this bill. Finally we had a spoken word poet, who did such a powerful poem I think that was when I realised we were sending a spiritual message.

SR: Since that first meeting it has grown more and more ... Idle No More has exploded globally, using social media to share information as well as direct-action protests. What happened after that initial teach-in?

SMS: I think someone donated $100 to us and we got invited to speak in Regina after people heard what we were doing in Saskatoon. I took off to Regina the following weekend with Jessica. The people who invited us secured a venue; it was appropriately at the First Nations University of Canada. They co-ordinated the event and coffee was donated. There were about 100 people that came out to hear about the government's plans and proposed legislation. Again, it was a mix of non-indigenous people and indigenous peoples. What a mix we were too! Our speakers sent a powerful message again; our spoken word poet came and shared their powerful poetry. The Regina group was a quiet group of thinkers, their questions relevant and insightful. The beautiful sun shone into the room, such a contrast to the dire topic being discussed. We wrapped up the meeting in a thoughtful and contemplative air.

Then again someone else donated about $75 and we were invited to North Battleford and Prince Albert and Louis Bull First Nation Alberta Treaty 6. I was already beginning to feel a stirring as we met in each town, city and community. I met with the elders in Alberta before we presented in Louis Bull First Nation. It gave me a sense of strength to stand and raise my hand to say "No More". This was enough.

It grew from there with people hearing about what was happening and information was being posted on Facebook, Twitter and YouTube. Next thing we knew there was an international day for Idle No More action, called on 10 December 2012, and it blew up after that. We knew we had to reach out to as many people as possible. We thought a national day of action would do exactly that. When we spoke of water and lands, it resonated with people from all different lands. "Idle No More" became known as our 'battle cry' to other indigenous peoples and non-indigenous peoples; it became our rallying call for support and help from our relatives all over the world. We became connected to others who were enduring the same genocide and colonisation. We no longer felt alone.

SR: How many days before it did you call for the action? There were many thousands of people in the streets around the world.

SMS: About one month. Three thousand people showed up in Ottawa at the houses of parliament. It was a magical time of strength and unity. I've never been a part of or seen such a show of power by indigenous and non-indigenous people. Yet it was prayerful and peaceful. Each of us understanding, feeling a sense of comradery while walking in the bitter cold and snow; it didn't diminish or deter each of us as we walked. I was in awe of our numbers; it was amazing. All across Turtle Island (Canada) were rallies, round dances and other peaceful acts of resistance. I can't describe those feelings of unity.

SR: You've mentioned that this was your first activism?

SMS: Yes, I've never been an activist before. I was happy and content to bury my head in a book and to focus on raising my family and studying our laws. I never considered myself an activist.

SR: Would you consider yourself one now?

SMS: In Canada there was a law passed that says that an 'activist' is equivalent to being a 'terrorist' – I hope our work is not considered that. I'm a defender of my homelands, the lands of my people. There was a report released outlining the federal government's new counter-terrorism strategy; Public Safety Canada[4] listed environmentalists among other "issue-based domestic extremists" that could pose a threat to the

Canadian state. They've referred to activists who defend our lands as "eco-terrorists". There are groups such as the Sierra Club Canada who believe "this portrayal is aligned with officials' attempts to silence environmental groups opposed to major energy projects like the Northern Gateway pipeline".[5] Once you label groups of people as terrorist then it triggers laws to begin criminalising acts of resistance.

SR: In the UK we've had very similar laws being passed and people are labelled as being "domestic extremists" if they question, protest or resist the state. What do you think the media's role has been in controlling what information people have about the new legislation and in not highlighting its full impacts? Have you noticed a difference between the media in Canada and internationally?

SMS: I can speak about the mainstream media in Canada – they have been outright racist and have distorted the message in Idle No More. The media called us "a bunch of jokers banging drums in the middle of the road" and said that we were similar to terrorists.[6]
The media has designated leaders to be spokespeople for Idle No More, but there are no leaders or spokespeople – it's all grassroots people. This has also been distorted by the mainstream media. We prefer to target and speak with grassroots media who put the true voice of Idle No More out there much more than the mainstream and commercial media.

SR: Why do you think the mainstream media distorts the message of Idle No More?

SMS: Their funding comes from corporations who have a vested interest in distorting our message. The corporations want to access our lands and extract profit from the natural resources and waters. Canadian Broadcasting Corporation[7] is a state-owned media company and its portrayals of Idle No More are not kind.

SR: What can people in London and the UK do in solidarity with Idle No More? A lot of British corporations are implicated in what is happening in Canada, for example.

SMS: Immediately write letters to your monarch. We signed our treaties with your monarch and not with the Canadian state.[8] The Canadian state is dishonouring the original treaties we signed, as sovereign peoples, with your crown. These treaties, which it's important to note were forced upon us, gave us some protection of our lands and waters. The reason the constitution was repatriated in 1984 was on the condition that Canada uphold the honour of the crown. We want your people to know that the Canadian state is not honouring your crown, in fact they are breaching the treaty terms and promises from which Canada was created. So, I would say, immediately write to your crown and urge your queen to act on behalf of her ancestors. You could also write letters to Stephen Harper letting him know that the people of London know now about what is going on. I would suggest starting rallies here as well and raising public awareness.

SR: Has the crown stated its position on this?

SMS: No there has been no response. In fact the crown's representative, the governor general, has signed off on the new legislation. That is part of the reason why I am in London, because the citizens here need to know and understand both the historic relationship and the ongoing colonial policies being enforced upon our peoples.

1. Conversation at This Is Not A Gateway Festival, 25 January 2013, Bishopsgate Institute, London, UK.
2. http://www.parl.gc.ca/content/hoc/Bills/411/Government/C-45/C-45_4/C-45_4.PDF.
3. Legal backgrounder: 'Bill C-45 and the Navigable Waters Protection Act (RSC 1985, C N-22)', Ecojustice, October 2012, http://www.ecojustice.ca/files/nwpa_legal_backgrounder_october-2012/.
4. Domestic-based extremism, deemed a threat to Canadian national security, is defined broadly: "... low-level violence by domestic issue-based groups remains a reality in Canada. Such extremism tends to be based on grievances - real or perceived - revolving around the promotion of various causes such as animal rights, white supremacy, environmentalism and anti-capitalism". See: http://www.publicsafety.gc.ca/cnt/rsrcs/pblctns/rslnc-gnst-trrrsm/index-eng.aspx.
5. http://www.sierraclub.ca/en/tar-sands/in-the-news/are-canadian-environmentalists-terrorist-threat.
6. http://www.sunnewsnetwork.ca/sunnews/straighttalk/archives/2013/01/20130120-081341.html.
7. http://www.g2mi.com/company_description.php?id=111.
8. http://www.canadiana.ca/citm/themes/aboriginals_e.html.

The Untold Story of the So-Called Latino

Colonial Cities Built on the Blood and Bones of our Nican Tlaca Ancestors

AWQAPUMA YAYRA COLQUE & NEMEQUENE AQUIMINZAQUE TUNDAMA

Before our continent Cemanahuac was branded as 'the Americas' by European invaders, we were one people, with a rich variety of civilisations, cultures and traditions. In the region that is now the colonial state of Peru lies evidence of our ancestors' genius in the city of Caral – structures and pyramids designed for astronomical purposes. This creative intelligence of our people in Caral was only the beginning of a series of large civilisations. In present-day Bolivia, you can still see the remains of the solar calendar that our Tiwanaku ancestors created in their main city. The peak of these civilisations combined was manifested in the great nation of Tawantinsuyu, where the political aim of the state was to eradicate poverty throughout our land.

The colonial republic of Colombia now governs where the exceptional Muisca confederation once existed. Our Muisca people developed a sophisticated commerce system in gold, emerald and textiles. The benefits of this trading network were felt by all members of this society.[1] The life of our ancestors is something to be admired. The poverty and violence that our people face in this region today is something that was not present prior to European contact. What are now known as Central America and the Caribbean islands were also places densely populated by our people, with societies varying from urban to tribal. The Taíno people were highly skilled in navigation, even at night, due to their astronomical knowledge.[2] As a result of their accomplishments, they had strong trading links with the Mexica (Aztec) and Maya civilisations.

In the north, the Mexica and the Maya had their heritages in the Olmec and Toltec civilisations. The Maya developed a complex writing system made up of more than 800 different symbols, and ingeniously created the concept of zero, more than 600 years before it was conceived in India. The Mexica, apart from their broad knowledge of astronomy, also made immense advances in the field of medicine; their medicinal capabilities exceeded those of the best European doctors of that time. Further to the north, we had the Mississippian people, who built astronomically aligned mounds, which supported schools, homes and temples. The Adena people constructed colossal public enclosures that spread out hundreds of feet across and reached seven stories in height.[3]

This is only a glimpse of our Nican Tlaca (indigenous) heritage, a heritage that was and still is being destroyed by Europeans. This destruction began in 1492 with the European invasion of Cemanahuac, and the subsequent genocide of 70-100 million of our people; 95% of our ancestors were killed in brutal and cowardly ways, mainly through the intentional use of smallpox and other European diseases. This is our holocaust. This is an account written by descendants of the 5% that survived; the 5% that were enslaved, raped, displaced, culturally castrated and subjugated under European rule, before and after the so-called independence of the European settler population in the early 19th century.

This is the type of information that has been hidden from us. For hundreds of years we have been told highly distorted accounts of endless wars and human sacrifice. In this chapter, we will not be delving into those highly complex aspects of our ancient societies. Not because we want to portray our people as pacifists; that would only go along with the Hollywood stereotype of the "harmful, peaceful, spiritual Indian". We are deliberately focusing on the part of our history that has not been shown to us. We will be telling you about the tremendous achievements of our people, how it was really destroyed and what we can do today to reconstruct our former glory.

Our ongoing genocide

European colonialism has taken various forms. From the start Europeans showed no respect for our human lives. They sought to steal our wealth and killed any of our people who resisted their genocidal rampage. Our holocaust, enslavement, rape and the theft of our lands are the most obvious aspects of this genocide. This inhumane treatment of our people is still evident today. In the colonial republic of Brazil, the white[4] landowners get away with murdering and displacing entire communities of indigenous people. Our people, the Guarani-Kaiowa, in what is now known as Brazil, are only one among many groups that suffer at the hands of European settlers. Their ancestral lands have been dispossessed, and they have been reduced to living on the side of motorways in reservations that have been assigned to them by the colonial government. In the colonial state of Chile, our Mapuche people are being relentlessly persecuted by the criollos (European descendants) and their henchmen.

The phrase 'Latin America' was coined in 1856 by a Chilean criollo called Francisco Bilbao; it replaced the label 'Spanish America' in order to include the French colonisers.[5] This name was forced onto our ancestors, who already had their own identity for thousands of years. Our people did not benefit from this term then, and we do not benefit from it now. The labelling of our land as 'Latin America' is just as offensive, arrogant and dehumanising as its previous name of 'Spanish America'. Both names transplant Europe at the heart of our identity and push our indigenous origins to non-existence.

We reject the label of 'Latin American' and/or 'Latino/a' because this is the name that the Europeans on our continent gave themselves after invading and looting our land, and murdering and enslaving our ancestors. Today this label serves as a slave brand that makes us property of the people who have oppressed us for the last 500 years. This term lumps the colonisers and the colonised in the same group, giving the invaders the right to live on our land, and live off our land. It makes us relate to the people who are exploiting us more than we relate to our own. Instead of embracing this colonial label, we should be despising it, and realigning ourselves with our indigenous roots, our Nican Tlaca identity.

It is at this point that our own people, in ignorance, reply: 'but we are not indigenous, we are mestizo, we also have European blood in us!' This is an automatic response that has been programmed into the minds of our people by the criollo-controlled education system. They teach us that our ancestors happily came together with the European colonisers and bonded in what was to become the beautiful 'mestizaje'. In reality, the European blood that some of our people may have is a result of hundreds of years of Europeans raping our grandmothers. To consider ourselves a mixture is an insult to the true history of our people; it is an offence to our ancestors who went through the terrible ordeal of being used as sex slaves to the European masters on the haciendas (plantations). We are like a child born from a raped woman, who has been named after the rapist; named after the person who committed a huge crime against our mother. Our people have been made to carry the name of the rapists who violated our ancestors and their descendants who continue their legacy, violating us and our land. Some of our grandmothers sacrificed their lives in order to avoid being raped. Yet here we are, celebrating the heartless actions that were carried out on our ancestors, claiming to be a fusion of cultures.

We say we're a mixture of two cultures yet we only acknowledge one culture: the European culture. We only speak the languages of the Europeans, we only practice the religions of the Europeans, we only wear the clothes of the Europeans, and we only have the haircuts of the Europeans. How are we a mixture, if we only acknowledge the European culture that is forced onto us? In reality, we are a colonised people, who have been tricked into thinking that there is a mutual cultural exchange going on. By believing in this illusion, we are justifying our genocide and accepting our subjugated condition. This is why we must not let the European blood that was raped into our family tree define us, in any way.

Eurocentrism even reaches those of our people who are genuinely seeking liberation from our oppression. The colonial education our people have gone through has not told us about our own heroes, our warrior ancestors, who fiercely fought off the European invaders for hundreds of years. People like Tupac Amaru II, Micaela Bastidas, Tupac Katari, Bartolina Sisa, Manco Capac II, Tundama, Aquiminzaque, Cacica Gaitana, Guaicaipuro, Anacoana, Galvarino, Lautaro, Cuauhtemoc, Emiliano Zapata, Hatuey, Agüeybaná II, Tecumseh, Geronimo, Crazy Horse, Sitting Bull, and so many more, are erased from our history books. Even when they are mentioned, they are not given the importance and respect they deserve.

This has led to our people looking to Marx and other Europeans for a method of explaining our persecution, forgetting the very important fact that these people developed their ideologies for the people of Europe. We have become experts at explaining the oppression of the European working class, while our own colonised condition is sidelined. The fact of the matter is, Marxism is built around the Eurocentric idea that industrial development is the exemplar of progress.[6] Therefore, Marx viewed our great civilisations that had eliminated poverty – something Marxism is supposed to achieve – as

The Great City of Tenochtitlan, Diego Rivera, 1945. Mural on the Palacio Nacional de Mexico, Mexico City

lacking in progress and essentially backward; a view that does not differ from the perspective of the European invaders. A view that, unfortunately, our own people promote too.

Our whole being is shaped by a foreign force, not leaving any room for economic, political, social, cultural, physical, psychological and sexual freedoms. We have no freedom from the colonisers' system that is put in place for the sole purpose of preserving their power over us. It is time for us to regain our dignity and become thinkers, warriors, for our people.

We are Nican Tlaca, the indigenous people of this continent. We are still here. We are the 5% of our people who remain, from the north to the south. This is still our land. Our rivers are still ours. Our mountains, our deserts, our valleys, our farmlands; they are still ours. They belong to no-one else. The Mississippi; it's ours. The Amazon; it's ours. The Ohio, the Colorado, the Andes, the Appalachians, the Sierra Madre. They are all still ours. All of the beauty and the wealth of our continent are still ours and no-one else's. We need to speak up. We are Nican Tlaca, the indigenous people of this continent. We will always be here. We have nowhere else to go.

Olin Tezcatlipoca, founder and director of the Mexica Movement

Nican Tlaca, in the Nahuatl language of the Mexica, literally means 'we the people here'. When the Spanish colonisers arrived in the lands of our Mexica ancestors, they asked them who they were, to which our ancestors replied: Nican Tlaca. This identity serves our interests as indigenous people of Cemanahuac, 'the western hemisphere'. We are aware that there are many names in many different indigenous languages that can be used and are equally as valuable. Our use of 'Nican Tlaca' is a way of unifying all of our people, from the north to the south; we are one people, indigenous to one continent. Today we waste too much time separating ourselves from one another. There are hundreds of different nations all over our continent but we must unite as one people to achieve liberation. As our great warrior-ancestor Tecumseh said: "A single twig breaks, but the bundle of twigs is strong." Our ongoing genocide can be physically destructive, but it can also be psychologically destructive. The use of the Latin American label, the illusion of 'mestizaje' and the focus on European culture and ideologies is a continuation of our holocaust. None of these things will lead us to liberation from colonialism. In fact, it refines and cements itself, making us dependent on all things European; making us perpetual slaves to the European master. By rejecting these colonial impositions and embracing our Nican Tlaca identity, we are regaining our human dignity as well as reclaiming our right to our continent and its riches (see image on previous page).

We are saying that we are the descendants of genius; of people who built cities that aligned with the stars, of people who could carry out brain surgery successfully, of people who constructed sewage systems and irrigation systems. We are asserting the fact that we are descendants of people who cultivated and engineered the corn and the potato, of people who had cities with running water, beautiful botanical gardens and immaculately clean streets, of people who were pioneers of mathematics and astronomy.[7] Our history, our identity, our culture, does not begin with the invasion of Cemanahuac 500 years ago. Our history, our identity, our culture, is thousands of years old and should be seen as a blessing, not a curse.

Nican Tlaca includes the mixed-blood and the full-blood as one people, with no connotations of superiority or inferiority; just the aim of breaking the European-created division between those of us whose ancestors were raped, and those of us whose ancestors weren't. The European blood that was raped into our people is a colonial scar that should serve as a reminder of what was done to our people and what we must fight against today, as the descendants of the 5% who survived the greatest holocaust in human history.

We reject all nationalities that were forged by the white settlers who sought to divide our land between themselves and divide us, the true owners of our continent. The European borders that have been politically marked onto Cemanahuac are a display of how much power the criollos have over us. We are not Colombian. We are not Bolivian. We are not mestizo/a. We are not Latin American. We are Nican Tlaca.

We are, in fact, descendants of genius and greatness. We are descendants of creative people, of honour and courage, a people of magnificent accomplishments.

Olin Tezcatlipoca

Cusco: the heart of Tawantinsuyu

Walking down the streets of the modern-day city of Cusco, you will come across cathedrals, churches, colonial buildings that look like they have been transplanted straight from Spain, statues dedicated to the founders of the colonial republic and the colonial flag. You will walk past walls that show the genius of Inca[8] architectural engineering, stones that could weigh up to a ton, fitted together with sharp precision. After centuries of challenges from the natural elements, such as earthquakes, these walls haven't moved one inch. In the distance you can see a giant statue of Jesus Christ that is ironically called 'the white Jesus'. There are neighbourhoods solely occupied by the wealthy criollos. Their flashy cars and intimidating mansions are protected by tall gates and hired security. This all feels out of place in a city that is mostly made up of poor Nican Tlaca.

The Nican Tlaca who live or work in the city wear European clothes and the Nican Tlaca who live in the outskirts wear traditional clothes, such as the *chullo* and the *poncho*. The traditional female clothing was not deemed acceptable to the Spanish invaders, and women were forced to buy long skirts, blouses, shawls and bowler hats. To this day, our Nican Tlaca women still wear these clothes, which are now considered 'indigenous', demonstrating the power the European settlers have over our culture. In fact, these settlers now view even these clothes as unacceptable as well; they would much prefer to see their subjects wearing jeans, shirts and trainers. The saddest thing about all of this is that our own people in the cities have taken on this same view; our perception moves with the perception of the coloniser.

The Inca Museum is housed in the mansion of a coloniser, Admiral Francisco Aldrete Maldonado, and generally is insultingly referred to as the Admiral's Palace. What is most offensive about this colonial mansion is that it was built at the start of the 17th century on top of an Inca palace that the Spanish attempted to completely destroy. Though it seems to celebrate Inca heritage, it is actually a display of the wealth that was stolen from our people by the Europeans. Like all institutions in modern-day Peru, it is owned and run by the criollos, the settlers that are mostly referred to as the oligarchy, the elite or the ruling class. Society has a clear division; it is split between the European descendants and their colonised puppets, and the mix-blood and full-blood colonised Nican Tlaca.

The first cathedral that was built in Cusco was constructed upon the base of the Wiracocha Inca Palace in 1539, only six years after the Spanish invaded the city. The interior is decorated with gold and silver that was looted from our land. Our ancestors were enslaved and forced to work in the mines of the Andean altiplano, in brutally harsh conditions, extracting gold and silver. The biggest mine was the Cerro Rico, in Potosi, and in three centuries the Spanish worked eight million human lives to death.[9]

Our valiant ancestors were considered to be disposable; lives that were replaced as soon as they died at the hands of the cruel Spanish slave master, who did not give them a moment's rest. The stolen gold was used to build and decorate the cathedrals and churches that, in turn, were used to destroy the minds of our people and, as always, used as an exhibition of European domination. Cusco was used as a regional base for the expansion of Christianity and colonial rule throughout the southern part of Cemanahuac.

Cusco was not always like this. It was once the heart of Tawantinsuyu, the centre that spread life to all the people of this honourable nation. In 1491, the Inca ruled the greatest nation on earth, larger than the Ming Dynasty in China, greater than Ivan the Great's expansion of Russia, bigger than Songhay of Sahel or the Great Zimbabwe of the southern African tablelands, larger than the cresting Ottoman Empire, greater than the Triple Alliance of the Mexica, indubitably bigger than any European state.[10] The Tawantinsuyu nation covered an amazing variety of terrain, from the rainforest of upper Amazonia to the deserts of the Peruvian coast and the 20,000-foot peaks of the Andes.[11]

The main aim of the Inca was to create a nation that was unified and to balance out the political and social differences that were among the groups who existed prior to the Inca expansion.[12] The Inca not only sought political unity, they also wanted to create a plurinational state that combined the region's economics, religions and arts.[13] Even the Peruvian criollo, Mario Vargas Llosa, who is no admirer of the Inca, had to praise them for managing to "eradicate hunger", something that "only a very small number of empires throughout the whole world have succeeded" in accomplishing.[14]

The unity that can be felt throughout the Andes today is due to the political genius of Pachacutec Inca Yupanqui, the ninth Sapa Inca, who reached out to smaller communities and convinced them to form a nation of millions under the centralised control of Cusco. It is important to add that this was not a relationship based on tyranny but a relationship based on co-operation, understanding, mutual aid and alliance. During Pachacutec's reign, he and his political aides managed to greatly improve the living standards for not only the people of Cusco, but for millions of people in the Andean region.

Creator
Lord of the Lake,
Wiracocha provider,
industrious Wiracocha
in shining clothes:
Let man live well,
let woman live well,
let the peoples multiply,
live blessed and prosperous lives.
Preserve what you have infused with life
for ages without end,
hold it in your hand.

Pachacutec

It is very restrictive when writing in a European language; the term 'reign' is not entirely accurate here. Each community that was linked to Cusco kept their own local leaders, culture, traditions and religions. Their ways of life were incorporated into the nation of Tawantinsuyu. The Inca would even set up shrines for the sacred objects of the newly integrated people in Cusco.[15] Pachacutec should be described as a leader, not a king. The early Spanish writers, never having witnessed something like Inca society, merely translated the titles of the Sapa Incas into something they understood: a succession of kings.[16]

There is also the issue of deliberate distortion of our history: "It should be recalled that Sarmiento's long history was commissioned by the Viceroy Toledo, who had instructed the author to demonstrate that the Incas were usurpers rather than rightful rulers."[17] This abuse of our heritage is something that has led many of our people to reject their Nican Tlaca identity and view it as something that represents totalitarian states. This misrepresentation was carried out in order to justify the European invasion and our holocaust, making the Spanish look like heroes coming to rescue our ancestors from a supposedly brutal regime. This type of rhetoric can also be found in today's society, when the British colonial government invade and destroy countries under the guise of humanitarian intervention.

What most history books don't tell you about is how the Inca leaders worked the land alongside the people and how they constructed roads in order to connect the different areas of their nation, placing major Inca cities along these roads, where food and clothing were stored and distributed among all the people.[18] We are not saying that this was a utopian society, we are merely demanding recognition of our ancestor's achievements.[19] We are warning you to avoid falling for the lies and the exaggerations of the Europeans. We must also remember that this nation was built out of the hard work of all our people, unlike the European states we see today, which built their nations through colonising, enslaving and exploiting people.

Under the European system that is prevalent throughout the world today, it is common for workers to go on strike in order to demand better working hours, wages or pensions. The Inca had managed to create a system that benefited them and the people that lived within their system. They developed a public service system that is nowhere to be seen in modern society. The *M'ita* was essentially a tax in the form of public labour, in which every taxpaying individual took part, working a certain amount of time every year for the betterment of the nation.[20] It was set up so that family life would be minimally affected, and the state ensured that the family would be taken care of in the absence of the *M'ita* worker, by making sure that there were enough people left at home and in the *ayllu* (community) to look after the fields and crops.[21]

There were also thousands of people assigned the task of cultivating food for the *M'ita* labourers. It was mandatory for a person to take part in the *M'ita* from the ages of 15 to 50, working only 65 days out of the whole year. Additionally, the Inca were very flexible when it came to what amount of time an individual had to share on their turn. It was this system that enabled the people to enjoy a society filled with high quality bridges, roads, schools, agricultural terraces, warehouses, temples and other public buildings. Land cultivation was also a major part of the *M'ita*. The village overseers would ensure that widows, sick people and wives of soldiers would be assisted in the working of their fields. There was also a form of taxation where the people would be expected to contribute some of their crops to the state, which in turn made sure that if there was any environmental damage to the crops there would be enough food in the Inca storehouses to be distributed to all in need.

The *M'ita* also enabled the construction of irrigation and water-management systems that were highly impressive. Irrigation waterways could be up to many kilometres long and at times were even stone-lined and covered.[22] The evidence of this great technology can be seen in modern day Cusco, still functioning as it did hundreds of years ago. In Cusco, entire river channels were straightened out and it has even been stated that the Tullumayor River, where it once flowed through Cusco, was completely paved.[23] The road system was another great achievement of our ancestors. It was one of the biggest in ancient times, being over 14,000 miles long.[24] Knowing that all of this was built through the collaboration between the citizens and the state, in what can be described as "institutionalized reciprocity",[25] is powerful reason for pride in our Nican Tlaca heritage.

As the Inca expanded their nation and incorporated more and more people within it, they had to meet the challenge of co-ordinating the activities of the people and the quantities of goods being transported throughout the land.[26] To do so they developed the *quipu*, which "consist[s] of a primary cord, usually a third to a half an inch in diameter, from which dangle thinner 'pendant' strings, typically more than a hundred, but on occasion, as many as 1,500".[27] This unique technology is "reminiscent of today's computer languages".[28] These *quipu*s would record the census, the stock of goods, numerical calculations as well as knowledge that was passed down from one generation to the next. The *quipu* has been described by Brian Fagan, an archaeologist at the University of California, as a pre-Columbian computer memory that stored precise information.[29]

Many of the foods people around the world enjoy today are native to and developed by our people on Cemanahuac; crops such as corn, potatoes, quinoa, oca, ullucu, many different kinds of beans and squash, sweet potatoes, manioc, yuca, tomatoes, chilli peppers, avocados and peanuts.[30] The agricultural work was carried out by both men and women, who worked together, as still practiced in the Andean region today.[31] Crops such as corn were engineered and cultivated by our ancestors in the 'Mesoamerican' region and were transported down to the south of our continent; there was trading between our people for hundreds and even thousands of years. In order for these seeds to be developed, instructions had to be given. Our ancestors communicated with one another despite the distances and language differences. Our people sometimes claim that if it wasn't for the Spanish language then none of us would have been able to interact, when there is plenty of evidence that directly contradicts this idea.

Our Inca people were highly skilled in construction, mathematics, agriculture, astronomy, medicine as well as the arts. The Inca textiles were colourful, complex and could endure any type of weather. The textiles were made in Cusco and distributed around the nation of Tawantinsuyu. Some of these have stayed intact for hundreds of years and have been found at very high altitudes as well as the coastal regions.[32] Our ancestors' creativity can be seen throughout all aspects of their society. Clothing did not serve one purpose only; it also helped to differentiate the different communities within the nation through the use of specific colours and patterns.

It is frequently said by Europeans and our own colonised people that our ancestors would still have been living in the wilderness, lacking any form of technological skill or political organisation, if not for the Europeans. This is simply not true. When we look at our Nican Tlaca heritage, it becomes all too clear that our people were highly knowledgeable not only in their tribal setting but also in their urban environment. The idea that we were small, scattered, feudal communities is what has been written in world history by those who only seek to make us feel inferior and to make the Europeans feel superior. This intentional distortion of our rich history does not allow us to believe that our people could have equalled and even surpassed today's technological advancements. Through looking at what was achieved by our ancestors, we can say, with confidence, that we were a people destined for more greatness until we were disastrously invaded and massacred through the deliberate use of smallpox and other European diseases, which were used as biological warfare.

Cusco was once the centre of this great nation of Tawantinsuyu. Now all that remains is what was left after the destruction carried out by the European colonisers, who replaced this wonderful city with a colonial one, from which they maintained and expanded the oppression of our ancestors through various institutions, such as the colonial government, the church, the military and the educational system. This subjugation is still going on today and it is being carried out by the descendants of those colonisers. We are here to challenge our enslavement through exposing the lies and omissions that have made our people ashamed to be Nican Tlaca. Cusco is just one example of many cities across our land that have experienced and continue to experience the violence and oppression of colonialism.

Our holocaust

The genocide that was carried out on our people in Cemanahuac was "the worst series of human disease disasters, combined with the most extensive and most violent programs of human eradication, that this world has ever seen".[33] As has been frequently said at our meetings, Hitler only dipped his toe in the pool of genocide while Columbus was swimming in it. At times, it is portrayed as a blessing in disguise, by both Europeans and ignorant Nican Tlaca. However, knowing what we know now about the Inca society that was destroyed by the European colonisers,[34] it must be clear that we suffered an unimaginable loss. Now take the time to remember that the Inca were only one of the civilisations that were taken from us.

The only people who benefited from our holocaust were the Europeans. While our people were flourishing, Spain and Europe as a whole were rife with violence, filth, betrayal and intolerance.[35] While Pachacutec and his descendants had strived to eradicate poverty from their land, the Spanish elite let their people starve to death and die of diseases.[36] These diseases were common due to the fact that the majority of Spanish people never bathed, "not once in an entire lifetime".[37] Street crime was a constant threat in most Spanish cities and outbursts of torture, murder and ritual cannibalism were common.[38]

It has been noted in the diaries of the colonisers that on arrival, many would ask themselves if what they were seeing was a dream.[39] Witnessing a land that was so different from where they were from, a land free from diseases, poverty and crime; a land where, despite large populations, there was abundance. The coloniser's did not have the humanity to respect it and learn from it. Instead, they saw it as an opportunity, something to 'take advantage of' in their depraved attempt to make themselves rich and powerful, and they did this using some of the most brutal methods known to mankind.

There is a great paradox at the heart of European colonialism. The colonisers left their native land of Europe with medieval mythical images in their minds of "dog-headed people", "races without heads and with faces in their chests" and other "bizarre semi-human beasts" roaming non-European lands.[40] However, to their regularly noted surprise, they came across highly sophisticated societies teeming with technological advancements, food cultivation, architecture and sanitation. Diaries of 'explorers' regularly note their amazement but also their desire and plans to exploit whichever resources they had come across. Their envy and greed resulted in Europeans immediately wanting it all for themselves. In order to rationalise and fortify their exploitation they invented racism; white supremacy. Disregarding the inconvenient truth, they developed this convenient preconceived idea of the 'savage creature' and imposed it on our people. The Europeans saw all the beauty of our land through eyes of evil greed, and they set about rendering our people, the very same people who had created these beautiful civilisations, as uncivilised and primitive.

It is critical to understand this, as it is the primary philosophy and rationale that spearheaded European colonialism and it continues to reinforce their ongoing occupations and genocides 500 years later. The rationale received a great amount of support, including in the work of Darwin and later Marx. This enduring logic is also the reason we face racist abuse daily in Europe and in our own lands.

The Europeans stole men, women and children from different nations and filled their ships with them, in order to bring them back to Europe and display them like animals in a zoo.[41] This was only the beginning. The European invasion plans were unfolded when Columbus returned with more Europeans on his second voyage. He landed on 'Hispaniola' (now known as the Dominican Republic and Haiti). The intentional use of infectious European diseases or, more appropriately put, biological warfare, was the main weapon the Europeans used against our ancestors.[42] Biological warfare was employed by Europeans as it would not have been possible for the regularly ill and weak Europeans to defeat our nations otherwise.

The Spanish invaders had "ferocious armoured dogs that had been trained to kill and disembowel" any Nican Tlaca that they came across. They stole, murdered, raped and tortured our people, trying to find out "the whereabouts of the imagined treasure houses of gold".[43] One of the many Christian missionaries reported that the Spanish soldiers would "test their swords and their manly strength on captured Indians and place bets on the slicing of heads or the cutting of bodies in half with one blow" and burn or hang captured chiefs.[44] They ripped babies from their mother's breasts by their feet and smashed their heads against rocks.[45]

This was not the only way they savagely killed our grandmothers' children. They "tore the child from the mother's arms and flung it still living to the dog, who proceeded to devour it before the mother's eyes ... When there were among the prisoners some women who had recently given birth, if the new-born babes happened to cry, they seized them by the legs and hurled them against the rocks or flung them into the jungle so that they would be certain to die there."[46] Such accounts might seem unbelievable; a defensive mind might think they are false accounts. However these are facts – facts regularly recorded, usually without any concern and as a 'matter of fact', in the diaries of the invaders and in their official documents.

This holocaust, this destruction of our cities and these malicious premeditated crimes that the Europeans committed and continue to commit against our people should motivate us to seek justice for what was done to millions of our men, women and children. They did all this to our ancestors and their European descendants continue their legacy today on our lands.

The machismo that can be seen in our men today is merely a manifestation of colonialism. This behaviour was taught to our Nican Tlaca brothers by the European invaders who saw our Nican Tlaca sisters as sexualised objects to be conquered. After whipping and beating the men, the Spanish would tie them up and make them watch while they raped their wives.[47] The women would be "thrashed" with a rope until they were too weak to resist any longer and violently raped.[48] This is why it is an insult to even suggest that we are a result of some romantic love story between the invader and our Nican Tlaca ancestors. It is time we threw the lies of Disney's *Pocahontas* away and educated ourselves on what really happened to our people.

The *M'ita* system that was once the driving force of the Tawantinsuyu nation was misappropriated and abused by the Spanish as a way to enslave our people. It came to be called the 'Mita'. It was mandatory for all Nican Tlaca to convert to Catholicism. They were then recruited to carry out gruelling work mining gold and silver to satisfy the greed of the Europeans, instead of working to improve the public services and structures for the people, as it was under the Inca state. Mita slavery was a ruthless colonial institution in which thousands and thousands of our people were forced to take part.[49]

The Europeans were shameless in their destruction; "The Spanish became so infuriated when *quipu* records contradicted their version of history that in 1583 they ordered that all knotted strings in Peru be burned as idolatrous objects".[50]

The usual response of those who bother to read up on this rarely told reality of what happened to our people and our civilisations is one of anger, frustration, sadness and helplessness. We must use these emotions as motivation to learn more and teach others about what we have learned. If we use our passion and knowledge in an organised and intelligent way, there is no doubt that, eventually, justice and peace will return to our beautiful Cemanahuac.

Two centuries of fake independence

Psychological warfare became the main tactic of the coloniser against our people. In the early 19th century, Nican Tlaca and African people who were slaves to the Europeans in their armies, mines and plantations knew full well that the wars they were forced to fight in, by leaders such as Simon Bolivar, were not their wars but the wars of their masters. However, today, two centuries after the republican criollo-led armies won their battles of independence from the Spanish crown, our people strongly believe that our ancestors and their African allies, happily and willingly got involved in the scramble over our land between two groups of Europeans.

From 1492, European royals controlled the colonisation of our continent. Later, the children of these original colonisers began to question the rule of the Spanish crown. They started to seek autonomy from the Spanish crown so that they would not have to share the riches they were stealing. They wished and fought to become masters of the continent themselves. It is crucial to understand that this was not an anti-colonial movement, it was merely a fallout and subsequent transition of power from one set of Europeans to another. Bolivar's very own words reveal this truth: "Though Americans by birth we derive our rights from Europe, and we have to assert these rights against the rights of the natives."[51]

To this very day, the criollos are asserting their illusionary rights over our genuine right to govern ourselves and our land. It is the descendants of the first European invaders who maintain power, control the media, military and loot our resources. A careful study of the political elite of the entire continent will confirm their shared European identity. Leopoldo Lopez, one of the opposition leaders in Venezuela and one who was involved in the attempted coup against our Nican Tlaca leader Hugo Chavez in 2002 and more recently in the violent protests against our brother Maduro, is a descendant of Simon Bolivar.

The idea that Bolivar and others like him are the liberators of our continent is, of course, a farce and a fairytale told by the criollos who, after independence from their Spanish crown, were equally as cruel and humiliating towards our people. We are rarely taught that "most of the leading revolutionaries, naturally including Bolivar, were associated with the creole, landed and slave-owning aristocracy".[52]

The fact that slavery in Colombia was legally abolished in 1851, a whole 41 years after there was so-called independence, is very telling of the nature of these supposed liberators and their quest for freedom. Another hero who is often worshipped by criollos, as well as by colonised Nican Tlaca, is Francisco de Miranda. He was a European settler who dreamt of giving the entire southern part of Cemanahuac the name 'Colombia'. The name was inspired by the fact that he thought "it was a historical injustice that the name Columbus was not given to the lands that he had discovered".[53]

Bolivar was a European settler, who came from a wealthy family that had made their living from the enslavement of our Nican Tlaca people, as well as our African brothers and sisters, in the gold mines and sugar plantations. He had his own slaves during the battles for 'independence'; one of them, known as Pío, even tried to assassinate him. It was only after seeking help from the Haitian president, Alexandre Sabès Pétion, that Bolivar was embarrassingly forced to free his slaves as a condition of receiving military assistance. Despite the fact that Bolivar only freed the slaves in order to get what he wanted, the story is glorified in order to immortalise the lie that he is our liberator. Historians' attempt to forge a link between this European slave master and our people by recounting the story of the African slave-maid who was forced to look after him as a child; they frequently romanticise her as a motherly figure in his life when in reality, she was seen as a commodity to the Bolivar family.[54]

The creation of the 'independent' republics in the 19th century was a movement of freedom for the Europeans on our continent. It was they who took power of the political systems; political systems that were created by them and for them. Even after the legal abolishment of slavery, our Nican Tlaca ancestors continued to work on the plantations and mines of the criollos. They were given meagre wages that were swallowed back into the pockets of the Spanish through a taxation system that was conveniently put in place to recover losses made from our people's supposed freedom. This colonial system is still in place today, and it is evident that most of the heads of state are actually criollos, the descendants of the Spanish, the same people who have been oppressing us for the last 500 years.

Rebuilding our nation

We are a people who have been fiercely resisting white supremacy on our land for 500 years. The history of people like Tupac Amaru II and Micaela Bastidas should be an inspiration for us as Nican Tlaca of Cemanahuac. These are two ancestors out of many who genuinely fought for our liberation from European domination.

The fact that these true Nican Tlaca heroes of our people are overshadowed by European settlers such as Simon Bolivar, Francisco de Miranda and José de San Martin is a testament to colonialism's censorship of the true history and reality of our people.

It is only in the last 50 years that we have been able to recover our true heritage of genius, creativity, courage, honour and dignity. We have learned the truth about our civilisations and accomplishments, and we have learned of all of these European settler false heroes that were placed before us as our liberators. The truth is that these false heroes have been oppressing us and distracting us from our true and full humanity, from our path towards total and true liberation. Tupac Amaru II and Micaela Bastidas were in the struggle and in the battles for the total liberation of our continent. They gave their lives so that we could be free from all European settlers, from all European sympathisers, all European institutions, and all European ideologies. The fight must continue with us, their descendants. We are the descendants of that 5% of our people who survived our holocaust, who survived the killing of 70 to 100 million of our people, a holocaust that killed 95% of our population.

We need to realise that the false colonial identities of 'Hispanic' and 'Latino', the colonial borders and the colonial nationalities only serve as a continuation of that holocaust, in a genocide that is meant to divide us and make us weaker, with the long-term goal of assimilating us, erasing us from history, exterminating us. The wealth and freedom that the Europeans enjoy today on our beautiful Cemanahuac, and in Europe, depends on that genocide. The continued flow of our wealth to the Europeans is dependent on our ignorance and oppression. Our people's ongoing enslavement to ignorance and to European interests is meant to keep us in the exterminating machinery that is European colonialism and its acts of genocide.

Our only solution to this seemingly unavoidable extermination of our people is to obtain and disseminate knowledge of our true heritage and to present clarity on our true Nican Tlaca identity. We must do this in an organised manner that brings about actions that demand justice for our people, and that ends in the total liberation of our people. It is not enough to dress, dance and sing Nican Tlaca. It is not enough to speak Nican Tlaca languages. We must liberate ourselves through educating ourselves and our people, and rebuilding our own cities and political, economic, social and cultural institutions under one Nican Tlaca nation.

Onwards Nican Tlaca, our destiny is in our hands.

1. H. Henderson and N. Ostler, 'Muisca settlement organization and chiefly authority at Suta, Valle de Leyva, Colombia: A critical appraisal of native concepts of house for studies of complex societies', *Journal of Anthropological Archeology*, 24, 2005, pp. 148-178, http://www.docentes.unal.edu.co/hhhenderson/docs/HendersonandOstler.pdf (accessed 23/02/14).
2. M.P. Imbert, 'The Possible Influence of Astronomy of the Culture of Ceramic-Age, Pre-Columbian Inhabitants of Greencastle Hill in Antigua', *History in Action*, 1(1) 2010, http://uwispace.sta.uwi.edu/dspace/bitstream/handle/2139/11062/Article%206%20-%20astronomy_Cerami.pdf?sequence=1 (accessed 20/05/13).
3. D.E. Stannard, *American Holocaust: The Conquest of the New World* (Oxford: Oxford University Press, 1992).
4. By white we mean European, including the Irish, Welsh and Scottish, and Eastern Europeans who practice Judaism. This is because all Europeans, no exceptions, took part in the colonial invasion of our continent and therefore, all took part in the genocide of our people and the construction of white supremacist power over us.
5. G.E. Fox, *Hispanic Nation: Culture, Politics, and the Constructing of Identity* (Tucson: University of Arizona Press Fox, 1997).
6. D. Bedford and D. Irving, *The Tragedy of Progress: Marxism, Modernity and the Aboriginal Question* (Nova Scotia: Fernwood Publishing, 2001).
7. C.C. Mann, *1491: New Revelations of the Americas Before Columbus* (New York: Knopf, 2005).
8. The more accurate term for our people who lived under the Inca state would be Runa, as Inca was a term reserved for our leaders. However, since Inca is commonly used we will be

doing the same so as to avoid any confusion.

9. Eduardo Galeano, *Open Veins of Latin America: Five Centuries of the Pillage of a Continent* (London: Serpent's Tail, 2009).
10. Mann, *op.cit.*
11. *ibid.*
12. M.A. Malpass, *Daily Life in the Inca Empire* (Indianapolis: Hackett Publishing Company, 1996).
13. Mann, *op.cit.*
14. *ibid.*
15. Malpass, *op.cit*, pp. 33-34.
16. *ibid.*, p. xviii.
17. N. Davies, *The Incas* (Boulder: The University Press of Colorado, 1995) p. 148.
18. Malpass, *op.cit.*, p. xxii, p. 33.
19. Some of our people's achievements have been documented in E.D. Keoke and K.M. Porterfield, *Encyclopaedia of American Indian Contributions to the World* (New York: Checkmark Books, 2001).
20. Malpass, *op.cit.*, p. 51.
21. *ibid.*
22. *ibid.*, p. 65.
23. J.H. Rowe, 'Inca Culture at the time of the Spanish Conquest', in J.H. Steward (ed.), *Handbook of American Indians*, Vol. 2 (Washington: Smithsonian Institution, Bureau of American Ethnology Bulletin, 1946) p. 233, http://www.lib.berkeley.edu/ANTH/emeritus/rowe/pub/rowe.pdf (accessed 21/05/14).
24. J. Hyslop, *The Inka Road System* (New York: Academic Press 1984) p. xiii.
25. Malpass, *op.cit.*, p. 31.
26. *ibid.*, p. 54.
27. Mann, *op.cit.*, p. 345.
28. *ibid.*
29. *ibid.*, p. 346.
30. E.D. Keoke and K.M. Porterfield, *op.cit.*
31. Malpass, *op.cit.*, p. 43.
32. J. Quilter, *Treasures of the Incas* (London: Duncan Baird Publishers, 2011) p. 196.
33. Stannard, *op.cit.*, p. 54.
34. Europe is often glorified and seen as the bringer of 'civilization' as is evident in Eduardo Galeano's *Open Veins of Latin America, op.cit.*, p. 16: "There was something of everything among the natives of Latin America: astronomers and *cannibals*, engineers and Stone Age *savages*. But *none* of the native cultures knew iron or the plow, or glass, or gunpowder or used the wheel *except* on their votive carts. The civilization from across the ocean that *descended* upon these lands was undergoing the *creative explosion of the Renaissance*: Latin America seemed like another invention to be incorporated, along with gunpowder, printing, paper, and the compass, in the *bubbling birth of the Modern Age*. The *unequal development* of the two worlds explains the *relative ease* with which *native civilisations succumbed*." (authors' emphasis added).
35. Stannard, *op.cit.*, p. 57.
36. *ibid.*, p. 58.
37. *ibid.*
38. *ibid.*, p. 61.

39. "When we saw all those cities and villages built on water; and the other great towns on dry land, and that straight and level causeway leading to Mexico, we were astounded. These great towns and shrines and buildings rising from the water, all made of stone seemed like an enchanted vision from the tales of Amadis. Indeed some of our soldiers asked whether it was not all a dream. It is not surprising therefore that I should write in this vein. It was all so wonderful that I do not know how to describe this first glimpse of things never heard of, never seen, and never dreamed of before." This is a quote from Hernal Diaz Del Castillo, '*The Conquest of New Spain*', 1565, in M. Wood, *Conquistadors* (Oakland: University of California Press, 2002) p.15.
40. Stannard, *op.cit.*, p. 198.
41. *ibid.*, p. 66.
42. "Europeans may not have known about microbes, but they thoroughly understood infectious disease. Almost 150 years before Columbus set sail, a Tartar army besieged the Genoese city of Kaffa and then the Black Death visited. To the defenders' joy, their attackers began dying off. But triumph turned to terror when the Tartar khan catapulted the dead bodies of his men over the city walls, deliberately creating an epidemic inside the city. The Genoese fled Kaffa, leaving it open to the Tartars. But they did not run away fast enough; their ships spread the disease to every port they visited.
Coming from places that had suffered many such experiences, Europeans fully grasped the potential consequences of smallpox. 'And what was their collective responsive to this understanding?' asked Ward Churchill, a professor of ethnic studies at the University of Colorado at Boulder. 'Did they recoil in horror and say, "Wait a minute, we've got to halt the process, or at least slow it down until we get a handle on how to prevent these effects?" Nope. Their response pretty much across the board was to accelerate their rate of arrival, and to spread out as much as was humanly possible."
C.C. Mann, *op.cit.*, p. 131.
43. *ibid.*, p. 69.
44. De Las Casas, in A Collard (ed.), *History of the Indies* (London: Harper & Row, 1971) p. 94.
45. Stannard, *op.cit.*, p. 71.
46. De Las Casas, quoted in T. Todorov, *The Conquest of America: The Question of the Other* (Oklahoma: University of Oklahoma Press, 1984) p. 139.
47. *ibid.*, p. 139.
48. Stannard, *op.cit.*, p. 204.
49. Ward Stavig, 'Continuing the Bleeding of These Pueblos Will Shortly Make Them Cadavers: The Potosi Mita, Cultural Identity, and Communal Survival in Colonial Peru', *The Americas*, 56(4) 2000, pp. 529-562.
50. Mann, *op.cit.*, p. 345.
51. Bolivar, 1951, quoted in M.G. Miller, *Rise and Fall of the Cosmic Race: The Cult of Mestizaje in Latin America* (Austin: University of Texas Press, 2004) p. 8.
52. D. Bushnell, *The Making of Modern Colombia: A Nation in Spite of Itself* (Berkeley: University of California Press, 1993) p. 44.
53. W. Ospina, *En Busca de Bolivar* (Bogota: Grupo Editorial Norma, 2010) p. 42.
54. *ibid.*

Geographies of Racism and Inequality

Peruvian Household Workers Navigate Spaces of Servitude

KATHERINE MAICH

They eat meat, and you say to them: "Could you give me a bit of meat for my rice?"
"No, there are eggs over there," they tell you, "there are eggs in the fridge."
And they get the meat.
Juana, 28, household worker, Cusco

Se necesita chica para casa. Cama a dentro. (Girl needed for house. Live in.)
Paseo de la Republica, Lima, Peru, November 2012

Peru[1] is currently understood as one of the fastest growing neo-liberal economies in South America, one whose wealth and political power is highly concentrated in the capital, creating an extremely centralised nation and fuelling a massive rural to urban labour migration. The country's history is a storied and profound one, as along with India, China, Mesoamerica, Egypt and Mesopotamia, Peru is considered a "cradle of civilization"[2]. Just north of Lima, the city-state of Caral is now understood to be the site of a highly organised and complex society dating back to 2600 BC, well over 4,000 years prior to the more popularly recognised Incan construction of Machu Picchu, near Cusco.

Centuries later, after years of trade relations, geographical fluctuation and fluidity between numerous indigenous cultures during many epochs, including the Pre-Ceramica, Inicial de la Ceramica, Formativa, Auge, Fusional and Imperial periods, the Spanish Conquista era began after

Francisco Pizarro captured Atahualpa, the Incan king, and occupied Tumbes in northwest Peru. Through violence and co-optation, the Spanish colonists extended and enforced their power throughout Peru, concentrating resources and wealth in the capital of Lima, *la Ciudad de los Reyes* (the City of the Kings). Thus, an entirely new system of colonisation took hold, shifting forever the trajectory of Peru as well as other nearby occupied lands throughout the entire continent. Indigenous cultures were systematically exploited and purposefully undermined by European colonialism. Land was stolen and pre-Columbian tribute systems were altered as the members of the indigenous population were subjected to practices of *repartimiento* (distribution) by paying tribute to the *encomendero* (agent), who extracted funds and labour from those subjected to this colonial legal system.[3] Lacking other economic alternatives, indigenous women were often forced into providing *servicio personal* (domestic service) in the homes of Spaniards where their bodies were regularly subjected to the physical, sexual and verbal abuses of the colonial domain.

Criollo (of Spanish descent) political leaders José de San Martín and Simón Bolívar are often thought of as 'liberators' of parts of South America and Peru though the Peruvian War of Independence of 1821, though in fact they also utilised violence to further their own self-interest in contested power struggles over land, wealth and resources, thus casting suspicion on their quest for 'independence'. Frustrated with having to confer with the crown in the 'old world' and with sharing the spoils of the occupation, the Spanish settlers revolted. The crown was determined not to lose the profits and resources that they had become accustomed to, and thus a bloody and brutal war began. By gaining independence from the crown, the Spanish settlers obtained the power and control of the occupied lands for themselves. Though 1821 marked the establishment of an official 'independence', Peru was still reeling from forced cultural, religious, political, social and economic changes enacted by the colonists and settlers. And this colonial legacy lives on in modernised forms – the practice of domestic work is one example of the continuity between a colonised past and a contemporary, colonised present. As Susan Socolow notes:

> *In the 16th and 17th centuries young Indian women were taken from their villages to work as domestics in nearby urban centers. By the 18th century, the opportunity for domestic employment was a major factor in attracting*

poor rural women to the city ... throughout the colonial period, in-migration of female domestic labor, whether forced or voluntary, was a major factor in producing a sexual imbalance in the region's urban population. Domestic service drew young single women to the city and provided employment for up to 75 percent of them.[4]

Due to the effects of geopolitical shifts, forced migration and rapid urbanisation throughout the country in the years since, economic opportunities continue to remain sparse in the rural reaches of Peru, and thus many indigenous internal migrants are forced to relocate and find work as *trabajadoras del hogar* (household workers) in Lima. However, just as during the era of official colonial rule, once there, they are situated within an extremely vulnerable and isolated context. These women's work is highly gendered, private and contained within the intimate space of the home, where threats of verbal, emotional and sexual abuse, isolation and discrimination based on race, ethnicity, gender and class continue to persist in daily life.[5]

Profoundly entrenched European colonial relations persist in the apartments and homes across wealthy districts of the capital, yet contemporary Limeño society considers itself as moving 'ever so forward' by pushing costly 'modernisation' projects, developing its booming tourist industry, and promoting its global culinary fame.

It is notable that much of Peru's tourism caters to wealthy English-speaking vacationers from the west, mainly travelling from the United States, Canada and the UK. A number of backpackers also circulate throughout the country, staying in cheap hostels and teaching English or volunteering with nonprofit organisations. However, Peru's tourist push encourages the bulk of moneyed tourists to visit the indigenous sites of, among others, Caral, Cusco, Sacsayhuaman, Machu Picchu, Chan Chan and other re-discovered, 'unspoiled' lands of the pre-Incan Lima, Moche, Chimu and Incan civilisations. Tourist companies approach Iquitos (the largest city in the Peruvian rainforest and the fifth-largest city of Peru) as a means to exoticise the *selva* (rainforest) and its residents. All-inclusive packages boast "brief sightseeing of Iquitos, boat trip by the Amazon River, lodging in 2 jungle lodges, meals, visit to Yagua natives, hikes, shamans, birdwatching, canoe ride, dolphin spotting and more".[6] However, that tourist money is siphoned back into profit-ventures and private companies. The excavation of the

Moche's Huaca de la Luna (Temple of the Moon) in the ancient Moche capital city of Cerro Blanco near Trujillo is on hold due to 'lack of national funds', but condominium construction continues across the street from Huaca Pucllana (the Moche's great pyramidal temple) in Lima's densely populated Miraflores district, with only a thin strip of asphalt separating pre-Incan ruins from the new marble floors of the upper class. "You don't even have to trek into the Andes," *Time Magazine* states in its review of the top "10 Things to Do" in Lima. Indeed, an upmarket restaurant shares the property of the ruins, serving 'haute cuisine' "to make your visit even better ... [t]here's nothing like dining while taking in 1,500-year-old views."[7]

My intervention and positionality

As a sociologist and workers' rights advocate in the US, I first travelled to Peru in 2011 and reached out to household workers' organisations and unions in order to learn about the effects of the Household Workers' Law (*Ley de los Trabajadores del Hogar*) passed on 12 May 2003 by the Peruvian Congress under President Alejandro Toledo, the first indigenous president to be democratically elected in Peru's history. Previous experience[8] had revealed that most household workers are denied basic labour rights, and therefore I wanted to study how and when the law impacted on this particular population.

After years of organising by Peruvian household worker groups and women's organisations, and after several iterations, the final version of the Household Workers' Law specifies working conditions around privacy in the home, proposes schedules for frequency of salary, guarantees vacation time and social security benefits, and obligates employers to pay for educational access for school-age workers (household workers below the age of 14 are prohibited). However, the law does not specify a minimum wage for household workers (as laws do for all other recognised workers in Peru). Instead, it stipulates that a household worker's wage is only legally required to be "of mutual accord", which frequently creates a situation in which young migrant girls from the provinces work for extremely low (and sometimes no) wages in Lima. According to this law, household workers are only granted half of the vacation days of other workers (15 days rather than a full month) and they are not required to receive a formal written contract with their employer (the contract can either be in written or, much more commonly, in verbal form).

Since ethnographic research has historically been problematic and oppressive, I paid attention to situatedness and embedded power structures while employing a critical feminist lens in an attempt to confront the problematic past, paying keen attention to the insider/outsider lines of differentiation and racial, economic and social power.[9] Bound up within our varied standpoints or 'lifeworlds' are lines of advantage, privilege and difference, and they are enacted differently in particular contexts, especially with regard to the power dynamics of conducting research.[10] As Nancy Naples cautions: "Feminist ethnographers [must] emphasize the significance of locating and analyzing particular standpoints in differing contexts to explicate relations of domination embedded in communities and social institutions."[11]

With that reflexivity in mind, when establishing contact with the groups in the hopes of gaining organisational access, I positioned myself as a labour researcher and PhD candidate in sociology with a focus on labour and gender, clearly expressing my politics and interest in advancing domestic workers' rights. I also used social networks of Limeño and *extranjero* (outsider) friends and contacts in Lima, inquiring whether I could meet and, if granted consent, interview their current or former household worker. This privileged access was predicated upon exercising my social capital 'correctly' with these employers to explain my project in a non-threatening, diplomatic way, and when successful, allowed me to speak with workers who were isolated and largely unaware of the existence of household workers' organisations. Wearing my blue *chaleca* (jacket) from El Hogar de Rosita, one of the prominent household worker advocacy organisations, I also approached household workers in parks where they often gather together to care for their employers' children, parents or dogs and create social space.

The intersectionality of my educational capital, social class and race was complicated in Lima; as a highly educated, middle-class (by Lima standards, I rented my own apartment in a well-off district), white, non-native, Spanish-speaking woman from a university in California, I enjoyed a great deal of access, as nearly everyone opened up to share a story about their thoughts on the Household Workers' Law. These stories, direct from the lived experience of household workers, advocates, lawyers and employers, spoke to each other's experiences and built on each other to demonstrate particular themes. They reveal how geography and architecture delineate neighbourhoods, space inside the home, and even how and what food is consumed, thus reproducing the deep roots of colonial relations inside middle- and upper-class Limeño homes. In highly centralised Peru, this colonial legacy is demonstrated in a number of ways: it is lived out through race and class relations, limitations on or access to future trajectories, and via spatial relations, with space as both a social construct and as a material manifestation of power.

Additionally, my paper examines implications of attempts to regulate these relations, since Peru passed national labour protections for household workers over ten years ago, though with negligible improvements in their lives. The law holds tremendous internal contradictions, yet it potentially presents a challenge to longstanding colonial legacies that permeate intimate labour relations in the home. How do the implementation and specifics of this legislation come to bear on the lives of those it attempts to protect, offer benefits to, or bring into political inclusion? The law can seem like a very distant tool of privilege rather than of justice when lived out as only a formality. Thus, I begin by asking, can the law intervene? How and when, and with what consequences? However, because this law is premised upon a legal system that is colonial in nature, I also ask, whose law is this, who does it belong to, and who does it 'protect' – those populations it regulates, or in fact, those in positions of power who shaped the law to their own benefit? My contribution here allows us to utilize a case study of domestic work to investigate how a colonial legal system fails to work for the benefit of those it was originally designed to oppress.

This essay explores the deeply ingrained nature of colonial relations in contemporary Limeño society, highlighting the gendered, racialised and class-based practices of household work and child labour. Based on ten months of in-depth interviews and participant observation-based fieldwork in Lima between 2012–14, driven by the desire to understand and interrogate the dynamics of household labour in Lima in its current form, this essay investigates the nature of the spatial divisions that mark distinctions of discrimination in the street, home and body. This research lays bare the embedded structural racism at play in Lima, demonstrating that colonialism lives on and much needs to be done to end oppressive practices.

Colonial relations lived out: *paso a paso*, sip by sip, bite by bite

Geography and architecture segregate everything: from that which is within the home for *cama adentro* (live-in) household workers, to which neighbourhoods *cama afuera* (live out) household workers populate, to the particular elevator or door they use to enter their employer's home, and even down to the spoon, fork, knife, table, and quality and quantity of food used for meals. Cecilia, a 52-year-old household worker from Jumbilla in the province of Bongará, said emphatically:

Yes, there is, there is discrimination ... for example, in the home! You can't sit on the furniture of the employers, you can't eat in the dining room of the employers, you can't use anything, you have to use your own bathroom. To eat, you have your own plate, and separate spoon. You can't use theirs. You have to enter the apartment through the service door if the house has one. You can't go through the main entrance, or otherwise, it's bad ...

Cecilia

Cecilia's sentence "*Entras por la puerta de servicio, si la casa tiene* (You have to enter the apartment through the service door if the house has one)" illuminates the importance of architecture in the reproduction of colonial relations inside the home. While some homes and apartments do not have a separate service entrance, most do, and others have separate *ascensores de servicio* (service lifts) specifically for the maids and other workers, while the apartment residents themselves enjoy the privilege of an exclusive elevator. Other structural issues of apartment design affect how predominantly indigenous workers occupy the space itself.

Now the apartments are smaller. If they don't have a room, we change in the ironing room, that's where we change. Each time the houses are getting smaller ... and to use the private employer's bathroom is impossible. Yes, this is the problem now. In many houses they just don't let maids use the bathroom ... because, well, they have their reasons. Well, sometimes they think we are sick with the plague, or that we are going to steal things.

Cecilia

Suspected theft is prevalent in discourses around trust with employers, though laced with irony as these employers themselves, usually criollo, are the contemporary 'settlers' squatting on land violently appropriated by their European ancestors from the very indigenous people subjected to doing domestic work in the intimate space of their home. Cecilia's obligation to eat with a separate plate and spoon, set aside from the family's cutlery, signifies deep-rooted hierarchy and racialised fear of 'mixing' and 'contamination' by a 'lower' racial group. Further employer discourses are laden with racialised stereotypes around cleanliness and character directed at women from the provinces, reminiscent of racial segregation and Jim Crow legislation in the US in the mid-20th century. This racist legislation designated specific, lesser-quality space and facilities solely to be utilised by black people in the US, just as predominantly brown and black household workers in Peru are relegated to using certain bathrooms, sitting on certain furniture, and eating off their own plates, lest they potentially 'touch' the employers' belongings (except to clean them, of course).

The paradox continues. Those who must 'do the dirty work' of cleaning up other people's messes and restoring impeccable order to the home are considered 'dirty,' 'sick,' or 'lesser'. As Frantz Fanon remarks, "[t]he perpetrator is the black man; Satan is black; one talks of darkness; when you are filthy you are dirty—and this goes for physical dirt as well as moral dirt".[12] This is reminiscent of Edward Said's reminder that there are no "empty" spaces in the world; that which is symbolically represented as shadowed or dark is equated with dirt, gloom, despair, lack of worth and filth. "You would be surprised at the number of expressions that equate the black man with sin," Fanon states. And this extends into the realm of consciousness and morality as well with a "dark/bad=black" and "light/good=white" division occurring. Fanon explains: "Moral consciousness implies a kind of split, a fracture of consciousness between a dark and a light side. Moral standards require the black, the dark, and the black man to be eliminated from this consciousness."[13] This contradictory positionality is embodied in the household workers who are considered 'unclean' and 'untrustworthy' by their employers and yet are responsible for cleaning these very people's most intimate spaces.

Cecilia's words also point to changes in the structural design of homes, apartments and condominiums for workers. As apartment sizes get smaller, workers are the ones whose bodies must be flexible as they make accommodations, such as changing into their uniforms in the laundry room or foregoing use of the bathroom during the entire day's shift, often of 12 hours or more.

Another interviewee, Juana, described the situation regarding restricted food and nutrition, and of being forced to eat food of a lower quality than the food she prepared for her employer's family. Live-in workers are highly dependent on eating food inside their employer's home as they spend the entirety of their existence there, save for the legally required yet not necessarily granted rest day (usually Sundays). The Household Workers' Law stipulates that employers must provide accommodation and nutrition for their workers according to the level of financial comfort the employer enjoys. However, the kind of food household workers are allowed to eat as well as how it must be consumed, exemplifies further the normalisation of their devaluation inside their employers' homes.

Yes. But the treatment was awful, and they don't give you dinner or a snack, for instance. I only have breakfast and lunch until the following day that ... you wake up at 5:30 in the morning without any fruit, without ... just lunch until the next day. Yes, so you have to work in the house without dinner. And they don't appreciate you, you see.
And if there are sandwiches, if you serve the table ... For some reason not many people show up, and sometimes some of the guests only eat the ham or the meat and leave the bread, no? So the boss tells you: "Eat the leftover bread" when the guest has already eaten the ham, or has eaten another part ... That is abuse!
Juana

Other women describe being only allowed to drink tea as breakfast in the morning while preparing a large meal for the employer's family, or being told to eat chicken bones, or nothing at all. Lidia, 48, from San Pedro de Lloc in the region of La Libertad along the northern coast of Peru, told me about the worst part of her job, the impossible expectations of employers and cost displaced onto workers.

Sometimes, the poor girl has to be Wonder Woman, even if she's sick, she needs to show up everyday, but there is a limit, isn't there? And it's a big sacrifice on us. And they exploit us.
Lidia

These comments and experiences point to the deep internalisation of racism which views the household worker as existing as a corporeal being, having the very basic human needs of hunger and thirst, occasional illness, and yet having no other means of recourse to address these needs while positioned inside the employer's home. Herlinda, 51 years old and from Cajamarca, echoed these sentiments of being trapped and left with only substandard sustenance.

But ... they don't leave me anything to eat. They don't tell me if there's meat, eggs or anything in the fridge. And if I touched it, on Sunday they ask: "I left a bit of steak there, have you touched it?" Imagine that.

So, she protested a day where I ate a bit of chicken, the employer. I told her: "Señora, there was nothing to eat for lunch, I ate it." Because I stayed to wash the babies' clothes, their room, bedroom, toy room, I was cleaning everything until three o'clock ... She complained that why had I done with the chicken! So, from then on I didn't touch anything. She told me: "There is pasta; you could have done something with butter." What is pasta with butter? Just pasta and fry them with butter, nothing else.

Herlinda

"What is pasta with butter?" speaks to the irony of the fact that Herlinda is expected to cook delicious, nutritious and satisfying meals for the family, but the employer (who would most likely fire Herlinda if she served the family pasta with butter) demonstrates that she believes Herlinda to be deserving of less – less quality, less food, less nourishment, less dignity as a human being. Deeply rooted race and class differentials take hold through the kind of meal that is offered, how it is made available, and visual class distinctions take hold through what food is eaten, how it is served, and where it is consumed ('servants' quarters' vs the main, centralised family kitchen space).

Inequality through design

For an empirical example of the way that space is constructed to reproduce these geographies of inequality, Daniela Ortiz de Zevallos, a Peruvian artist of Spanish descent, utilised her racial and class position to create a project entitled *Habitaciones de Servicio (Maids' Rooms).*[14] Employed to film wealthy families on holiday at Playa de Asia, a popular beach resort near Lima, Ortiz witnessed marked distinctions in terms of space and clothing in this exclusive setting where young children frolicked. She was given strict instructions, which she followed, to "take care to ensure no housemaids appeared in the footage".[15] The contradictory role of housemaids – absolutely required to do the work of caring for the children and yet made invisible and ignored through zero presence in the video footage – captured the artist's imagination and inspired her to launch several projects exploring the ramifications of subtle and overt racist practices against household workers in Peru. Ortiz examined the geographical layout of 60 homes in Lima constructed between 1930–2012 through photographs, blueprints of the floor plan layout, and made a spatial comparison of the dimensions of the maids' quarters and the other bedrooms. These homes are not *tabulae rasae*. They are the foundation and entrenchment of historical patterns of racist discrimination and servitude. Ortiz's project highlights and challenges the implications of elite architectural practices as they replicate and reinscribe colonial relationships in the home.

As Edward Said states, "Decolonization is a very complete battle over the course of different political destinies, different histories and geographies, and it is replete with works of the imagination, scholarship, and counter-scholarship."[16] Benjamin Orlove similarly notes in his article on race, geography and 'postcolonial Peru': "colonial orderings emphasized historicized racial differences among persons within a relatively balanced and homogeneous space, while postcolonial orderings stressed naturalized regional differences among places within a homogeneous, though covertly racialized, population".[17] This social and political landscape of racialised hierarchies is still blatantly at work in contemporary culture in Peru, denoting space according to value in the elite homes of 80 years ago and today.

The continuity of the size of servants' quarters from 1937 to 2007, as well as the distance between the 'servant's room' and the rest of the home, is striking. Furthermore, separate entrances denote a value distinction, as household workers must enter by the service entrance, unless an employer specifies otherwise. Indeed, even in the most modern construction projects happening across Lima's districts of San Isidro, La Molina, Surco, Miraflores and Jesus Maria, large-scale condominiums and high-rise apartments still include *cuarto de servicio* (servants' quarters) in the floor plan, complete with an attached, closet-like bathroom and often no windows. Ortiz presented her work formally but also, in guerilla fashion, distributed copies of a poster from the installation that read: "*Habitaciones de Servicio. No hay excusa para su ubicacion y dimensiones* (Servants' Quarters. There is no excuse for the location and dimensions)" around Lima and architecture schools in an effort to disseminate a critique of the normalised maltreatment of household workers, confined to live in tiny pockets of the spacious mansions that they maintain in pristine condition.

Delineation of space: the two worlds of Peru

During my Spanish lesson this afternoon, we were practicing the imperative. My teacher, Rocio, told me to use as an example how I would talk to my empleada [housemaid] ... you know, what commands I would give her.
Johanna

Beyond the structure of the house and designed inequality, discourses carrying racism, classism and gender-based discrimination flow freely and pervasively around the city. Johanna's teacher, Rocio, a Peruvian with strong Andean features who teaches Spanish lessons to visiting tourists and expatriates, urged her to get comfortable with the imperative tense by imagining a conversation with her maid. In this exercise, Johanna, 31, a white French Canadian volunteering in Lima, is taught how to 'command' a fictional household worker, revealing how culturally acceptable it is to speak to household workers as though they are a subordinate class. Additionally, it demonstrates the perhaps reluctant, complicated complicity that the teacher has in equipping foreigners with linguistic tools that perpetuate discrimination in attempts to relate or show classed and racial alignment with the learner.

These discourses become materialised with regard to the limited future options household workers in Lima have due to the nature of their work being contained inside the home. Cristiana, a Limeña friend who has been involved in household worker advocacy and empowerment for years, explained some of the limitations placed on household workers in Lima. She described Lima's dual-class society in terms of the way that specific jobs allow particular access to education, decent pay, security and future advancement, whereas other jobs offer no access to those options. A 37-year-old organiser who has been running theatre groups, population education workshops and reproductive rights courses for adolescent and adult household workers for the last ten years, Cristiana notes, "There are two worlds in Lima. There is the world of the *trabajadoras del hogar* (household workers), and there is the world of their employers."

Discussing these two worlds further, she elaborated about the lack of possibilities for any kind of educational advancement for household workers living in their employer's home.

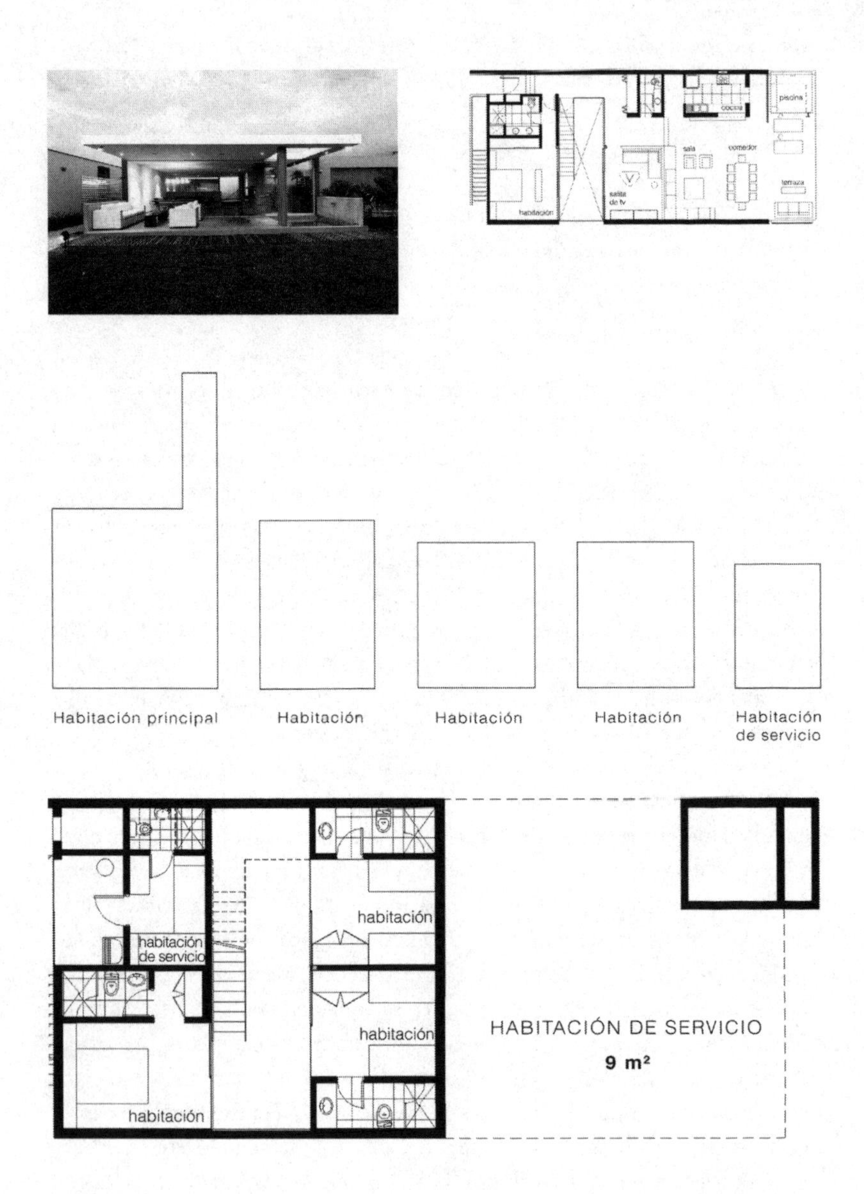

Casa La Isla, constructed in Lima, in 2007, Daniela Ortiz de Zevallos

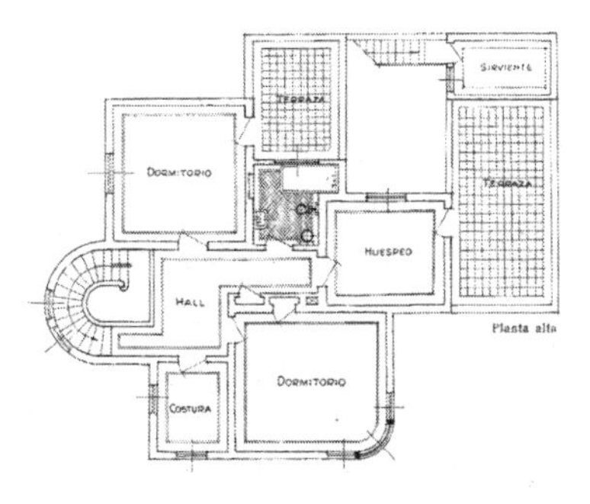

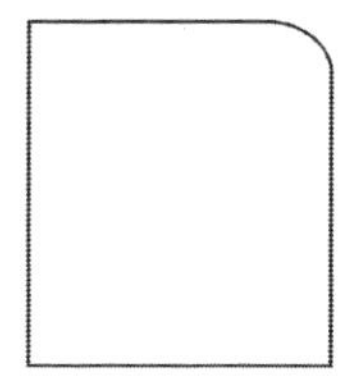

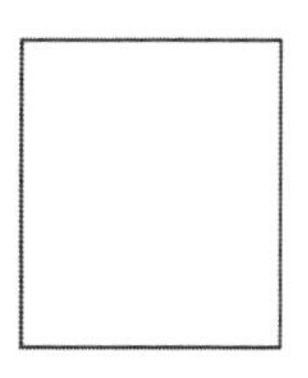

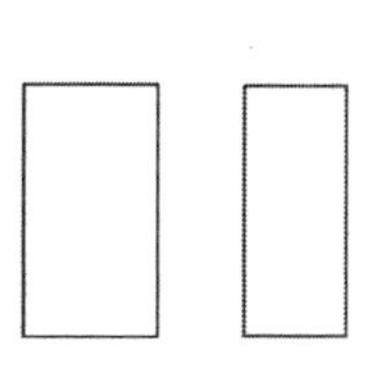

Habitación principal

Habitación

Habitación

Habitación de servicio

Habitación de servicio

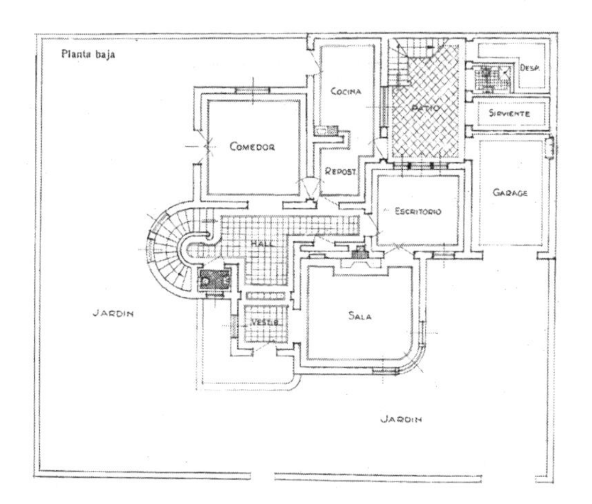

HABITACIÓN DE SERVICIO

7,5 m²

As compared to Casa Rycroft,
constructed in Miraflores, Lima, in 1937
Daniela Ortiz de Zevallos

What you have here is that issues of discrimination and racism come together. Look, domestic work is a profession, is a job, where racism and discrimination come together as part of it. This isn't the case in other kinds of work.
Cristiana

Similarly, Vanessa, a longtime feminist lawyer and domestic worker advocate from Lima, conveyed how inherent racism is within Limeño society. Her organisation works to raise consciousness on the Household Workers' Law, but this racism in household labour, along with gendered and class-based discrimination, continues.

Racism is very strong in America Latina. Speaking of the importance of decolonising relations of power, racism is a heavy part of this relationship. It isn't just class exclusion, but also race, and gender. For this reason, the job of household work demonstrates more than any other the intersection of oppressions. I believe this is a really important dimension to domestic work, because it speaks to the type of work, the type of employment situation, the type of home, the space of the home, and the type of society we have.
Vanessa

In the same way that Fanon, in *Black Skin, White Masks,* understands the power imbued in language – how speaking French presumes the collective consciousness of the French including all of its overt and covert racism – those in Peru who speak Spanish as either a first or second language (with an indigenous language being primary) point to another moment of colonial distinction. Fanon posits: "To speak means to be in a position to use a certain syntax, to grasp the morphology of this or that language, but it means above all to assume a culture, to support the weight of a civilization."[18] Vanessa's comment about household workers' oppression demonstrating a particular kind of society is powerful, hearkening to Fanon's notion of the collective unconscious (as "the sum of prejudices, myths, and collective attitudes of a given group") being culturally acquired (rather than genetically) and thus reinscribed through the reproduction of these oppressive relations in the home.

This intersection of oppression is demonstrated on the streets, when workers wear pure white or light blue uniforms while pushing strollers or walking dogs, and it is also manifested in their treatment within the home. Indigenous Peruvians are demeaned as *campesinas* (peasants), *chicas* (girls), and *muchachas* (girls) – for instance, household workers being called 'girls' even when they are well into their 50s and 60s – and other terms of disrespect, while the utter, requisite respect of *Señor* (Sir), *Señorita* (Miss) or *Señora* (Madam) is demanded by the employer's family at all times – and is so ingrained that nearly anyone else they encounter in the home besides a fellow household worker becomes a *Señorita* or a *Señor*. In addition, because of their darker skin colour and Andean features, language also functions to further entrench colonial modes of thought, practices and cultural understandings. This is witnessed throughout Lima's civil society, as household workers are regularly restricted from entering private clubs and even certain beaches. These racialised tropes are holdovers of colonial-era delineations of space that preserved certain areas for criollo privilege, and they manifest themselves in dress code requirements. Even those indigenous Peruvians wearing the most on-trend, expensive clothing who show up at exclusive clubs with an attractive ensemble of friends are often socially discouraged and denied entry. A young Limeño friend told me a story of covering up his friend's denial at a club by pretending that they were both too drunk to enter in an effort to protect his friend's feelings against the normalisation of racist policies that allow this abusive system to continue.

Regulating marginality, regulating discrimination? *La ley y sus descontentos* (The law and its discontents)

Roselia, a former housemaid who began working at the age of seven in her hometown of Cajamarca, smiled and kindly asked, "*Amiga, tu nombre*? (Friend, your name?)" "*Luz, como*... (Light, as...)" the 16-year-old household worker gestured up at the dim light, flickering high above us in El Hogar de Rosita, the old home in Lima's Jesus Maria district. "*Luz*, ok, *perfecto, de Huaraz* (Luz, ok, perfect, from Huaraz)." Roselia, who now runs advocacy programmes and workshops for newly-migrated household workers, jotted down a couple of notes and moved on to the next worker, also young, also from the provinces. Aprons and *gorros* (caps) still in place from the morning's cooking class, the group of nine household workers from the south, the *sierra* (mountains) and the *selva* (forests), gathered around the table together to discuss the 18 articles of Law 27986, the Peruvian Household Workers' Law.

Roselia works with thousands of household workers each year, some of whom are new to Lima and fresh from the provinces while others have lived and worked in other people's homes for years. As the group talked about the law together, Isabel, 29 years old and also from Cajamarca, commented on some of the internal contradictions.

Hmm … the law says one thing and it is impossible for the employer to follow. For example, say the person should work for 8 hours – this can never happen! Never. If you get up at 7 in the morning and start to work, you cannot be done yet; working until 7 is 12 hours. No, it's impossible. This part of the law is really bad…
Isabel

As discussed elsewhere[19], Isabel's recognition of the fact that working hours can hardly be regulated inside the home points to a failure of the state to recognise the constant, repetitive, eternal nature of reproductive labour. However, in the last ten years, Peru has joined the growing number of South American countries advancing laws for formerly unrecognised and unprotected workers, a modern twist on a law that usually prefers to look the other way regarding household workers[20]. Only 0.1% of those workers enjoy the protections of a written contract.[21]

Other women attending the law workshop tell stories of internal migration, a common factor shaping the lives of those leaving the provinces to find work in Lima. Aimalinda, a 27-year-old from Huancabamba, left her family in the highlands of Piura province tucked in the far eastern edges of the country and migrated to Lima at age 13, where she lived with and worked for the same family until age 19. "And how was your relationship with your employers?" I asked. She instantly described the slavery-like treatment that she suffered for seven years. "*Ellos no me pagaban* (They didn't pay me)," Aimalinda explained. They didn't pay her because she lived with the family and she didn't have to pay rent, even though, of course, she was living only to work constantly for the family. Now things are better; from 3–8pm Aimalinda takes classes, but during the day she cares for her employer's young child and 90-year-old grandmother. "She's equal to a baby," Aimalinda mused. The benefit to her of living in is that she doesn't have to worry about commuting for 1–2 hours each way from the poorer districts of Lima to the central districts where the majority of wealthy employers are concentrated. Aimalinda is now paid S/.400 per month (roughly US$160), clearly more than her nonexistent salary for seven years, yet less than half of the already low Peruvian minimum wage. The law can do nothing for Aimalinda with regard to this payment, since all that it requires is a mutual agreement between the employers and the employees, vs a set, defined bottom line.

El Hogar de Rosita takes on the task of diffusing information to women working and hidden inside of the home. Most are new to the sprawling, chaotic city of Lima with its 43 districts, and yet all too familiar with mistreatment, either by relatives or strangers. A radio programme broadcast by El Hogar de Rosita at 8am on Saturdays gives news about the workshops, decent jobs and the sense of community offered at this little oasis on a quiet side street in a working-class district. They recognise that these women have been conditioned to accept poor working conditions and justification for abuse and lack of pay because of the structural setup of migration and dependency, while architecture and employment practices continue to reproduce the dynamics of colonial relations. Truly, this population has been disciplined, scattered and dispersed into "compact groupings of individuals wandering about the country in unpredictable ways"[22].

A window display with maid's uniforms and Christmas decorations, Miraflores, Lima, Peru, February 2014

Lima's future: modernising inequality?

The more material wealth becomes concentrated in the hands of the elite, the more domestic work becomes deeply entrenched, and the more extreme, polarised race relations that recall colonial policies, practices, approaches and understandings are further ingrained. The pervasive nature of structural inequality remains, lived out through the street, the home and the body.

In thinking about attempts of an oppressed, subjugated population to move toward full social and political inclusion, the law is not enough to right centuries of wrongs and to launch structural challenges against deeply embedded racism. The law remains one tool among many that fail these internal migrant household workers confronting Lima's contemporary colonial climate, even as broad-based efforts are made elsewhere to decolonise and disentangle the deeply-rooted social hierarchy and elite class understandings that pervade much of Peruvian culture. As the so-called 'sophisticated' skyscrapers in districts across Lima are constructed everyday, elegantly entrenching and reproducing colonial power relations through employment practices inside the home, the misguided national quest for modernity remains embedded in racism and inequality.

* Thanks to Sofía Mauricio, Blanca Figueroa, and Victoria Maraví in Lima, Peru; KC Wagner at the Worker Institute of Cornell University; and Nicolás Sacco at the University of Buenos Aires for their dedicated work and encouragement of this project. Thanks also to the Inter-American Foundation's 2012–13 Grassroots Development Fellowship faculty and fellows for their intellectual support.

1. For the purposes of this paper, the colonial name Peru is used to describe the lands in this particular western region of South America. The name was 'bestowed' on this land in 1522 by the Spanish crown which first called these Incan lands 'Peru' after Biru, an indigenous ruler who lived in the region that is now called the 'Bay of San Miguel'. This name was 'legalised' in 1529 when the Spanish crown designated the captured lands as the province of Peru. Under Spanish occupation, the lands were first called the Viceroyalty of Peru, which then became the Republic of Peru after the later Peruvian War of Independence.
2. Museo Larco, Lima, Peru, 'Culturas y Mapas de Tiempo', http://www.museolarco.org/coleccion/culturas-y-mapas-del-tiempo/.

3. Susan Migden Socolow, *The Women of Colonial Latin America* (Cambridge: Cambridge University Press, 2000).
4. *ibid.*
5. Rhacel Salazar Parreñas, *Servants of Globalization: Women, Migration, and Domestic Work* (Palo Alto, CA: Stanford University Press, 2001); Evelyn Nakano Glenn, 'From Servitude to Service Work: Historical Continuity in the Racial Division of Paid Reproductive Labor', *Signs*, 18(1) 1992, pp. 1–43.
6. Paseos Amazonicas "Amazon Jungle Tours", http://www.paseosamazonicos.com/amazon_tours.htm.
7. Lucien Chauvin, 'Lima: 10 Things to Do', *Time Magazine*, http://content.time.com/time/travel/cityguide/article/0,31489,1977548_1977464_1977441,00.html (accessed 22/06/14).
8. My previous experience includes working as a job dispatcher at an immigrant workers' centre in the Mission District of San Francisco in 2008–09; organising with domestic workers in Guatemala City between 2009–11 in order to challenge the state on the implementation of the recently passed maternity coverage law; and volunteering in New York and California from 2012–14 with a domestic employer organisation that seeks to enforce codes of conduct among domestic employers.
9. P.H. Collins, 'Learning from the Outsider Within: The Sociological Significance of Black Feminist Thought', *Social Problems* (Special Theory Issue), 33(6), 1986, pp. S14–S32.
10. Donna Haraway, 'Situated Knowledges: The Science Question in Feminism as a Site of Discourse on the Privilege of Partial Perspective', *Feminist Studies* 14(3) 1988, pp. 575–599; Saba Mahmood, *The Politics of Piety: The Islamic Revival and the Feminist Subject* (Princeton University Press, 2005); and Nancy Naples, *Feminism and Method: Ethnography, Discourse Analysis, and Activist Research* (Oxford and New York: Routledge, 2003).
11. Nancy Naples, *ibid.*, p. 21.
12. Frantz Fanon, *Black Skin, White Masks* (New York: Grove Press, 1967) p. 165.
13. Frantz Fanon, *ibid.*, p. 170.
14. Daniela Ortiz, 2012. *Habitaciones de Servicio*, http://habitacionesdeservicio.com, http://daniela-ortiz.com/index.php?/projects/maids-rooms/. 'Casa Rycroft', http://habitacionesdeservicio.com/casa-rycroft/.
15. Marcelo Expósito, http://marceloexposito.net/pdf/exposito_danielaortiz_en.pdf.
16. Edward Said, *Culture and Imperialism* (New York: Vintage Books, 1993) p. 219.
17. Benjamin S. Orlove, 'Putting Race in Its Place: Order in Colonial and Postcolonial Peruvian Geography', *Social Research* 60(2) 1993, p. 301.
18. Frantz Fanon, *op.cit.*, p. 18.
19. Katherine Maich, 'Marginalized Struggles for Legal Reform: Cross-Country Consequences of Domestic Worker Organizing', *Social Development, Democracy and Human Rights in Latin America*, Special issue of Social Development Issues, forthcoming 2014.
20. Merike Blofield, *Care Work and Class: Domestic Workers' Struggle for Equal Rights in Latin America* (University Park, PA: Penn State University Press, 2012).
21. Conferencia sobre el Convenio 189 del OIT, Lima, Peru, 13 December 2012.
22. Michel Foucault, *Discipline & Punish: The Birth of the Prison* (New York: Vintage, 1977).

Tales from the City of Gold 2010-2013

JASON LARKIN

2563

POTOMAC ST

STOP

Visualising Addis Ababa

Deconstructing Privilege-Making Narratives

CLARA RIVAS ALONSO

'Construction projects' are dramatically fracturing the landscape of Addis Ababa and real-estate billboards about: site specific and regional urban development plans are springing up all over the Ethiopian capital. The contrast between this advertising industry imagined city and the 'real' city of building sites is striking: 'global'[1] neo-liberal images of glass and metal violently contradict indigenous ways of using and producing space, particularly urban space.

This essay addresses the means by which Addis Ababa is being physically and imaginatively re-constructed by new globalised real-estate narratives; a city undergoing extensive conversion via new, largely alien, urban developments. With the aid of interviews, I seek to critically approach the global discourse placed on real-estate billboards that encourages and also attempts to justify the changes.[2] I argue that this discourse promotes the internalisation of the transformation and further stratification of the urban fabric. In order to offer an insight into the current urban processes at play, it is necessary to highlight both the recent history – a late-19th-century emperor's choice of the area to establish 'his' capital city; Europe's colonial "scramble for Africa" movement of invasions and occupations; post-independence neo-colonialism – and current hegemonic influences on the city's development. This will hopefully enable the understanding of the present context of a city under breakneck-speed construction.

Historical and contemporaneous struggles

According to urbanists interested in post-colonial theories and frameworks[3], Addis Ababa pushes the boundaries of what 'city' or 'urbanity' means, and further, proves that the concept of 'city' is open and flexible inasmuch as there are infinite indigenous ways of creating and reproducing spaces. Different understandings of the use of urban space take place through the re-appropriation of colonial symbols and the diversification of 'healthy' formal and informal economies in the face of local and global institutional developmentalism. Practices considered 'rural' in western urban conventions, such as herding, co-exist with newly built shopping centres where security guards protect spaces devoid of any activity. These recently introduced spaces remain eerily silent whilst a growing (but hardly a majority) middle class becomes more visible in advertisement narratives as possible consumers. In the meantime, the impoverished, who historically inhabited the central parts of the city in what are considered by some as 'informal dwellings' (later formalised as *qebele* housing), are pushed to the outskirts, far from work and their existing communities. Newly built condominiums do away with previous social, cultural and labour networks.

Addis Ababa stands as the result of local, regional and international struggles. An Ethiopian state was formed in the 19th century, expanding its borders and annexing populations. It was hierarchical in nature and, as with all empires, the different Ethiopian emperors, from Tewodros to Menelik, struggled to formalise and settle the borders of their empire. Ethiopian rulers had long been in contact with foreign forces, establishing relationships of convenience (mainly to secure arms) that could and would be broken whenever necessary. When at times Ethiopians had sought European support against Sudanese or Egyptian invasions, European powers would also turn against them. They had to wrestle with the forces of European colonial imperialism keen to take over the lands and with the peoples who had no wish to belong to anyone's empire. Egyptian, Sudanese, British and Italian forces, at different moments and with varied intensity, all posed a threat to the successive emperors' attempts at establishing an Ethiopian Empire. It could be argued that the strong external pressure forced the *negast*[4] to consolidate an imperial power in order to face down European expansionism. These struggles are imprinted in the walls and spatial use of the city, and are another reason for the preservation of its material and immaterial heritage in the face of large-scale urbanisation.

With the completion of the Suez Canal in 1869, the region very quickly gained the interest of European colonialists, effectively starting the devastating "scramble for Africa". "This was the genesis of the Anglo-Italian collusion over Ethiopia: the Italians were desperate to control Ethiopia, and the British were ready to support them as long as they acted as a watchdog of British imperial interests."[5]

Addis Ababa, or New Flower as it translates from Amharic, was founded in 1886/87. Emperor Menelik had used the surrounding Entoto Mountains as his base in his strategic attempt to undermine the different challenges to his imperial ambitions,[6] and his wife Taitu (1851-1918) chose the site as an appropriate place to create a settlement. The nearby thermal springs of Filwoha were already famous for their therapeutic waters and in use by the Oromo peoples and others seeking their beneficial effects.[7] After the Imperial Palace was constructed in 1886, the city started to grow mainly as a combined military and palatial settlement,[8] at the centre of an expanding country and a state in formation.[9] It is understood that groups of migrants came to Addis invited by Menelik, namely Greeks, Armenians and Indians, bringing knowledge and experience of their own vernacular urbanisms, thereby developing the city further with the use of both local and foreign materials.[10] The Oromo peoples were eventually subsumed into the growing city,[11] a situation that remains controversial and contested up to today. Internal struggles such as that undertaken against the Oromo peoples or the incorporation of territories such as Gambella under the umbrella of the model of a multi-ethnic federal republic are some of the issues that demonstrate the need to deconstruct institutional history in order to examine the narratives of historical events from those in positions of power able to write them. Nevertheless, a focus on the foreign powers' ambitions and their consequences sheds light on the mapping of contemporary colonialism and post-colonialism.

In 1896 the Battle of Adwa took place:

> *As a counter-current to the sweeping tide of colonial domination in Africa, it shocked some as it encouraged others. It forced observers, politicians and businessmen to reassess their positions ... The racial dimension was what lent Adwa particular significance. It was a victory of blacks over whites.*[1]

It was during the following years that Addis went on to become the recognised capital of the Ethiopian Empire. Filled with the symbolic importance of overcoming European attempts at colonising it, the city stands to lose much more than just old buildings for the sake of entering the world market: its indigenous and exceptional networks of social interaction will be subjugated to the homogenising landscape of western urban capitalism happily and wilfully applied by a local elite.

Ethiopia was never colonised. It was, however, occupied by the Italian fascist forces for five years from 1936. The brutal Italian understanding of occupation involved deploying spatial and economic segregation of the urban population along racial lines. Their urban project was not completed, but its legacy is still present.[13]

Subsequent regimes neglected the living conditions of the 80% living in informal housing, whose needs have been partially addressed both domestically and internationally.[14] Informal housing areas were institutionalised as part of the so-called *qebele* housing, thus allowing the state to exert powerful and often unilateral administrative control over all dwelling spaces. Currently, the portrayal of a city in full-blown neo-liberal explosion seems to toy with the absurd when the needs of the overwhelming majority relate to basic services such as sewage systems, access to electricity and safe water, and above all to participatory decision-making practices and protection of human rights.

Economic imperialism, neo-colonialism and Ethiopia

Whereas the legacies of the Italian occupation and British 'influence' are evident in the names and shapes of some of the spaces in Addis Ababa, there are other more contemporary aspects of foreign influence. It is important to highlight the ongoing social, cultural and economic relationships that western and more recently Chinese elites have expanded and entrenched within Ethiopia's elite. With this awareness, it is easy to see how Ethiopia's elite are attempting to build a city ideologically and visually reflecting western narratives of 'development' and 'progress'.

As host to the seat of the Organisation of African Unity (now the African Union) since its creation in 1963, Addis is often referred to as 'the diplomatic capital of Africa'. In urban terms, this representation goes beyond the discourse; the impact of being a so-called 'diplomatic city' on the social and urban fabric is profound. Vast areas of land along the valleys that make up the city were provided for foreign embassies and informal housing settlements quickly sprang up around them. Under the current massive development schemes, the social fabric of this *qebele* housing, with its small shops and bars, has been torn apart to make space for bulldozers and cement trucks. Neighbourhoods such as the French Embassy quarter have been wiped out in order to give way to the construction of a bridge and motorway, with no account taken of either the previous use of land by its dwellers or the impact on the landscape.

The development of luxury housing and the steep rise in rents and leases owe much to the representation of Addis Ababa as the diplomatic capital of Africa. But this representation obscures the reality of the city, which is comprised of a small diplomatic elite among other privileged classes (usually related to the current ruling party), a growing middle class and a majority of poor people. While condominiums spring up and private gated luxury villas are constructed, people's homes and small businesses in long-established 'informal settlements' are demolished. These opposites of the housing spectrum are divided by a chasm hardly bridgeable unless solid social and housing policies are adopted.

International 'diplomacy' impacts directly and indirectly on the city fabric. China has built the newest African Union building in Addis as a 'gift' to Africa. China is also involved in the construction of roads, railway and tramway lines in both city and across the country. Events such as the celebration of the 50th anniversary of the African Union have encouraged and increased construction of the neo-liberal city. For example, the area of Bole Road earmarked for the AU celebrations was finished in record time to satisfy government requirements; speed was prioritised over safe building conditions.

The current 'scramble' for land in the region, under the deceptive label of 'economic investment', has profound implications for the city. The Ethiopian government's leasing of land to India and other Asian 'investors' for the mass cultivation of sugar and roses has been widely criticised and reported.[15] Its construction of the controversial Grand Renaissance Dam project, carried out by Italian constructors Salini Costruttori, will create human and ecological havoc, not to mention the human rights implications of supporting a government that forces the population to 'donate' one month's salary towards the dam's construction.[16] Under the banner of agricultural support and funded by UK aid, the UK has been paving the way for companies such as Unilever and Monsanto to access new lands and markets:

> *The reforms required of African countries will make it much easier for companies to get hold of large tracts of farmland. In Ethiopia for example, a scheme is being set up to fast-track investors' access to land.*[17]

African lands are yet again seen as ripe for discovery/exploitation/manipulation/incorporation for neo-liberal western interests and profit.

One of the human consequences of this 'economic investment' is rural to urban migration. Removed from their lands and homes, people are forced to move to Addis Ababa in search of work and means of survival, putting pressure on the entire urban infrastructure and social fabric.

Narratives in public space

The names of urban spaces and places provide fertile ground for de/reconstructing histories. Addis Ababa's streets and main avenues hold official names, but many smaller streets and alleys lack signposting.[18] In the era of seemingly universalised Google maps and satellite navigation, the lack of street names stands as a rebellion of sorts. Furthermore, even the spaces that are named are, more often than not, normally referred to locally by a completely different name. If we asked for the way to De Gaulle Square, it would be hard to find a local person who knows where it is. But if we asked for Piazza, as it is commonly known, everyone would be able to give us directions. Both names clearly reference European interventions and highlight a critical point in the process of claiming and territorialising lands. To quote Kwame Ture:

> *One of the characteristics of the European settler colony is that, when the European arrives, they change the name. They change the name. They change the name for two purposes. They want to obliviate the history of the past, number one, and, number two, they want to legitimise their existence as the true owners of the land. That's very important. Very, very important.*[19]

The names of the city's streets and squares reveal varied attempts of urban authorities to reflect history according to Ethiopian institutions. One of the most popular thoroughfares is Churchill Road, as both traffic and pedestrians fill the wide lanes of this avenue. And around Churchill Road, the neo-colonial elite city administration considers it suitable to honour or allow the honouring of the likes of General Cunningham, General Wingate and Queen Elizabeth II. Mexico Square is named for Mexico's stance in the League of Nations regarding the Italian occupation of Ethiopia. The vast market area occupying much of the north west of the city is still known as Mercato, an obviously Italian remnant.

With the furious pace of construction in areas around Bole Road, the changing names indicate a revised political geography of sorts: Ethio-China Friendship Road and European Union Peacock Park stand out among streets named after other African countries. Roads that were already named (Ethio-China Friendship Road was previously known as Wollo Sefer) are turned into symbols of contemporary alliances; the city turns into a tool for its own historical rewriting.

Eviction and exclusion in Addis Ababa

These institutional alliances tend to disregard the needs of the majority – a common trait in countries aligning with practices of capitalism and neo-liberalism. The clearance of social housing and 'upgrading' of land for profitable enterprises have taken (and are taking) place globally. In the case of Ethiopia, state-controlled media and official discourse cannot fully cover up the reality of the abrupt divide between the possibilities of the few and the majority. Supported by western powers, the government that aligns itself with the elites and has no problem in using violence whenever necessary[20], is the same government that is shaping the city to suit its will and interests.

Another example of urbanism as political tool in the Ethiopian context are the uprisings led by Oromo students in universities in Addis Ababa and the Oromo region at the beginning of May 2014.[21] The uprisings have been explained as a reaction to the expansion of Addis Ababa's city boundaries into Oromia and the threat to urban tenure rights. It could also be read as a strategic move by the government to identify and neutralise student activists ahead of the 2015 elections. Whatever the case, as official accounts and institutional information cover up the reality of a brutal regime, the 'unconfirmed' reports of numerous students being killed can be trusted.[22]

And I am personally able to confirm the internet is being censored – by whom it is difficult to say.

When an area dedicated to small butcher shops near the Sheraton Hotel, south of Arat Kilo, was demolished and its dwellers evicted, the authorities used the institutional green and yellow fences to block the entrances. Some weeks later, the women of the area came back to the ruins of their houses and mourned the space and the homes they had lost as if it were a funeral: cries and black dresses became the visible expression of citizens' discontent. Tellingly, one of the most efficient forms of self-organisation in Addis is the *iddir* or social funerary associations, which have, in some cases, been able to negotiate with local authorities the terms of local area upgrading programmes. A skeleton of its old self, the area near the Sheraton now provides refuge for homeless families who make do without water, electricity or even solid walls to keep them warm.

This brief contextualisation provides a backdrop for the real-estate advertising billboards that have been placed all over Addis Ababa. The size, regularity and design of these advertisements are injecting a very particular narrative of urban development throughout the city.[23] They stand out from building sites without buildings to be seen, from the side of glass towers overlooking slum areas, from the sides of streets and on the top of green and yellow walls. All repeat the same message: urban development in Addis is going ahead, it is not for the benefit of the majority, and it is transforming the city based on the idea of a imagined 'modern western city'.

Imagining privilege: Addis billboards and dwellers in conversation

There are different mechanisms that attempt to capture the space that we now so easily call 'the city'. City dwellers can produce different imaginings of collectivity (even if that collectivity is based on the western neo-liberal regime's assumption of individualism). Institutional policy produces other collectivities normally aimed at creating docile citizens and enriching the politicians and their friends. Media goes on to aid the institutional project or impose other imaginations that intertwine with dwellers expectations, realities and dreams of the city they inhabit. It is thus that the images and language reproduced in billboards offer a glimpse of the struggle between the language of power and the space available for managing citizens' expectations.

It is also thus that the abyss between reality and the institutional dream can be identified once the voices of dwellers respond to those narratives.

In Addis Ababa, this abyss latent within the discourse is supported by a very real spatial division between developing and renewal areas and the rest of the city, between the spaces where the hegemonic discourse materialises in the shape of high rises and the spaces where dwellers have been actively involved in their development.

The reading of these billboards is supported by interviews with some Addis Ababa dwellers.[24]

Proliferation of spatial borders

Unfinished building behind green and yellow fences in the area of Kazantchis in south east Addis Ababa, Clara Rivas, 2013

The green and yellow fences delineate the renewal areas in Addis, bordering spaces all over town. In this particular area in Kazantchis, Guinea Conakry Street draws both a conceptual and physical boundary between traditional local business (low-rise cafes, bars and shops) and the future shape of the city (buildings such as the Intercontinental Hotel). The space the Intercontinental stands for, that eventually will engulf the rest of the street, is a private space, accessible only to those with the means. The key to open this space is (unsurprisingly) capital. The very exclusive nightclub (Liquid Lounge), on the side of the Intercontinental, mirrors the night bars on the opposite side of the street. Both sides stand for similar pleasure-seeking activities but those frequenting these places belong to opposite sides of the class and race spectrum. The traditional bars and shops with roofs of corrugated iron host social activities with no class-specific approach. *Tej bet*, or houses where the locally made honey liqueur is drunk, have traditionally provided a space for socialising. This social practice involves *azmari* singing, a popular cultural medium that gives an accurate, if normally satirical, snapshot of Ethiopian social woes and foes. If the other side of the street is indeed the shape of things to come for Addis Ababa, the *azmari* and places such as the *tej bets* will face an uncertain future, torn between disappearing or becoming caricatures of themselves, nicely branded for touristic revenue purposes.

What the writing conceals

Real estate billboard advertising luxury condominiums in front of an unfinished building behind green and yellow fences in the area of Kazantchis, Clara Rivas, 2013

These days the city has two faces. There are places that are considered to be areas of the high-class people and there are places which are taken as places for the non-privileged groups. If things continue the way they are now, then, at the end of the day, the urban division will escalate to the point of no return.
Daniel

The discourse on almost all the real-estate billboards clearly stems from the European-American neo-liberal agenda imposed around the world. Firstly, luxury ought to be the main aim of city inhabitants. From an urgent need for improved living conditions to luxury condominiums – the difference is an abyss hardly possible for the majority of the population of Addis Ababa to bridge. This distance and the desires it promotes are bound to make the general population feel alienated in the future Addis, where the major constructions and developments will tell them their needs are not catered for.

When I was taking this photograph ('AZ Real Estate's Luxury Condos are on sale') the police made themselves known. In a very similar way to how the security and big brother culture protects the private rather than the public, the protection of urban renewal sites in Addis Ababa is a priority.

Images detached from the city

No I don't think they truly represent the real Addis. Instead, they anticipate the aspiration of people for future Addis in relating with western major cities. For instance, if you go to Bole, around Dembel, you find New York Café with the symbol of the liberty statue that reminds me of New York City, and so many more. In my opinion, they lack some originality.
Israel

A common feature in the language and images on the development boards is the lack of reality surrounding the building depicted. There is nothing that gives away where the building is supposed to be constructed. There are no references to the neighbourhood that eventually will provide the network and support all neighbourhoods provide. This is another tool to induce a certain detachment from what the city has come to mean so far.

One of the clear markers in the social racial[25] divide of Addis Ababa is that those who can afford it mainly travel by car; it is very uncommon to see white people walking. As Addis is being pushed to become an international business and political hub, the activities in the streets, which provide the lifeline for many, might eventually decrease and turn into localised or marginalised forms of urban living, whilst gated areas and private shopping centres spread.

Projected future vs the infrastructure of the present

Well, I can say that the images promote urban division than cohesion. As I told you before, the city is divided into so many groups. Each group tends to promote its own culture. That is why there is no common culture that unites us to be 'Addis Ababans'. So, while making the billboards, a businessman/businesswoman from each group tries to promote the culture of that specific group which he/she belongs to. Even if the billboards are trying to address people from other groups, the message is displayed based on the norms specified in the source's group culture. Therefore, from my point of view, these billboards have self [group] promoting effect rather than creating cohesion among different groups.

Wonde

Cables, eucalyptus scaffolds and precarious working conditions define the majority of present urban renewal projects. Cranes, scaffolding and half-way-there high-rise buildings have become the everyday landscape of many parts of Addis. The future result will undeniably be the product of these conditions, precarious urbanism devoid of all the attributes that have until now given character to Addis Ababa.

Imposing unobtainable lifestyle dreams

The billboards found in the city, not only the ones found in the construction areas, do not reflect Ethiopia culture and way of life at all. Even if the country's constitution clearly stipulates that the working language of the country is Amharic such billboards used a language of different countries. It seems that they are trying to communicate [with] other people rather than the city native dwellers.

Daniel

I feel that they address only to those who could primarily understand English. I see identity crisis, target missing, erratic, and less meticulously organised billboards.

Zereay

Billboard advertising the new development of Dembel City Center
Shopping Centre in Bole Road, Gabriel J. Turkairo, 2013

Dembel stands as the first shopping centre or mall in Addis Ababa. It is currently undergoing expansion. The message conveys a certain number of assumptions. Firstly, and part of the narrative across the board, the use of English implies an educated and/or foreign audience, excluding in one stroke all the rest of dwellers who might not have had access to a certain type of education. Furthermore, it adds to the idea that English is indeed the necessary global language essential in order to function as part of the privileged classes. One of the interviewees offered a solution:

Yes, it is for me/locals and for other people as well. I think it is because Addis is not only the capital of Ethiopia but also the Headquarters of [the] African Union and also other international organisations which makes the target audience to be both local and international community. So I do believe messages on the billboards should be presented both in local and foreign/English language. But usually you don't see that happening. Most messages on the billboards particularly around major construction sites lack comprehensiveness. They completely ignore the local audience.

Israel

From Shabby to Chic, witness the transformation

Referring to Addis as 'shabby' conveys a wish to change the city into something different (bigger, shinier at least). It presents the idea that the old buildings, centre and housing are places and architectural forms that Addis Ababa ought to turn her back on.

In my view, yes, it's all to the community in general aiming to show the new improvements of the city so that the government will get acceptance of the community for the sustainability of [its] power.

Habtish

The aim is to change Addis into somewhere 'chic'. We are presented with a skyline of a so-called chic city, which should have a series of skyscrapers and no people around to use them or confuse the idea of the city. City dwellers are told to "witness the transformation" – being explicitly excluded from the decision-making process, city users can only look on as the city is turned into something else completely. This already lays the ground for how city users are supposed to behave once the 'transformation' is complete, i.e. look on now and, after it is finished, use it as you are advised to, as the space organises you to behave.

The buildings are erected on the spaces once held by the poor urbanity. The poor feel hopeless to access in these buildings due to financial disparities.
Zereay

The Dubai in Addis

They reflect the dreams/visual of a city in UAE, I feel, as they largely lack the Ethiopic aesthetic impressions.
Zereay

The majority of building aesthetics in Addis clearly refer to the urban horizons created in cities like Dubai, which are open about their hopes of apeing western development models – but with a local twist to the design of buildings, for example. This leads to a reflection on the relationship between the city and so-called urban landmarks. In the case of Dembel, the promoters present the silhouette of a group of buildings, a skyline that can be identified as a city. This is quite common in these projects. The issue in this case is that it is not possible to identify any city. The skyline is imaginary. It only sends the message that a city of skyscrapers is under construction. Here is the dream. Furthermore, the skyline is ambiguous, it can also be interpreted as a typology of buildings: there are five towers in decreasing size. This seems to convey the notion of a catalogue demonstrating the different building types the promoters are able to construct.

I always wonder why the people who prepared them fail to see Addis's beauty and historical realities. All seems trying to reflect facts on pictures of other countries, especially the Middle East countries like Dubai. Let alone the billboards, even the design of the buildings does not have any Ethiopian or African touch. The majority of the people that I know feel uneasy about all these facts. The things that are happening to the city are done just with a clear political motivation rather than thinking [about] the everlasting effects of the measures that are taken. Sadly to say, if things go this way, Addis will lose all her natural beauty

and historical significance not only to the city dwellers [but] even to those Africans who considered the city to be an African capital.
Daniel

The billboard provides no reference to Addis, which has several prominent buildings that were once the pride of the city. The Addis Ababa City Hall was used as a cover picture for the official booklet of the 100th anniversary of the foundation of Addis Ababa in 1987. It was then the landmark of Addis as a capital. Now this building seems to be absent from the new urbanism as if the promoters not only deny Addis's existing 'identity', but also forget to propose a renewed identity based on popular or recognisable buildings.

This suggests an atomised city, as illustrated by the billboard featuring the Burj Al-Arab look-alike. Burj is one of Dubai's landmarks. It seems the promoters are saying that everything is possible in the new city. New Addis will be like a new Dubai, a brand new city of skyscrapers in the imagined heartland of a 'united Africa'.

(An open) Conclusion

I imagine Addis in 2020, a city which is only for the first–class society, because most of the poor people at this time they move far away from the central city due to the construction of buildings and infrastructures like railway and hotels construction.
Mohammed

Lots of development, very fast growth and very big city with too many people. But all that will depend on who we have as a gov … Addis can be the same as 20 years ago. The changes made didn't really change people's minds or lives really. All this new development doesn't add much to people's lives. It seems more like doing something that is less needed to cover for the important thing that you are not willing to do.
Lydia

2020, I imagine Addis as a very crowded city. Currently, the rural urban migration is very high. I don't think this pattern would decrease in 2020. And I also imagine that

there will be no green areas left, if the construction continues at the current pace.
Wonde

A city of 'concrete jungle'!
Zereay

Addis in 2020, seven years from now. I do not think much will differ from the present look that it has. Many of the big projects in the city somehow are behind their estimated time, so I do not think that many differences will be there. But if things continue this way, I think, at the end of the day, the city will have a double face. Both the old and new faces will be the marks of the city.
Daniel

Of course there will be division between the different urban classes like the rich and poor. These new buildings tend to change the former networks of sociability, organised around the cheap qebele *houses, with the neighbourhood associations (*mahaber*) that provided the modest dwellers with basic livelihoods (selling drinks or food...) and 'social security' (see the* iddir*).*
Mimi

I would personally want to see the government making effort to narrow the gap between the rich and the poor in many ways, for instance on the building of residential construction targeting the poor dwellers. I also want to see radical improvements of the sewerage line construction.
Habtish

Taking into account the needs of the majority of Addis dwellers, it is difficult to understand or appreciate the assumption that an urbanism based on western skyscraper construction (best exemplified in the case of Dubai) is a suitable model of city development. Yet, as the model for the neo-liberal city, it continues being reproduced both physically and in the social imaginary of growing cities. It is a model many in 'the west' also don't sympathise with due to the process of alienation and inequality it embeds. Furthermore, when buildings are the product of the working conditions of a place such as Dubai, the city becomes the product of an ideology, following the rules of the market and the dictatorship of capital, leaving the welfare of thousands of city inhabitants out of the picture, let alone those exploited to build this new city. Thus, the presentation of an urbanism in the image of Dubai as a wonder of the world, let alone the model to follow, remains at least questionable.

As seen in cities that have experienced rapid growth (past or recent), capital-led urbanism solidifies social and racial divisions and entrenches the stratification of society into economic classes. City-building thus reflects the social and cultural appropriation of space by the ruling classes, classes that in the Ethiopian case reproduce a global system of discrimination, with the approval and support of western institutions.

The western neo-liberal discourse also becomes international: the priority is not the construction of a more egalitarian city, based on spatial exchanges occurring at the same social level. The city being built, both in effect and in the imagination, perpetuates the system of the privileged and hassle-free exploitation, from Addis to Istanbul via London. In this context it becomes imperative to build networks of information and communication, and thus exchange knowledges with those involved and affected by urban changes, in order to effectively deconstruct the ideology and imaginary of the neo-liberal paradigm and overthrow it once and for all.

1. When using 'global' this article is referring to the western-engineered ideology that imposes one exclusive way to understand the world: a borderless privilege-producing network of capital flows.
2. In order to deconstruct the neo-liberal regime that suffocates the lives of different peoples all over the planet, I believe it is of extreme importance to highlight how its transformation and implementation in different parts of the world obliterate indigenous production of urban spaces. As a white westerner living in Addis Ababa, I consider it a responsibility to work towards a critique of those narratives, born in western imaginations and taking over cities like Addis.
3. Tim Edensor and Mark Jayne, 'Introduction', in Tim Edensor and Mark Jayne (eds), *Urban Theory Beyond The West* (Abingdon: Routledge, 2012) pp. 1-27. This introduction is particularly effective in compiling some of the trends within urban theory that reclaim the narrative of cities from western theorisation.
4. The emperor was referred to as *Negus nagast*.
5. Bahru Zewde, *A History of Modern Ethiopia 1855-1991* (Addis Ababa: Addis Ababa University Press, 2002) p. 73.
6. It was strategically important due to the mountains' orientation towards the south: Menelik was in the process of unifying the southern lands of the country. He also sought legitimacy as the area had provided camps to medieval rulers. Bahru Zewde, *op.cit.*, p. 68.
7. Fasil Giorghis and Denis Gerard, *The City & Its Architectural Heritage: Addis Ababa 1886-1941* (Addis Ababa: Shama Books, 2007) p. 34.
8. Paul B. Henze, *Layers of Time: A History of Ethiopia* (London: C. Hurst and Co., 2000) p. 154.
9. Paul B. Henze, *ibid.*, p. 153.

10. TEDxTalks: Architect: Fasil Giorghis at TEDxAddis, http:/youtu.be/9V7CRdz8Kz4 (accessed 20/03/13).
11. The Oromo Peoples are the largest ethnic group in Ethiopia. The Oromia Region is one of the nine regional states in Ethiopia, with Addis Ababa as its current capital.
12. Bahru Zewde, *op.cit.*, p. 81.
13. Areas such as Mercato were redefined as 'indigenous market' and transferred to a different area of the city, whilst neighbourhoods such as Kazantchis were for the use of Italian elites.
14. UN Habitat, 'Condominium Housing in Ethiopia: The Integrated Housing Development Programme', 2011, http://www.unhabitat.org/pmss/getElectronicVersion.aspx?nr=3104&alt=1 (accessed 27/05/13).
15. William Lloyd George, 'World Bank told to investigate links to Ethiopia "villagisation" project', *The Guardian*, 19 March 2013, http://www.guardian.co.uk/global-development/2013/mar/19/world-bank-ethiopia-villagisation-project.
16. http://www.internationalrivers.org/campaigns/ethiopia-sdam-boom (accessed 02/06/14, when it had not been censored yet).
17. http://www.theecologist.org/News/news_analysis/2343978/uk_aid_is_financing_a_corporate_scramble_for_africa.html (accessed 20/04/2014).
18. Yosef Teferi, 'Where the Streets Have No Name', in Zegueye Cherenet and Helawi Sewnet (eds), *Building Ethiopia. Sustainability and Innovation in Architecture and Design* (Ethiopia: EiABC, 2012) pp. 87-89.
19. http://americanradioworks.publicradio.org/features/blackspeech/scarmichael-2.html.
20. Hardly mentioned in western media, the riots that followed the Ethiopian government's meddling in the country's Islamic Council elections are one of the many examples of the undemocratic nature of the Ethiopian state. Yet, as a key ally in the Horn of Africa, western states continue to create alliances with the current government, turning a blind eye on issues of legitimacy, equality and human rights.
21. http://thinkafricapress.com/ethiopia/addis-ababa-sleeping-beauty-no-longer-student-protests-police-response-oromo?utm_content=buffer4f1c7&utm_medium=social&utm_source=facebook.com&utm_campaign=buffer (accessed 09/05/2014). This article was available in Ethiopia for three days until the government blocked its access.
22. http://www.hrw.org/news/2014/05/05/ethiopia-brutal-crackdown-protests (accessed 09/05/2014).
23. Selamawit Wondimu, 'Ignoring the Signs', in Zegueye Cherenet and Helawi Sewnet (eds) *op.cit.*, pp. 81-86.
24. Interviewees expressed their critical views on the billboards, and discussed to what extent they agreed with this development. They were asked the following questions: (1) How do you imagine Addis in 2020? (2) Do you think the current urban changes will benefit the poorest urban dwellers? (3) Do you think the billboards placed in major construction sites (in Kazantchis, Bole, etc) are for you or are they trying to communicate to other people? Who do you think they are for? What do you think about the use of English on the messages? (4) Do the billboards represent the real Addis Ababa in your opinion? Otherwise, what kind of city do you think they are trying to portray? Do the images remind you of any other city? (5) How do you think people in general react to the images of the new Addis shown in these billboards? (6) Do you think the images foster social cohesion or promote urban division between the different urban classes? (7) What changes would you like to see implemented to improve your city? What would make the city more equal and fair for everyone?
25. It's a racial divide inasmuch as the majority of western foreigners have access to better conditions than the locals. Still, the privileged class is composed by a local elite and foreigners of many different nationalities, including other African countries.

Creating Subjects

Citizenship in a Private City

PERSIS TARAPOREVALA

Nestled in the hills of western India, the 'private' city of Lavasa is under construction and is implicitly changing the discourse on citizenship in the democratic landscape of India. This paper defines a private city as one that is owned, developed and governed by a private company, and its focus is to understand the political repercussions of creating a city that is governed by a non–state entity, with special reference to citizenship.

The governing structure in India is essentially divided into three strata – national, state and local (urban/rural), with elected government bodies at each level, and in discussing issues of citizenship and disenfranchisement, this paper specifically refers to the local context. As Lavasa is only partially inhabited, the arguments presented are speculative. However, given the legal and social legitimacy the city enjoys in India, it is essential to pose questions and examine the potential fallouts of a privately governed city.

The thesis rests on the understanding that space is more than a 'geometric' or 'neutral' geographic concept – it is a political concept constructed by humans through their interactions with the space.[1] The governance structure of Lavasa is analysed through Ferguson's idea of 'depoliticisation' wherein the political aspects of a development project are ignored and lead to deeply entrenched political changes.[2]

Relevance of studying private cities in India

The McKinsey Global Institute (MGI)[3] report, titled 'India's Urban Awakening:

Building Inclusive Cities, Sustaining Economic Growth', attempts to spell out the demographic future of India.[4] It states that there will be an exodus from rural to urban areas on an unprecedented scale and that urban India does not have the capacity to absorb these people. The report begins with a series of figures to contextualise the importance of creating new cities in India. It says that by 2030 the estimated urban population will rise to 590 million, up from the 2008 estimate of 340 million. India has only 42 cities which can accommodate over a million people and the report predicts that the nation will need 68 such cities in total. These urban areas will generate 70% of new employment in India and will create class-based changes as the population of middle-class families will rise from 22 million to 91 million. Failure to use this window of opportunity would cause the already crowded cities of India to collapse under the weight of their expanding populations and increasing demand on resources. This would lead to a reduction in investment in India and negatively impact the growth of the economy. In short, increasing urbanisation is inevitable and could be used to improve social and economic conditions in India and a failure to create new cities to house and facilitate living space for the growing population would result in chaos.

The MGI report states that it is imperative to locate and start utilising USD 2.1 trillion to build these cities. It encourages increased private investment in or the privatisation of urban development and governance through more flexible forms of public-private partnerships (PPP). These are considered essential to create spaces of economic growth and to deal with the burgeoning urban population.

It is important to note the Indian context in which the city of Lavasa is being promulgated – where new cities are viewed as solutions to social and economic problems of existing urban spaces and where the private sector is encouraged to take on roles that were previously undertaken solely by governmental bodies. Legal and political structures have been created to allow private companies to own and govern cities such as Lavasa. The city is being developed with the direct support of the state-level government of Maharashtra and is promoted as a vehicle of sustainable and comprehensive socio-economic development.

The concept of the private city is new in India and only a couple of cities, such as Jamshedpur and Lavasa, follow this model. However this paper argues that India's Industrial Townships and Special Economic Zones (SEZ) also function like private cities and, as such, there is a sizable number of these privately governed spaces.[5] Furthermore, there are plans to create the Delhi–Mumbai corridor with cities that may utilise such forms of urban governance.[6] As privately governed cities are viewed as a strong solution to urban problems, it becomes increasingly important to understand the repercussions of allowing this form of government. While there has been a fair amount of discussion on the environmental impacts and issues of land rights that are associated, there is little written on the political ramifications of private cities.[7]

Notions of citizenship

Debates on democratic citizenship, including the formula utilised in the Indian Constitution, are based on the premise that humans are autonomous intelligent beings with the right to participate in the processes of their governance.[8] The legitimacy of democracy depends on the notion that government is "of the people, by the people and for the people"[9] and there is growing concern that the rise of neo–liberal economic policies, with an increased emphasis on private participation in traditional government roles, will affect various political aspects of life, including citizenship.[10]

In considering democratic governance, it is important to distinguish between 'active' and 'passive' citizenship. Active citizens take part in public deliberations on the personal and common good of people and are interested in who governs them.[11] They are concerned with which policies are adopted and why, and are prepared to exercise power themselves if needed. They receive benefits from the state but also decide how the benefits and burdens, rights and obligations are to be spread. All citizens have the legal right to engage in these processes.[12] Passive citizens, in contrast, are recipients of certain benefits of state[13] but are not involved in a political community and do not take part in decision–making aspects of citizenship.[14] This paper argues that the inhabitants of Lavasa are disenfranchised at the local level and through a series of processes are transformed into passive citizens.

The creation of a private city

Lavasa is being constructed by Lavasa Corporation Limited (LCL), a public limited company and a subsidiary of the Hindustan Construction Company, an infrastructure development firm that focuses predominantly on large-scale projects like nuclear and hydel power plants, highways and bridges.[15] It could be argued that the city has been designed like a large-scale infrastructure project, with service provision at its core and efficiency as the supporting structure. What is lacking is a deeper understanding and implementation of the political facets of democracy within the structure of governance in the city.

In order to better understand the process of depoliticisation in Lavasa, it is essential to understand the role and function of LCL. Lavasa is not formally categorised as a 'city' by the government of India, but as a "notified area under the Special Planning Authority" (SPA) which is the governance body of the area.[16] LCL has been officially designated by law as the SPA of Lavasa and thus the entire authorisation of the city rests on the existence and functioning of LCL. The SPA is primarily comprised of individuals chosen by the private company LCL and this leaves little room for civic engagement in local governance, disenfranchising the citizens of Lavasa and moving towards a form of passive citizenship.

In terms of creating a private city, this paper analyses three aspects of the process of creating Lavasa: (1) the structural plan and the local inhabitants, (2) changes in the Indian legal system to allow for the existence of privately governed cities, and (3) the marketing strategy in order to give indications of the form of citizenship experienced by its inhabitants.

The built environment and the people

The city is located amongst seven hills, on the backwaters of the Warasgaon Dam, an area with a concentration of 20 villages that were primarily concerned with subsistence farming.[17] The Lavasa master plan describes a city that covers 25,000 acres (approximately 100 square kilometres), however LCL currently owns only 12,500 acres (approximately 50 square kilometres).[18] The SPA is in dialogue with local villagers, who are primarily people from Scheduled Tribes (communities officially identified as indigenous people by the government of India)[19] as well as upper-caste Hindu communities and government institutions that own the remaining 12,500 acres of land.[20] The original population of the villages that constitute the 25,000 acres was estimated at 3,000 people in the 2001 Indian census.[21]

The main advantage of Lavasa, as put forth by LCL, is that it is a planned city so it can create enough diversity in terms of green zones, educational institutes, housing and economic centres to allow for a better quality of life than what is available in the over-populated, polluted and chaotic urban centres in India.[22] The master plan divides the city into four zones on the grounds of utility, namely 'town centre', 'commercial', 'luxury' and 'education centre'.[23] Each zone has its own architectural style. Only the first phase, which comprises apartments, small villas, water-based sports facilities and other tourism industries, is near completion. The structures are bright and are modelled on the Portofino Italian Riviera.[24]

Lavasa is marketed as a city where dealing with administrative systems will be easy, efficient and effective, and is viewed as respite from the otherwise inefficient and corrupt administrative systems that dot the urban areas of India.[25] What is extraordinary is that LCL has not publically released any document that explains what the exact functions of the SPA are, who the board consists of and on what merit they were chosen, thus the governing body limits the role and powers of the residents. This movement towards passive citizenship in Lavasa is partly a consequence of the wider 'crisis of legitimacy' – the phenomenon where faith in government institutions and structures is falling into disarray and the idea that corporate governance and global capital could be the solution to the problems of the state.[26]

The city prides itself for having the facilities of a gated community with private administration, security, efficiency, cleanliness, order and structure while not promoting the social inequalities that gated communities create, such as heightened social fragmentation and class-based inequalities.[27] The city has luxurious mansions but states that it also provides cheap housing for economically disadvantaged sections of society. The veracity of the affordable housing could not be determined as LCL did not share where the housing facilities were located in the city.[28] The company states that they provide free health check-ups and education to the villagers who resided in the notified area before the city was under construction.[29] The feedback from the villagers regarding these facilities has been mixed as the health check-ups were dismissed as unhelpful, however the school was appreciated by the local community. In order for Lavasa to live up to its claims of being inclusive, there would have to be a more visible attempt at providing quality infrastructure to the local community within the notified area. In terms of existing and planned structures that were available for the researcher to study and observe, Lavasa seemed to segregate people based on economic background and could potentially allow for an urban bubble that is disengaged from people who are not within a particular socio-economic spectrum.

Similar arguments are used when discussing the environment. LCL states that it is conscious of the need for a healthy ecology within the city and is working towards maintaining green zones and undertaking various plantation drives.[30] However, the SPA has received major critiques revolving around land rights and environmental degradation. First, the company was accused of not following due processes of law to create the city. Second, with reference to land rights, some of the villagers claimed that their land had been built on without their consent and that they were under constant physical threat and often lost access to water and resources because of their stand against the city.[31] Third, there were records of cheques bouncing and the use of underhand techniques to change the names on land records. Fourth, there were claims that some portions of land that LCL had bought were not allowed to be transferred for commercial purposes as they were portions that belonged to Scheduled Tribes or were reserved for redistribution to underprivileged sections of society.[32] Fifth, there were claims that LCL had quarried and constructed on more land than they were allowed to, which arose from the lack of several required permissions from the central government that had been provided for by the Maharashtra State government.[33] This barrage of criticism created the image of a city that was partially an unauthorised construction, built through methods of coercion and force, along with a disregard for the environment and the law of the land.

The National Alliance of Peoples Movements (NAPM), a human rights network in India, raised these issues with several government bodies, and the Union Ministry of Environment and Forests (MoEF) investigated the project. In November 2010 the MoEF found that LCL had violated several laws regarding land use and acquisition. It stated that the environmental violations that NAPM had pointed out were true, but other claims were neither ratified nor denied by the state. Rather than terminate the project, the government decided to present the company with the option of adhering to a new set of rules and paying a fine to the government.[34] In November 2011, LCL was granted conditional permission to continue with construction and has since moved ahead with the project.[35]

The legal construction

The question arises of how such a privately governed body exists within a democratic framework, and the answer lies in the Maharashtra Regional and Town Planning (MRTP) Act (1966). Since the mid–1990s, a series of changes to that particular law has facilitated the construction of a city owned and governed by a private company.

All planning and development of land in the state of Maharashtra is subject to the MRTP Act (1966). This act not only regulates land use but also constitutes regional planning boards and development authorities to undertake town planning schemes and construction activity. It provides guidelines that control who can undertake these roles and to whom they are accountable. According to the MRTP Act (1966), the Western Ghats were "afforestration zones" and, as such, no construction could take place. In 1996, however, a notification in the official gazette stated that tourist resorts/holiday homes/townships could be developed in Maharashtra by changing the green "afforestation zone" into a "hill station" area. The notification provided a set of "Special Regulations" which controlled the size and nature of the project. This included restrictions like no excavating of hills, no felling of forests, and set a limit of 2,000 hectares on the size of such hill stations. It stated that the area was to be governed by a Special Planning Authority, a planning and infrastructure building committee, and to be constructed predominantly by state government members, with the ultimate authority vested in the Collector of Pune.[36]

By May 2001, the LCL–designated area encompassing the 20 villages was declared appropriate to be changed from an "afforestation zone" to a "hill station" area.[37] The regulation controlling the size of a project was removed from the MRTP Act (1966). On 27 June 2001, the Maharashtra State government allowed a private company to invest in and start constructing this hill station.[38] This company was Lake City Corporation Private Limited, a precursor to Lavasa Corporation Limited.[39] The area was still under the control of the Collector of Pune. Between 2001 and 2004, the rules on land size and mining regulations were loosened and much more felling and construction was allowed in this previous green zone.[40] In June 2008, a notification stated that the request from LCL to form a Special Planning Authority was sanctioned.[41] This is when the right to govern Lavasa shifted from central or state government to a privately owned company. Lavasa's SPA was constituted by people chosen by LCL with the one exception of the Director of the Town Planning Department of Pune[42]. At this point Lavasa formally became a private city with a predominantly private governing body with limited accountability to its residents.

Marketing strategy

Through its website, advertorials and social media, Lavasa Corporation Limited projects the city as an example of utopian living, social inclusion and decentralisation of governance with a clear increase in power to the local governing body. This image is developed through LCL's marketing strategy. The publicity has been conducted through multiple routes, which include advertorial articles (advertisements in narrative form) in newspapers and through their social media outlets. The strategy was simple - to build a need for corporate governance in the urban sphere. LCL partnered with Bennett Coleman & Co. Limited, a mass media company that owns one of the largest circulating English newspapers in India, *The Times of India,* and that had bought a stake in LCL. *The Times of India* ran a series of articles called "Urban Longings" which provided opinions on the insufficiencies of urban infrastructure and continuously equated better urban living with greater access to resources.[43] The articles were distinctively quiet regarding improving political participation and associated civic aspects of urban life.

The website, Facebook page and Twitter account provide information on how LCL wants to depict the creation of Lavasa and the ethos it is trying to portray. Its methods aim at sparking interest in the project by distributing information about the construction and facilities, and utilising virtual spaces to exonerate the company from the allegations of irregularities in the legal procedures for creating the city; but it also uses these spaces to attempt to create a sense of community. Through competitions, quizzes and discussions on the problems of urban life and the need for global cities and infrastructure, LCL could build Lavasa's brand value, while also making people feel involved in the process of creating the city. Thousands of people participate in this sphere, ranging from land owners to holidaymakers. However, this seemingly open forum has inbuilt exclusionary systems. In addition to need for access to the internet, the online fora are only active in English and require users to have a working knowledge of the language, something the original inhabitants of the villages would have had little to no access to.

While the city is promoted as a form of decentralised governance, the SPA does not account for participation, citizenship rights, elections, representation or other aspects of governance that are normally associated with decentralisation, and it does not uphold the principle on which decentralisation is based, i.e. increasing participation and power of local people in their governing institutions. Thus, while the discourse of decentralisation is used to justify the construction of the city, it is not really an example of decentralisation. It is merely a delegation of power away from democratic institutions towards corporate entities

Political ramifications of Lavasa

The SPA has the right to take decisions about the governance and planning of the city. This includes infrastructure development, land usage, providing utility services of water and electricity, and undertaking permitted development activities such as tourism, shopping complexes, hotels, educational institutions, sports facilities and transportation and communication hubs for the city. All the activities undertaken by the SPA have to be in accordance with the regional plan for the area and the SPA does not have the right to relax any of the development control regulations. The SPA is accountable to the Town Planning Department of Pune and must submit plans to them for approval.[44] This raises a few questions, the most prominent being: if the Special Planning Authority is accountable to a government body (Town Planning, Pune), does that affect the rights of the residents, at the local level, at all?

Structure and functions of the Special Planning Authority

The answer lies as much in the role of the Special Planning Authority as in its structure. The SPA in Lavasa, conflates two roles: the role of a governing body and the role of a planning body. The former is supposed to administrate and govern an area, and is legitimised by the fact that it is elected and is accountable to the citizens who live in the area. The latter functions as a development authority and usually consists of appointed technocrats. Combining these roles, Lavasa's Special Planning Authority is simultaneously the governing and the planning body of the area. By taking on the function of governing Lavasa, the SPA has taken over the role of an elected body and directly affected democratic government at the local level, resulting in a dilution of citizenship and a form of governance that disempowers citizens.

Beyond its role, the SPA's structure disenfranchises people because Lavasa Corporation Limited chooses who constitutes the SPA.[45] The residents cannot vote for candidates for the SPA and cannot participate in government by standing for election. This loss of political rights is indicative of passive citizenship. Privileges are held by only a few and most residents no longer have the right to participate in the governance and functioning in their city, thereby becoming passive inhabitants.[46]

There is also a conflict of interest as the Special Planning Authority consists of people chosen by the private company that has business interests in the area. In the absence of accountability to the people, if the company chooses to administrate and govern so as to benefit the company over the needs of the residents, the voices and needs of the people might be sacrificed to corporate interest and profit.

Even though the SPA is accountable to one government official (the Director of the Town Planning Department of Pune), this does not counteract the processes of disempowerment it has unleashed on the people it governs. Thus the SPA, as it exists in Lavasa, turns citizens into subjects.

Effects of contract on citizenship

Since this is a study of citizenship it is imperative to analyse the relationship between the citizen and the company. It is too early to make claims about how citizenship is functioning within the city because Lavasa is still under construction and only partially inhabited. However, a critical study of the contract and lease agreement between Lavasa and its customers is useful to clarify the legal nature of the relationship between the citizen and the company.

The contract has multiple sections stating that Lavasa Corporation Limited, at all times, has the right to issue and change guidelines, fees and prices, and even to authorise changes in people's houses.[47] The lease also states that the customer acknowledges the legitimacy of the guidelines created by LCL and agrees to follow these guidelines, knowing that they can be changed whenever the SPA deems appropriate.[48]

According to this document, Lavasa Corporation Limited can transfer its authority to any nominee that the company sees fit. This third party or nominee will then undertake all the powers and functions attributed to LCL and, in turn, can charge customers fees, maintain and manage all facilities and amenities and also undertake functions related to the general management and supervision of the city.[49] The contract also states that the customer cannot object to the appointment of such nominees.[50]

The customer cannot sell or lease out the property without getting consent from and paying a fee to LCL.[51] LCL can terminate the contracts of individuals if they are termed a nuisance by other residents or by the company itself. There is no explanation of what constitutes being a nuisance.[52]

The city of Lavasa has no court. In case the customer decides to press charges against Lavasa Corporation Limited, the contract stipulates that this can only be done through processes of arbitration in Mumbai, that LCL has the right to choose the arbitrator, and that all proceedings have to be conducted in English.[53]

Thus, the rights of individuals are compromised at various levels under the rules in the contract created by LCL. It impinges on their ability to take decisions for themselves in and around their living spaces and forces them to obey all decisions taken by the company, all the while financing the city and the governing body. The company has sweeping rights over the lives of its citizens: it has the right to evict, to fine, to determine the use and design of land, and to change the governing body and the rules, while controlling the rights of people to object to these processes. Should the residents feel the need to seek justice, their right to protest and their chances of getting a fair hearing are compromised because the company has control of the location, the language and the choice of arbitrator in any legal action. The citizens' rights and responsibilities within Lavasa are thus 'legally' restricted and there is little space for a politically active citizenry that is interested and capable of providing an opinion on the city's laws, policies and governance structures.

The combined effects of the structure and role of the SPA and this contract and lease agreement are that residents lose the substantive aspects of citizenship including civil, social and political rights.[54] Citizens cannot vote for the governing body and they cannot protest against decisions taken by the city. The right of people to be recognised as autonomous citizens who can actively participate in the governing processes of their city is changed into a legal status where residents within the zone are 'customers' subject to the rules and authority of a private company.[55] This legal and contractual understanding of the role and status of the people of Lavasa makes them passive subjects and not active citizens.

Conclusion

The events unfolding in Lavasa are not unique to the city. The status of the SPA in Lavasa is based on policies regarding Special Economic Zone Authorities laid down in the Special Economic Zone Act (2005) and the policy on Industrial Townships, which allow private companies to own, develop and govern areas.[56] The Special Economic Zone Act could lead to similar outcomes – creating subjects rather than citizens, along with issues of lack of accountability and conflicts of interest – affecting the governance of these areas. In fact a person who resides in a Special Economic Zone is referred to as an 'occupant' not a citizen, thus creating a new ambiguous legal space. The role and rights of the citizen are known but the role and rights of the 'occupant' are not. Through this vagueness, citizens could play out passive, obedience-based roles and become subjects.

Although there are only a few cities that are discussed as private cities in India, there are numerous private cities in the form of Special Economic Zones. There are currently over 900 approved Special Economic Zones in India and more private cities are planned along the Delhi–Mumbai Industrial Corridor. These development enclaves are rationalised on the basis of economic growth while simultaneously undermining the democratic foundation of the nation and the sovereignty and rights of the citizen. With hundreds of these potentially privately governed areas dotting the nation, this model of urbanisation is swiftly replicating itself across the Indian landscape.

While the issues of environmental justice and land rights with regard to Lavasa have been discussed in the public sphere, the political changes have been left untouched. This process of depoliticisation,[57] or disregard of the political aspects of development projects, has created deeply entrenched political changes in the region and as India undertakes a movement to create more privately governed bodies, both as Special Economic Zones and Industrial Townships, it is important that these aspects of built environment be assessed. The argument in favour of private governance is rooted in ideas of enhanced access to resources and private cities as solutions to the over-burdened existing urban centres, and while these are worthwhile objectives they should not eclipse the democratic foundations on which the Indian nation functions.

In conclusion, this paper is the starting point of a discussion on the political ramifications of the privatisation of governance. A city like Lavasa, and the trend in urbanisation it reflects, concern much more than better facilities and streamlined hassle-free administration – it has deep consequences for governance, the quality of citizenship and democracy in India. It is a substantive move in a direction that will change the citizens of a sovereign and independent country into mere subjects. It is in the spirit of the Constitution as a tool of empowerment and laws and policies in India as a means of empowering the people that this thesis was written.

1. David Harvey, *Spaces of Global Capitalism: towards a theory of uneven geographical development* (London: Verso, 2006); David Harvey, *The condition of Post Modernity: an enquiry into the origins of cultural change* (Oxford: Blackwells Publishing, 1990); Henri Lefebvre, *Rhythmanalysis: space, time and everyday life* (London and New York: Continuum, 2004); Henri Lefebvre, *The production of space* (Oxford: Basil Blackwell, 1991); Christopher Tilley, *A Phenomenology of Landscape Places, Paths and Monuments* (Oxford: Berg Publishers, 1994); Swapna Banarjee-Guha, 'Shifting Cities: Urban Restructuring in Mumbai', *Economic and Political Weekly*, 37(2) 2002; Swapna Banarjee-Guha, 'Space Relations of Capital and Significance of New Economic Enclaves: SEZs in India, *Economic and Political Weekly*, 43(47) 2008.
2. James Ferguson, *The anti-politics machine: "development," depoliticization, and bureaucratic power in Lesotho* (Cambridge: Cambridge University Press, 1990).
3. McKinsey and Company Inc. is a global management consultancy in the UK, which works with government bodies, private companies and other organisations on development concerns. While McKinsey has no *stated* ideological leaning they seek pro-private and pro-market solutions. The McKinsey Global Institute is affiliated with the management firm.
4. Shirish Sankhe et al., 'India's Urban Awakening: Building Inclusive Cities, Sustaining Economic Growth'(McKinsey Global Institute, 2010), http://www.mckinsey.com/insights/urbanization/urban_awakening_in_india.
5. R.N. Bhaskar, 'The New Cities Of India', *Forbes India: Business.in.*, 30 November 2010, http://business.in.com/printcontent/19662 (accessed December 2010).
6. J. Fontanella-Khan, 'India, the "nation of villages" faces an urban future', *Financial Times, Future of Cities Special*, 9 September 2009, http://www.ft.com/cms/s/0/9670af02-c50f-11df-b785-00144feab49a.html (accessed 18/12/10).
7. Ayona Datta, 'India's ecocity? Environment, urbanisation, and mobility in the making of Lavasa', *Environment and Planning C: Government and Policy* 30(6) 2012, pp. 982–996; Kumar Sambhav Shrivastava and Arnab Pratim Dutta, *Lavasa Exposed*, Down To Earth (1–15 April 2011), http://www.downtoearth.org.in/content/lavasa-exposed; Akshay Deshmane,

Who is Monitoring Lavasa, Down to Earth (31 August, 2013), http://www.downtoearth.org.in/content/who-monitoring-lavasa; Sakshi C. Dasgupta, *Lavasa Above the Law*, Down to Earth (15 March 2011) http://www.downtoearth.org.in/content/lavasa-above-law

8. Rajeev Bhargava, *Politics and ethics of the Indian Constitution* (New Delhi: Oxford University Press, 2009); Sunil Khilnani, 'Indian Constitution and Democracy' in Eswaran Sridharan and R. Sudarshan Zoya Hasan, *India's living constitution: ideas, practices, controversies* (London: Anthem Press, 2005).
9. Durga Das Basu, *Introduction to the Constitution of India* (Columbia, Mo: South Asia Books, 1984).
10. R. Mohanty and R. Tandan, 'Introduction: Identity, Exclusion, Inclusion: Issues in Participatory Citizenship' in R. Mohanty and R. Tandon (eds), *Participatory Citizenship: Identity, Exclusion, Inclusion* (New Delhi: Sage Publications, 2006).
11. Michael Walzer, *Obligations: Essays on Disobedience, War, and Citizenship* (Cambridge, Mass: Harvard University Press, 1970).
12. Bhargava, *op.cit.*, 'Introduction'.
13. Rajeev Bhargava and Helmut Reifeld, *Civil society, public sphere and citizenship: dialogues and perceptions* (London: Sage, 2005).
14. Bhargava and Reifeld, *ibid.*
15. While 65% of the company is owned by the real estate subsidiary of Hindustan Construction Company (HCC) called HCC Real Estate Ltd., it is also partially owned by Avantha Group, Venkateshwara Hatcheries, Mr Vithal Maniar, Hincon Holdings Limited, Bennett Coleman & Co. Limited (The Times Group) and Axis Bank Limited.
16. Security and Exchange Board of India (SEBI), Lavasa Corporation Limited, *Red Herring Draft*, 2010.
17. Lavharde, Verge, Bhode, Pathershet, Bebatmal, Palase, Admal, Padalghar, Dasave, Wadavali, Sakhari, Bhoini, Mugaon, Koloshi, Ugavali, Dhamanhol and Gadgale from Mulshi district; Mose Bk, Saiv Bk and Varasgaon from Velhe taluka.
18. SEBI, *op.cit.*
19. Constitution of India 73rd Amendment, article 342, 1992; Interim Report of the People's Commission of Inquiry, 20 April 2009, http://www.indiaenvironmentportal.org.in/files/Interim%20Report%20Apr%2020-2009.pdf.
20. Interim Report, *ibid*; Personal interview with Lavasa City Manager Scott Wrighton, 18/08/10.
21. *ibid.*
22. Personal interview, *ibid*; Personal interview with Lavasa Senior Vice President Marketing Anuradha Paraskar, 08/10/10.
23. Lavasa Corporation Limited, 'Electronic Brochure, Lavasa City', http://www.lavasa.com/high/files/Lavasa_EBrochure.pdf (accessed 2010); Personal interview with Lavasa Senior Manager Urban Design Anubandh Hambarde, 13/08/10.
24. *ibid.*
25. *ibid.*
26. John Gaventa, 'Perspectives on Participation and Citizenship' in R. Mohanty and R Tandon (eds), *op.cit*; Colin Crouch, *Post Democracy* (London: Polity Press, 2004); R. Kothari, *Politics in India* (New Delhi: Orient BlackSwan, 2008); Keith Faulks, *Citizenship* (Oxford: Routledge, 2000); Walzer, *op.cit.*
27. S.M. Low, 'The edge and the center: Gated communities and the discourse of urban fear', *American Anthropologist*, 103(1) 2001, pp. 45–58.

28. Lavasa Corporation Limited, 'Electronic Brochure, Lavasa City', *op.cit*; Personal interview with Lavasa Senior Manager Urban Design Anubandh Hambarde 13/08/10; Personal interview with Lavasa Senior Vice President Marketing Anuradha Paraskar, 08/10/10.
29. *ibid.*
30. *ibid.*
31. Interim Report, *op.cit*; Personal interviews with villagers in the notified area, 15 August – 10 September 2010.
32. *ibid.*
33. *ibid.*
34. Ministry of Environment and Forests, 'Final Directions: Show Cause Notice Section 5 of Environment (Protection) Act 1986 for violation of the provisions of Environment Assessment Impact Notification 1994 as amended 2004 and 2006 by M/s Lavasa Corporation Limited, Vikroli (Mumbai: Government of India, 2011).
35. http://moef.nic.in/downloads/public-information/Lavasa_order_Ph_1.pdf.
36. The department and person in charge of all civil and administrative activities at the city level, http://www.puneonline.in/Administration/Local-Government.aspx.
37. These changes were made between the department of urban development, town planning and the state environment department. Notification No. TPS – 1800/1004/CR-106/I/2000/UD-13.
38. Notification No. TPS-1800/1004/C.R. 106-1/2000/UD-13.
39. This was the previous name of LCL. It started as Pearly Blue Lake Resorts Private Limited in the year 2000 and finally came to be LCL in 2004.
40. SEBI, *op.cit.*
41. Notification No. TPS-1808/449/CR-93/08/UD-13.
42. Pune is the closest city to Lavasa.
43. http://www.lavasafuturecities.com/urban_longings.html.
44. SEBI, *op.cit*; MRTP Act (1966).
45. SEBI, *op.cit.*
46. Faulks, *op.cit.*
47. The Agreement to lease of lot-cum Agreement for Sale of Villa (sections 5.5, 13.1-3, 16.4); The Agreement to lease of lot-cum Agreement for Sale of Villa (section 24.s).
48. The Agreement to lease of lot-cum Agreement for Sale of Villa (sections 5.5, 13.1-3, 16.4).
49. The Agreement to lease of lot-cum Agreement for Sale of Villa (section 12, 16.3, 38).
50. The Agreement to lease of lot-cum Agreement for Sale of Villa (section 12, 16.3, 38).
51. The Agreement to lease of lot-cum Agreement for Sale of Villa (section 20.1, 22.1).
52. The Agreement to lease of lot-cum Agreement for Sale of Villa (section 29.3.i, 29.3.iv).
53. The Agreement to lease of lot-cum Agreement for Sale of Villa (section 26).
54. James Holston and Arjun Appadurai, 'Cities and Citizenship', *Public Culture* 8(2) 1996.
55. Bhargava, (2009) *op.cit*; Khilnani, *op.cit.*, p. 67; The Agreement to lease of lot-cum Agreement for Sale of Villa, *op.cit.*
56. Ministry of Law and Justice (Legislative Department), 'The Special Economic Zone Act, 2005', in *The Gazette of India* (New Delhi: Government of India, 2005).
57. Ferguson, *op.cit.*

London's Debt To Slavery

KATE DONINGTON & NICOLAS DRAPER

It has been understood, even within the United Kingdom, that London was essential to the financial structure of British colonial slavery. The reciprocal question, how important was colonial slavery to London, has been obscured by the density of London's history, its role as capital city – as centre of the court, of government, of commerce, of the law, of public life – and its explosive growth (especially south of the river) in the 19th century, all combining to render the impacts of slavery difficult to trace or muddled. In the absence of an articulated empirical data set, the generally accepted argument amongst academics and others shaping the official narratives of London has suggested that slavery is not relevant to understanding the history of London or even, quite remarkably, of the City.

In stark contrast, a dissenting discourse outside dominant cultural institutions, including universities, has existed which says that London was built on the work and blood of slaves.

The two discourses at present have no common forum and no common body of evidence. Despite the 2007 'London, sugar and slavery' exhibition at the Museum of the Docklands and the Fen Court memorial unveiled in 2008, the standard synoptic histories of both London and the City of London are completely silent on slavery.

A small team at University College London applied for and received an ESRC research grant that allowed us the time in the British National Archives in Kew to investigate the records of the Slave Compensation Commissioners and other associated documents. The Slave Compensation Commissioners' documents reveal one of the UK's most remarkable cultural and also financial facts: when slavery was 'abolished', thousands of absentee slave-owners in Britain, as well as in the Caribbean, received compensation for the 'loss' of their 'property in enslaved people. Between 1834 and 1838, the British state paid £20 million to the colonial slave-owners, a sum equivalent to 40% of total annual government expenditure in the 1830s.[1] The compensation would be worth some £16 billion in today's money. The 800,000 enslaved people themselves received nothing.

This database, which reveals all the recipients of this compensation, including British Prime Minister David Cameron's family, is now accessible to everyone via www.ucl.ac.uk/lbs. As well as identifying the absentee slave-owners, the database records hundreds of specific 'legacies' of slave-owners in British politics, business, the built environment, culture, philanthropy and intellectual traditions. For London, these 'fruits' of slavery range from the foundation of mercantile dynasties to the demand that sustained new areas of urban development (notably in Marylebone and Bloomsbury), from the establishment of new financial institutions to the founding of philanthropic bodies, from cultural accumulation to the funding of new educational institutions such as King's College.

Our aim is certainly not to celebrate the slave-owners and their legacies but rather to make visible the presence of slavery in many areas of London life – past and present today.

George Hibbert

Almost 1,000 individual slave-owners and 150 merchant firms named in the database lived or operated in London. London was the biggest single concentration of both *rentier* and mercantile slave-ownership in the British Empire. George Hibbert had vast interests in both. By virtue of his political role as a pro-slavery advocate he is a striking example of the connections of slavery to London. But he is not an isolated figure. Instead, he is representative of a whole class of absentee slave-owners and colonial merchants who transmitted the profits of slavery into the heart of the capital. Researcher Kate Donington has developed the following walk, which anyone in central London can undertake with this guide.

It is possible to get a glimpse through this one individual, George Hibbert, of how London was and remains inextricably entangled with the European enslavement of Africans and the European colonisation of Africa and the Americas.

Slavery & London: A Guided Walk

This guide is designed to take you on a walk through the London of George Hibbert MP (1757–1837). Hibbert was a West India merchant, a ship-, dock-, plantation- and slave-owner. He was also a leading political supporter of slavery. He lived and worked in London and traces of his presence can be found across the capital, from Bloomsbury to the City of London, and from the West India Docks to Clapham Common. The Hibbert family owned, managed and financed plantations in Jamaica and some of them lived on the island.

This guide focuses on the metropolitan branch of the Hibbert family in order to explore the links between London and slavery. The impact of slavery is highly visible in the Caribbean but its influence on Britain has been less well documented. This guide focuses solely on the sites associated with slave ownership as opposed to abolitionism – this is a deliberate decision. Slavery was part of the fabric of Britain. The exploitation and suffering endured by enslaved Africans enabled Europeans to consume desirable tropical commodities, produce profits, expand markets, build an empire and develop the imperial centre. Slave-ownership was a common and unremarkable way of life for 250 years. Slave-owners occupied positions of political, financial, social and cultural power. They invested heavily across London in a variety of institutions. In highlighting this history, this guide aims to raise awareness of some of the ways in which slavery permeated the historical geography of London, helping to form the metropolis we know today.

City of London Map

overleaf: Gardener Map of London, 1827, Senate House Library, London

Regent Canal
Towing Path
Frog Lane
City Road
Wenlock Cott.
London Mills
H O X T O N
Whitmore Pl.
Orchard Pl.
Crescent Pl.
Old Street
Artillery Ground
Bunhill Fields Burial Ground
Finsbury Circus
West Smithfield
Charter House
Holborn Hill
Fleet Street
Cheapside
Cornhill
Tower
St. Catherine
Goodmans Fields
Blackfriars
London Bridge
Borough Road
Westminster Road
Trinity Church
Great George St.
Toll Gate
R
T
H

Providence Row
Cambridge Ter.
Acton Lock
Hackney Foot Path Br.
Ash Grove
Clifton
Lark Row
Wolverley Pl.
Cambridge Pl.
Fish Pond
Three Colts Tea Gardens &c
Barn Place
Oldford Road
Bonners Hall Br.
Kings Arms Row
Bishop Bonners Hall
Lock
Oldford Road Bridge
Globe Cottage
Globe Lane
The Drift Way (a Foot Path)
Turnpike
Bearbinder Lane
GLOBE TOWN
Old Bethnal Green Road
Patriot Sq.
Patriot R.
Ponds
Twig Folly
Church
Towing Path
Regents Canal
Fly Pl.
Regent Pl.
Mile End Lock
Jews Bur.
Wharfs
York Pl.
Hough P. H.
Bow Road
Rope Walk
Maritime Alms House
Cow Houses
Bow Common
Foot Path
Stepney Foot Path
Wades Pl.
Jews Burial Ground
Belle Vue Pl.
Fullers Alms Ho.
Trinity Chap.
Crown R.
Johnsons Lock
Chambers S.
Trafalgar Square
Stepney Green
Mans Row
Easmount Terr.
Stepney
Rhodes Well Com.
Dows Corner
Eastfield Street
Kings Palace
Alms Ho.
John Str.
Lock
Mary St.
LIME
Copenhagen
Limehouse
THE COMMERCIAL ROAD
Mercers Pl.
Roberts T.
Devonport St.
James Place
Gas Works
Basin
Rope W.
St. Anns Ch.
East India
Cornwall St.
Fields
Rope Walk
DOCK
LONDON DOCK
Basin
Mill Yard
Shadwell Dock
Stone Stairs
Globe Stairs
Entrance of the Regents Canal
Limehouse Bridge Dock
Dukes Shore
Limehouse Dock
The Pageants
Limehouse Hole Stairs
New Crane Stairs
King and Queen Stairs
Cuckolds Point
Queens Wharf
Brewery
Morris's Causeway
Greenland Stairs
Mill Wall Stairs
THE POOL
GRAND SURREY OUTER DOCK
Island
Rotherhithe
Church Stairs
King Stairs
Princes Stairs
Red Bed
GRAND SURREY INNER DOCK
Foot Bt.
Ship Yard
Kings Tobacco Grounds
Randalls Rents
Greenland Dock
Bedford Pl.
Claremont Place
Colours Place
Work Ho.
Seven Islands
Augusta Pl.
THE
THAMES
ROTHERHITHE
LIMEHOUSE

George Hibbert
right: George Hibbert, by Sir Thomas Lawrence, oil on canvas, 1811, Museum of London

Portland Place, W1B 1QE
above: View of Portland Place, by anon., aquatint on paper, c.1814 , City of London, London Metropolitan Archive

George and Elizabeth Hibbert lived at 38 Portland Place, now 78–81. The family also owned a large residence on the north side of Clapham Common which housed George's botanical collection. They had 14 children, with one son dying in infancy. Portland Place was home to a number of absentee West Indian planters and their families. This provided the Hibberts with an immediate business and social circle. Close to the City of London where George worked, it was fashionable, expensive and spacious. The house was adorned with George's valuable collection of books and art.

George Hibbert was an avid collector and he also dealt in art. Using the profits generated through his involvement with the West Indian plantation economy, he spent thousands of pounds on improving his collections. His book collection included Martin Luther's own translated and signed German

Bible as well as various rare vellum editions. In 1829 the sale of George Hibbert's book collection lasted 42 days with 40,000 volumes changing hands. The final sales' estimate reached £23,000. In the same year he also sold some of his art collection, including works by Rubens, Rembrandt and Turner. This money helped him to renovate his country house at Munden, Hertfordshire.

St George's Bloomsbury, Bloomsbury Way, WC1A 2SA
left: View of St George's Bloomsbury, by George Shepherd, watercolour on paper, 1811, City of London, London Metropolitan Archives

George Hibbert and Elizabeth Fonnereau were married at St George's Bloomsbury in 1784. Elizabeth came from a well-connected Huguenot family; her father was Philip Fonnereau, an MP and a Director of the Bank of England. Elizabeth's relations were also involved with the slavery business. Her sister Mary-Ann married into the Thellusson family, some of whom were involved in the West Indies. The family had links to London's biggest slave trading firm, Camden, Calvert & King. Marriage brought with it the promise of land and property. Elizabeth was due to inherit Munden House in Hertfordshire from her uncle, Rogers Parker. George remodelled the house in 1829 when the couple came into possession of the property. Munden is still the residence of the Holland-Hibbert family today. The marriage represented the merging of religious, financial and mercantile interests. However, Hibbert's private letters reveal a deep affection for his wife and children. He spent some of his leisure time writing plays and poetry for his family.

Ibbotson Hotel, Vere Street, W1G 0DJ
overleaf: Debenhams department store is now situated on the former site of the Ibbotson Hotel, photograph by Trenton Oldfield, 2014

George Hibbert was a business associate of the Jamaican planter Simon Taylor, who was thought to be the richest man on the island. They corresponded for two decades, discussing sugar duties, the Haitian Revolution, and the threat of abolition. Taylor lived in Jamaica but when he was in London he had his letters delivered to the Ibbotson Hotel. The Ibbotson was a favourite West Indian haunt and the Society of West Indian Planters and Merchants sometimes met here to discuss the political and economic issues of the day.

DEBENHAMS
DEBENHAMS
DEBENHAMS

British Museum, 96 Euston Road, NW1 2DB
bottom left: British Museum, photograph by Trenton Oldfield, 2014

George Hibbert not only sat for portraits by both John Hoppner and Sir Thomas Lawrence, but was also an enthusiastic collector and dealer. He sometimes worked in partnership with fellow West Indian slave-owner and art collector Sir Simon Haughton Clarke. His collection included prints by Leonardo da Vinci, Rembrandt van Rijn, Paul Rubens and Adam Elsheimer. Prints from his collection can be found at both the British Museum, London, and the Fitzwilliam Museum, Cambridge. In 1809 he sold off 10,000 items from his collection; the sale lasted 14 days.

Freemason's Shakespeare Lodge, Covent Garden Piazza, WC2E 9DD
above: View of Covent Garden, by Thomas Sandby, engraver Edward Rooker, engraving on paper, 1777 , City of London, London Metropolitan Archives

Hibbert became a Freemason in 1796 and resigned his position in 1807. Membership of the Freemasons offered him access to their social,

THE LONDON INSTITUTION,
FOR THE ADVANCEMENT OF LITERATURE, AND THE
FOUNDED BY SUBSCRIPTION A.D. 1805,
DIFFUSION OF USEFUL AND POLITE KNOWLEDGE;
by THE RIGHT HON. SAMUEL BIRCH, ALDERMAN, and then LORD MAYOR OF LONDON.

The Figures by T. Rowlandson — Architecture by J. Shephard
Engraved by R. Reeves
PATRIOTIC DINNER.
PATRIOTISCHE MAALTYD.

cultural, political and financial networks of influence. From 1773 the Shakespeare Lodge was located in the Shakespeare Tavern on Covent Garden Piazza, an area well-known for its vice and excess. *Harris's List of Covent Garden Ladies*, published between 1757 and 1795, was a 'directory' of prostitutes living and working in the Covent Garden area. The document stands as testimony to the scale of misery concentrated in London over the period.

London Institution, Finsbury Circus, EC2M 7AB
top left: The London Institution, 1819, City of London, London Metropolitan Archive

The London Institution was designed to raise standards in science and the arts among "the middling sort". Its founder members included a number of West India merchants and absentee planters. The President Francis Baring and four Vice-Presidents George Hibbert, Beeston Long, Richard Neave and John Julius Angerstein were associated with the slavery business. Henry Thornton, a prominent abolitionist was a manager for the institution.

London Tavern, Bishopsgate, EC2M
bottom left: The London Tavern, 1809, City of London, London Metropolitan Archive

The London Tavern was an important social space for the West India interest in London. The Society of West Indian Planters and Merchants met here regularly. As Chairman of the society, Hibbert would have been very familiar with the Tavern. It was from here that William Innes delivered a speech in 1789 entitled "The slave trade indispensable" in refutation of William Wilberforce's first parliamentary move to end the slave trade.

Guildhall, Gresham St, EC2V 7HH
overleaf: Guildhall, photograph by Trenton Oldfield, 2014

In 1798 George became Alderman of Bridge Within Ward in the City of London. He resigned in 1803 with a view to entering parliament and achieved this in 1806, just in time to oppose Wilberforce in parliament during the slave trade abolition

debates. The aldermen were drawn from London's financial and mercantile elite. Many of them supported the slave trade, for example in 1789 Alderman Newnham complained to parliament that London would be a scene of ruin if the trade were to end. Newnham's portrait is on display in the Guildhall Art Gallery.

Bank of England, Threadneedle Street, EC2R 8AH
overleaf: The Bank of England, M W Barre

Samuel Hibbert, George's nephew and partner in the Hibbert merchant house, was one of a number of Directors of the Bank of England with links to slavery: Philip Fonnereau, Richard Neave, Samuel Bosanquet, William Manning and Beeston Long. At the end of British colonial slavery the government paid the slave–owners £20,000,000 in compensation. Recipients had to visit the National Debt Office of the Bank of England to sign for and receive these payments.

Mincing Lane, EC3R
right: Commercial House on Mincing Lane, City of London, London Metropolitan Archive

Mincing Lane was a centre of commerce during the period. George Hibbert's counting house was close to that of his friends Francis Baring and John Julius Angerstein, the father of Lloyd's. The three men represented three key

Plate V

LONDON.

The Custom House, burnt down. Feb.y 12, 1814.

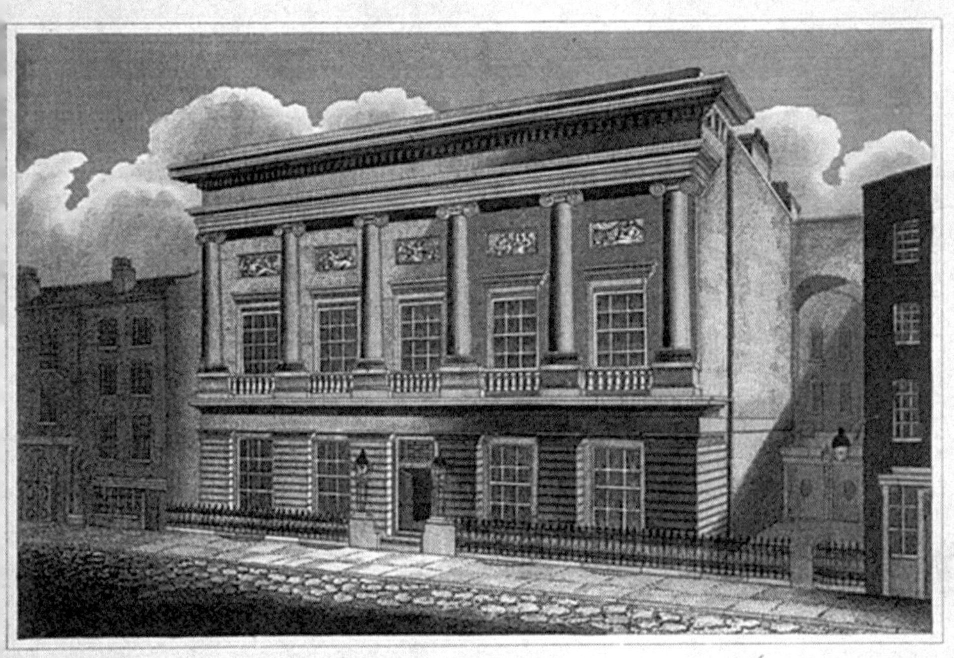

Commercial Hall, Mincing-lane, now used as a Custom House.

London, Published as the Act directs May 28, 18[illegible] by G. Jones

areas of the slavery business: mercantile, finance and insurance. Angerstein underwrote insurance taken out on both enslaved people and Caribbean produce like sugar. The insurance industry flourished as goods and people were moved across the globe. The enslaved often resisted their transportation making the journey treacherous. To encourage investment in what was a risky trade, insurance was offered as security.

Lower Thames Street, Custom House, Sugar Quay, EC3R 6DU
above: View of Custom House from the Thames, 1799, City of London, London Metropolitan Archive

When sugar arrived at the Port of London a duty was paid to the government at Custom House. The sugar duties represented a significant proportion of the revenue raised from colonial commodities. The payment of duties gave the West India interest the ear of the government. The Hibbert family owned private quays close to Custom House on Lower Thames Street prior to the opening of the West India Docks in 1802.

Acknowledgements

This guide was researched by Katie Donington, Research Associate for the Legacies of British Slave-ownership project at UCL. The research was made possible by the 'The Legacies of British Slave-ownership' project at UCL, which is funded by the ESRC. The guide has been paid for by the Beacon Fund at UCL. Images have been supplied by the London Metropolitan Archive, Museum of London, National Portrait Gallery, Senate House Library, Trenton Oldfield and David Perdue. Additional information has been supplied by Nick Hibbert Steele.

Additional resources

David Beck Ryden, *West Indian Slavery and British Abolition 1783–1807.*
Nicholas Draper, *The Price of Emancipation: Slave-Ownership, Compensation and British Society at the End of Slavery.*
David Hancock, *Citizens of the World: London Merchants and the Integration of the British Atlantic Community, 1735–1785.*
Kenneth Morgan, *Slavery, Atlantic Trade and the British Economy 1660–1800.*
Christer Petley, *Slaveholders in Jamaica: Colonial Society and Culture During the Era of Abolition.*
Eric Williams, *Capitalism and Slavery.*
'London, Sugar, Slavery' at the Museum of London in Docklands. A permanent exhibition exploring London's relationship to slavery.
Website by Nick Hibbert Steele which explores the Hibbert family and their involvement in Caribbean slavery, http://www.georgehibbert.com/.
Legacies of British Slave-ownership website, http://www.ucl.ac.uk/lbs/.

Why Are Our People Cleaners?

AWQAPUMA YAYRA COLQUE

In order for us to accurately explain what is happening today we must put it in context. We must look to the past to see how it shapes our present-day reality. We did not become exploited cleaners overnight. This is a result of hundreds of years of colonialism in all its forms; the most obvious here being the economic aspect of capitalism.

How did we end up here as migrants in the first place? Did we leave our homeland by choice? No! We were forced to come here. The police and military of governments across our land have scared us out of our ancestral homes, our family's lives and onto planes to Europe. And these governments are colonial governments, made up of criollos, the descendants of the Europeans who invaded our continent in 1492. How much has really changed?

Some of us were so poor back home that we had to leave, with the hope that we could find a better life here, a life where paying the bills and putting food on the table is not a heavy rock weighing you down, but a simple task in life. Something easy, something normal. Instead, we found ourselves still finding those things a challenge. Our qualifications, which we worked so hard to gain, back home, had to be thrown away and instead of being doctors or nurses, we are now cleaning the shit and piss of people training to be doctors or nurses. Our skills in law, journalism and sports are pushed aside to clean the buildings of institutions that treat us as if we are invisible and irrelevant. Our teaching talents are rendered obsolete; our pen must be replaced by a mop, our books are replaced by a bucket.

Why did we find it so hard economically back home? Why were we so poor? The usual answer is 'multinational companies'. But the fact is that these multinational companies have a nationality, an identity, they are all European.

There are British companies looting our land right this second. There are Spanish companies stealing our resources right this moment. There are French, German, Italian, Portuguese, Dutch, Russian companies on our land right now, taking the natural wealth out of our land and out of our hands.

These companies cannot be separated from those companies of the US and Canada, because who runs those companies? The European settlers of those two colonial states. Where is all the profit going? To Europeans in Europe and Europeans who have settled on our land, on the bones of our ancestors, on the blood of our *abuelos*. The only people who benefit from the current system of colonialism are the descendants of the first colonisers; that is why when we look at the ruling elite of all of our countries we see European faces looking back at us. If we were to put a large group of Spanish people living in Spain into a room as well as Santos and his family, Peña Nieto and his family, Piñera and his family, not one of these colonial presidents would stick out, as they are Spanish themselves. How much has really changed in the past 500 years if we are not being allowed to govern ourselves?

Colonialism never ended. It began in 1492 and it is still going strong in 2013. We had to leave our land because the criollos made it impossible for us to live there. Now we are here, as migrants, as cleaners, facing white supremacy in the workplace and all other aspects of society.

The British Museum exploits our people while making money from the artefacts they have stolen from all the people they have colonised around the world. We are the descendants of the Muisca, the people who created beautiful golden figurines – the figurines that are in the British Museum right now. They belong to us. That is our legacy, our heritage, our pride. Yet the closest we get to them is through a glass window that our people must clean.

I want to be clear; I am not undermining the role of cleaners in society. Cleaners are essential for the organisation of a city and should be valued. While this is something the people here cannot seem to grasp, our ancestors understood it perfectly. Prior to the European invasion, there were hundreds of cleaners in Tenochtitlan, keeping the city pristine, clearing the pavements so people could get to restaurants, barbers and other places without a problem. Unlike here, where education is not easily accessible for those who are on a cleaner's salary, our people made education mandatory for all.

Cleaners were not marginalised but a part of society, something vital to the function of our great civilisations, and were treated as such. Here in Europe, in this day and age, it is a whole different story. As our *Amauta* (teacher) Olin Tezcatlipoca has said to us:

The people who are now cleaners are people who could have been doctors, teachers, engineers, and other professionals, if not for colonialism that has robbed them of the wealth of their lands. Our people have proven themselves to be creators of civilisations, builders of large cities, architects of beautiful buildings, doctors who invented medical procedures and who developed medicines, and philosophers, poets and mathematicians. All of our possible genius has been stolen from us by the colonial and genocidal hands of the Europeans.[1]

We must begin to effectively resist the conditions that are being imposed on us. We must realise that we do not only deserve holiday pay, sick pay and better working conditions. We also deserve reparations and restitution for everything that has and is being stolen from our land and our people. We deserve and must start demanding an end to colonialism on our land because it is the ongoing colonial system that has put us in this place.

This will not happen overnight. In order to achieve decolonisation and true liberation for ourselves, education is necessary; self-education on our ancestors, our civilisations, our heritage of creative genius and the real reason we find ourselves in the mess we are in today. This education must be passed down to children, grandchildren, nieces, nephews, everyone. Education is crucial to liberation.

We may be exploited cleaners for now, but we cannot let ourselves be defined as that. Our ancestors were great warriors who defended their lives and our land from the invaders; we can be the same, until one day when we no longer have to say goodbye to our homelands, our friends and family to come to a European city and be cleaners. Our current situation is only a tiny part of millennia of mind-blowing achievements.

Throw those shoulders back, Nican Tlaca. We are a people of dignity, honour and strength. Hold your heads high, Nican Tlaca. Our liberation will come as long as we fight for it. Let us be more like the warriors that we descend from and make it happen sooner rather than later.

1. http://mexicamovement.blogspot.co.uk/2014/08/stolen-genius.html.

UK Securitisation Targeting 'Suspect Communities'

LES LEVIDOW & SALEH MAMON (CAMPACC)[1]

Governments across the world have put into place a strategy of 'securitisation' whereby potentially all societal conflicts are portrayed as threats of disorder or malign enemies. 'Security measures' have become pervasive, supposedly to protect the public from threats such as 'terrorism', 'extremism' and 'suspicious behaviour'. These threats are defined so broadly and vaguely as to encompass potentially any social or political activity. Following the high-profile 'war on terror' since September 2001, the strategy normalises special powers to intimidate, punish and criminalise individuals.

In the name of security, entire communities have been turned into suspects – subjected to surveillance, preventative measures, restrictions on movement, secret evidence and punishment without trial. Through this global securitisation strategy, socio-political conflicts have been depoliticised and turned into technical-legal tasks of preventing disorder. This strategy disciplines society by imposing compliance and silencing dissent.

UK securitisation initiatives have targeted urban populations for several reasons. Cities host high-profile events, such as intergovernmental conferences or the Olympics, which provide opportunities for protests to gain mass-media coverage. As a global city, London links state agencies with multinational companies, alongside migrant communities which have fled from oppressive regimes allied with the UK, as well as Muslim diaspora communities hostile to UK military intervention in Muslim countries. Their protests can embarrass or even impede the UK's global alliances, so 'security' measures aim to intimidate and deter dissent against UK foreign policy.

'Anti–terror' powers were legislated supposedly to protect the public from violence, yet the powers have been increasingly used to target political dissent. An example was the 2003 Defence & Security Equipment International (DSEI) arms fair in London's Docklands, where protesters were detained under anti–terror powers. It is less well known that such powers routinely target migrant–diaspora and Muslim communities.

Securitisation activities have been increasingly privatised by outsourcing functions that were previously carried out by state agencies. The British–Danish company G4S was designated as "official provider of security and cash services" for London's 2012 Olympics; the government outsourced responsibility and even made itself dependent on G4S for training police. Privatisation impedes efforts to monitor the abuse of state powers, as well as to hold individuals and companies to account.

Shortly before the 2012 London Olympics, military equipment was deployed to heighten public fear. The Ministry of Defence (MoD) sought to put missiles on the roofs of housing estates in East London, supposedly to protect the Olympics from terrorist attacks. The High Court ruled that the MoD had legal powers to site missiles wherever necessary for 'national security' as defined and judged by the government. Such operations are psychological warfare – frightening us in the name of protecting us – while protecting state–corporate alliances from protest.

What are the implicit political aims of 'security' measures? How can those aims be undermined? What are the prospects for collective resistance? After presenting critical perspectives on securitisation, this article analyses how such UK strategies target migrants and Muslims as "suspect communities", as well as how their response opens up prospects to develop broader communities of resistance.

Securitisation: critical perspectives

'Security threats' have a long history as a pretext for foreign aggression and domestic repression, especially by the British state[2]. After World War II, the US government formalised a doctrine of 'national security', exaggerating its own vulnerability to justify strategies for western global domination.[3] National liberation movements were demonised as proxies for 'the communist threat' in the Cold War context. Across the world, US–led alliances have supported regimes suppressing dissent through torture, disappearances and killings. 'National security' more generally has served an agenda to extend global control, to expand resource extraction, to demonise rival forces, to pre–empt political debate, and to silence dissent.

Since the 1990s, a broader securitisation agenda has been reducing more socio–political conflicts to 'security' problems. Such narratives emphasise malign threats as grounds for greater state powers as the necessary guarantor of security, thus undermining societal capacities and solidarities. By contrast, "human security" has promoted a people–centred approach addressing broader threats such as economic inequality, poverty, diseases, human rights abuses, environmental pollution and natural disasters, argues the jurist Richard Falk.[4]

These contradictory agendas are illustrated by foreign aid. Western powers have increasingly justified their military intervention as an essential prerequisite for development aid to be effective; the military even distributes aid in order to gain local support. Opponents have criticised such blurring of roles, while counterposing a "human security" approach to development.[5]

Likewise the phrase 'energy security' blurs two different meanings. It can mean reliable, affordable, everyday access to energy for individuals and communities, or it can mean elites' control over resources and the force necessary to maintain such control. When promoting energy security in the elite sense, "securitising everything tends to generate more insecurities" in a self–perpetuating cycle.[6]

As a critical framework for analysing state power, 'securitisation' originated in the mid–1990s. Social scientists identified how the security agenda is used to construct a 'threat–defence' sequence in the military sector. This framework can also help us to understand a broader securitisation process in society as a whole. Here politicians and the mass media manufacture existential threats for society. This helps to justify urgent extraordinary measures.[7] Such measures in turn can reinforce the construction of a threat to a society's existence. The attempt to securitise everything then renders all things potentially terrifying.[8]

As a critical–analytical framework, securitisation draws on general theories of how social communication is deeply strategic. When invoking or even analysing security, the language used "operates as a mediating instrument that brings social practices into a particular communicative, institutionalised framework", thus "speaking and writing about security is never innocent," argues Jeff Huysmans.[9]

In the EU since the 1980s, many politicians have warned that migration destabilises domestic integration and endangers public order. Since the 1990s, EU policy has linked migration with threats of crime and terrorism within a national security framework. Migrants and asylum seekers are portrayed as a threat to national identity and welfare provision, thus feeding the "negative politicisation of immigrants, asylum-seekers and refugees as an illegitimate presence and scapegoat," argues Jeff Huysmans. Within a wider debate, this strategy has stigmatised such groups and questioned their legitimate membership of western European societies.[10]

EU security discussions imagine a society that is united internally but is perpetually threatened by external foreign forces: "Securitisation constitutes political unity by means of placing it in an existentially hostile environment and asserting an obligation to free it from threat."[11] Likewise EU counter-terrorism policy has identified new threats and devised new policy tools "to alleviate public problems defined as threats".[12]

Governments use new methods and powers to deal with perceived threats. After the state labelled some political organisations as 'terrorist' and banned them, special powers targeted individuals from communities suspected of having links with such organisations. Many have faced punishment without due process of law and have been prosecuted for alleged association. The securitisation paradigm continuously creates and circulates fear about existential threats through numerous minor "speech acts", and mundane everyday items, such as credit cards, letters, fertilisers etc., become symbols of terrorist threats.[13]

Such continuous insecurities help to justify exceptional powers and their routine application. EU elites have implemented:

> *... the political consensus around tough measures on 'illegal' immigration, special powers to combat terrorism, the creation of an international framework to combat organised crime, the embrace of new security technologies, the right of the state to place 'suspects' under sustained and intensive surveillance, and the securitisation of a host of new threats.*[14]

This political agenda blurs any distinction among potential threats and measures supposedly for countering them.

Entire city landscapes and everyday spaces are penetrated by the securitisation agenda. This shows a resurgence of colonial strategies and techniques that were used to control subject populations. New surveillance and control technologies become pervasive and permanent. They intensify during mega-events such as the Olympics and remain in place long afterwards. By conflating terrorism and immigration, migration *per se* is portrayed as "acts of warfare".[15]

This internal colonialism was noted by Foucault in the mid-1970s:

With its political and juridical weapons, colonization transported European models to other continents. It also had a considerable boomerang effect on the mechanisms of power in the West – through apparatuses, institutions and techniques of power. A whole series of colonial models was brought back to the West, [which thereby] could practice something resembling colonization, or an internal colonialism, on itself.[16]

His prophetic insight has become ever-more relevant. A large-scale, extreme case was the colonial counter-insurgency agenda in Northern Ireland during the 1970s-90s. The British state treated the Irish as a 'suspect community' throughout the UK. Under the 1974 Prevention of Terrorism Act, 'suspects' were detained in large numbers for potentially long periods without charge and were stigmatised by joint police-media campaigns; this pressure also served to blackmail them to become informers. This regime resulted in a "normalisation of special powers".[17]

This agenda extended "low intensity operations" from colonial counter-insurgency. Anti-colonial resistance was seen as "subversion and insurgency", which "can involve the use of political and economic pressure, strikes, protest marches, and propaganda, and ... the use of small-scale violence", according to a military strategist.[18] Colonial counter-insurgency emphasised 'security' measures such as systematic surveillance, intelligence-gathering, psychological warfare and intimidation against entire populations in order to separate them from insurgents. Within such low-intensity operations, in Northern Ireland and British colonies alike, legal frameworks played a crucial role:

... the law should be used as just another weapon in the government's arsenal, and in this case it becomes little more than a propaganda cover for the disposal of unwanted members of the public. For this to happen efficiently, the activities

of the legal services have to be tied into the war effort in as discreet a way as possible.[19]

Similar strategies have been turning migrant and Muslim populations into suspect communities, as described in the rest of this article.

Anti-terror regime: turning migrants and Muslims into suspect communities

As the war in Northern Ireland was subsiding in the late 1990s, hopes rose that the 1974 'emergency' anti-terror powers would lapse, but instead they were expanded. Securitisation strategies have elaborated new existential threats justifying broader anti-terror powers. The Terrorism Act 2000 made anti-terror measures permanent. Subsequently five more anti-terrorism laws have been put in place. In practice these powers have turned migrants and Muslims into suspect communities. For this political agenda, the ordinary criminal law would not suffice, so exceptional powers are necessary.

Criminalising association

Movements for national self-determination have often gained trans-national public support. UK government advisors identified such support as a problem, whose solution required broader, permanent anti-terror powers. According to a key expert report, a terrorist group looks internationally "for any ideological, political or diplomatic support it can manage to obtain; sub-state terrorism is typically the weapon of the weak". To counter such support, the UK needed permanent anti-terrorist legislation, argued the academic Paul Wilkinson.[20]

Accordingly, the UK Terrorism Act 2000 defined terrorism to include simply "the threat" of "serious damage to property", in ways "designed to influence the government" for a "political cause". This broad definition blurs any distinction between military, political and civilian targets. Organisations can be banned on the basis that their activities anywhere fit the broad, vague definition of 'terrorism'.

In early 2001 the Home Office banned 21 organisations. The list predictably included many organisations resisting oppression abroad e.g., the Kurdistan Workers Party (PKK), the Tamil Tigers (LTTE) and Hamas. At a CAMPACC public meeting, Tony Benn MP denounced the entire anti–terror framework, which signified:

> *... an agreement among the governments of the world that no government is to be challenged from inside with support from outside. That is what it is about – nothing to do with human rights, and very little to do with 'terrorism'. In a global economy Britain wants to trade with repressive regimes. And if they find that these regimes are complaining that there are people in London campaigning for Kurdish rights, for Tamil rights or for Kashmiri rights, then the British government is expected to respond.*[21]

By banning organisations as terrorist, the government "reduced highly complex political situations to simplistic caricatures that would disgrace a comic book," argued the solicitor Gareth Peirce.[22] These organisations were operating almost exclusively in their places of origin, so the government's political target was their legitimacy and verbal support within the UK. Today more than 50 organisations are banned in the UK. The decision is taken by the Home Secretary without any judicial scrutiny. Once an organisation is banned, there is no clear procedure to obtain evidential grounds from the government, much less a procedure to remove an organisation from the list.

The 2000 Act criminalised association as well as membership. It became an offence to organise or speak at a meeting of more than three people with the knowledge that a member of a banned organisation will be a speaker. It became illegal to support these organisations anywhere – politically, financially or any other way. 'Support' was conveniently left ambiguous; it could mean attending a meeting sympathetic to a banned organisation, or giving funds to its humanitarian programme, or simply wearing a t–shirt with its name. Under the statutory duty of disclosure, moreover, it became a criminal offence not to inform the police if you know someone who has engaged in such activities.

Terrorising communities

By creating such new crimes of association, the Terrorism Act 2000 directed suspicion and intimidation at entire communities. Such powers have targeted Muslim and migrant communities, many of which fled from oppressive regimes allied with the UK; their state's terrorism is sanitised by stigmatising any resistance as terrorist. It attacked the right of self-determination, as well as popular support across countries.

The new crimes of association have affected charities, their banks and the regulator, called the Charities Commission. Charities have been persecuted and disrupted. Interpal, which provides humanitarian aid in Palestine, twice found that its bank account was frozen while under investigation by the Charities Commission. Interpal was suspected of allowing its funds to reach 'terrorist' activities, presumably meaning Hamas. No evidence was found against Interpal, yet meanwhile the freeze undermined its operations and reputation.

Many migrants and Muslims have been subjected to arbitrary harassment when travelling abroad. Under the Terrorism Act 2000, Schedule 7 authorises severe powers: police can detain, question and search anyone for up to nine hours at ports of entry. Refusal to answer even one question becomes a terrorist offence. A detainee can be subjected to a body search and collection of biometric data such as fingerprints or DNA samples.

The official rationale for these powers is that they are necessary to determine whether someone is involved in terrorist activity. Yet the powers do not oblige officers to demonstrate any specific cause for suspicion against a detained individual. In practice, moreover, detainees are often asked questions about political activities or mundane personal details – even those which are well known to MI5 from wider surveillance activities – thus simply harassing detainees.[23]

The UK's proscription list is closely linked with its EU-wide counterparts. All EU member states are required to implement the December 2001 EU Council's Common Position on Combating Terrorism. This generated a Europe-wide list of banned organisations, whose bank accounts must be frozen by member states, without evidence that can be tested in public under due process.

The UK government has portrayed its measures as a difficult 'balance' between civil liberties and security, yet the securitisation agenda continuously expands the insecurity problem as vague existential threats:

It does not add up to a balanced consideration of what the 'balance' should be between freedom and security. However, that question may be unanswerable in so far as the measurement scales are not definable.[24]

Moreover, the false debate about 'a difficult balance' disguises the fundamental design and role of anti-terror powers to protect the state from political dissent.

Protecting state terror abroad

The UK 'terror list' and special anti-terror powers have several purposes. An official pretext is the need to pre-empt terrorist activities at an early stage. Given the vague definition of both terrorism and support for it, however, bans on organisations deny free expression and the right of free association, thus violating Articles 10 and 11 of the European Convention of Human Rights. The bans deter campaigns against oppressive regimes abroad, solidarity with resistance to such regimes, and even discussion about how to resolve conflicts there. Special powers are used for punishment without trial, as well as character assassination – regardless of any criminal prosecution, which remains rare. Indeed, juries have been rarely persuaded to convict political activists on terrorism charges.

The anti-terror framework also attacks the right to political asylum, while protecting state terror abroad. Prior to the 2000 Terrorism Act, many asylum seekers disclosed their association with a national liberation movement, as grounds for 'reasonable fear of persecution' by the regime that they had fled. Under the 2000 Act, however, such disclosure would lead to criminal charges. Their asylum claim becomes weaker without such disclosure. Thus all political refugees face a double bind. Many decide not to claim asylum, thus joining an undocumented invisible underclass, even more vulnerable to exploitation.[25]

Meanwhile regimes abroad more easily continue or intensify their oppression of civilian populations by associating them with terrorism. The UK's domestic securitisation complements analogous strategies by its allies abroad. Such regimes protect access to their country's resources for multinational companies and western governments, as well documented by many writers.

Britain's basic priority – virtually its raison d'être *for several centuries – is to aid British companies in getting their hands on other countries' resources.*[26]

To pursue this aim, UK policies have been "helping to make the world more insecure, unequal and abusive of human rights", as shown by Mark Curtis.[27] Perversely, insecurity is used to sanitise UK allies, while also demonising opponents there and in the UK.

Through such collusion, UK anti-terror powers serve as an instrument of foreign policy. These powers create a wide range of 'terror suspects' and entire 'suspect communities' - more than a million people from refugee communities associated with liberation movements. Anyone who associates with protest activity may be harassed or even criminalised for supporting 'terrorism'. UK anti-terror laws have been used to discipline, intimidate, frighten, silence and isolate migrant communities. Surveillance has targeted specific groups, thus contradicting official denials that any groups are investigated 'on grounds of their ethnicity'[28].

Despite being persecuted, UK migrant organisations have continued their political activities. Defiance gives practical content to the demand for repeal of 'terror' bans, while helping to undermine the bans in practice. This persistence broadens and links communities of resistance, as described next for UK Kurds and Tamils.

Kurds' persecution and resistance

The UK is complicit in the long-term suppression of the Kurds, especially in the recent phase deploying anti-terror powers to support and sanitise the oppressive Turkish regime.

UK collusion in persecuting Kurds

The UK has played a central role in attacking Kurds and creating a long-term basis for their persecution. After World War I, the UK and France agreed to partition Kurdistan into three countries: Turkey, Iraq and Iran. When Iraqi Kurds revolted against this plan, the UK bombed their villages with poison gas. Imposed by state terror, partition laid the basis for the long-term suppression of Kurds, their political aspirations and cultural identity.

The founding of the Turkish Republic in 1923 was based on an exclusionary constitution which enforced a single Turkish identity and put the military at the centre of state power. This was the basis for repressive programmes of violence and assimilation which denied the existence of Kurdish identity and of Kurds themselves. The Kurdish language and all expression of identity were banned. Kurdish opposition in the 1920s was brutally repressed and martial law implemented. Turkish forces deployed to the Kurdish regions destroyed hundreds of villages and engaged in the mass killings of Kurds.

A series of military coups in the 1960s and 70s culminated in a third military coup in 1980. This imposed martial law directed at leftists and those understood to be 'separatists', i.e. anyone advocating Kurdish national rights. Parliament was abolished. State-sponsored violence against leftists, and the Kurds in particular, saw thousands of people, arrested, tortured and imprisoned.[29] When tens of thousands immigrated to the UK after the 1980 coup, Kurds in particular were targeted by MI5 intimidation to serve as informers on their communities. There was greater collaboration between security agencies of the two countries.

Kurds targeted by UK anti-terror powers

When the UK banned the Kurdistan Workers' Party (PKK) (among 26 organisations) in 2001, this further helped to protect Turkey's state terrorism against the Kurds. Nevertheless protest and defiance began from the start. Kurdish groups mobilised 6,000 demonstrators to protest. Some wore T-shirts that said 'I am PKK', thus defying police to arrest them. None were, until two years later.

In 2003 some Kurdish activists were prosecuted for supposedly raising funds for the PKK. One defendant was invited to become a police informer in return for help with his refugee status; he refused this blackmail proposal. All the defendants were acquitted by the jury after hearing about Turkey's oppression of the Kurds.

Kurdish organisations faced greater intimidation from the police after 2008. Community centres have been insulted for displaying pictures of a 'terrorist', i.e. the PKK leader Abdullah Ocalan, who has been imprisoned on Turkey's Imrali Island since his 1999 abduction. The police have attempted to prevent free expression at Kurdish demonstrations, e.g. by suppressing the Kurdish flag or pictures of Ocalan. Police used Public Order laws on the pretext that such symbols could incite public disorder; Kurds have been especially targeted by such powers. Nevertheless community organisations persisted in their protest and organised legal observers with assistance from the Haldane Society.

A turning point came in October 2008, when millions of Kurds held protests throughout Turkey, Kurdistan and European cities in response to physical attacks on Ocalan. In London the police initially refused to permit any demonstration, so community representatives warned them about the consequences if Kurds could not protest in a peaceful way. Eventually the police gave permission but imposed a condition banning any flags supporting Abdullah Ocalan and the Kurdish Freedom Movement. Attempting to enforce that rule, the police had a large presence and numerous photographers from the Forward Intelligence Team (FIT).

Using a megaphone, however, one activist denounced the police for collecting intelligence for the Turkish military and then raised the Kurdish flag, followed by other demonstrators. Thus they defied the police restrictions and the ban on the PKK. UK Kurds have held more demonstrations flying the flag, rejecting the 'terrorist' label and demanding that the PKK be unbanned.[30] Indeed, they have acted as if there were no ban, thus undermining it.

Meanwhile the anti-terrorism police intensified their harassment of Kurdish activists and potential ones. Distributors of the Kurdish newspaper *Özgur Politika* were stopped by police under anti-terror powers and were questioned about their activities. Several houses were repeatedly raided, for no apparent purpose other than harassment. Anyone visiting a Kurdish community centre is warned about the consequences of such activity, thus deterring attendance at events there.

Anti-terror police and MI5 have intimidated many Kurds against visiting the Kurdish community centres, especially against participating in the management. These centres have provided community services on housing, immigration, schools, etc., and also run projects helping the elderly, women and children. All these services have been harmed by state intimidation.

In September 2011 an extraordinary large-scale operation targeted the renovation of the new Halkevi Centre. Anti-terrorism police confiscated all computers and financial records of funds necessary for completing the renovation. They also arrested numerous staff and contractors on 'suspicion' that grant money for the renovation was being used for terrorism. After an investigation lasting almost a year, no evidence was found to justify the raids and arrests. Despite these severe obstacles, the renovation was completed. The centre's property was returned about a year later.

In parallel with greater UK harassment of Kurds, around 2010 Turkey escalated its detentions of anyone supporting Kurdish demands for democratic freedoms, thus intensifying "its traditional politics of securitisation".[31] Detentions soon reached 10,000 people – half the global total of detentions under 'anti-terror' laws. Many detainees were put on trial en masse starting in 2012. Solidarity activists and lawyers served as observers there, reported back at public events in London, and linked Turkey's terror campaign with its UK counterpart against Kurdish communities. There is extensive co-ordination between the Turkish and British intelligence services in targeting Kurdish community activists.

Tamils' persecution and resistance

The UK is complicit in the long-term suppression of the Tamils, especially in the recent phase deploying anti-terror powers to support and sanitise the oppressive Sri Lankan regime.

UK collusion in persecuting Tamils

Persecution of Tamils has origins in British colonial rule over Ceylon. Having occupied the island from 1796, the British merged the Tamil and Sinhala nations into one unit for administrative convenience in 1833. Ceylon gained independence in 1948 with a Westminster-style political representation, despite protest from the Tamils, who comprised almost 30% of the population. Tamils were relegated to a permanent minority.

Within months of independence, the Ceylon government passed the Citizenship Act, which rendered stateless more than a million Tamils of Indian origin. The British had indentured them as cheap labour to work on tea plantations in the 19th century, especially in the up-country areas. The 1948 Act established a Sinhalese electoral majority there.

In 1956 Prime Minister Bandaranaike came to power on the twin platform of making Sinhala the official language and Buddhism the state religion. This language policy attacked Tamil livelihoods and achievement because English education had been a passport for social mobility into the professions and administrative services. Peaceful protests were crushed by the police; any attempts at reconciliation were suppressed by the Sinhalese reaction. There were widespread killings and dispossession of Tamils:

> *From then on the pattern of Tamil subjugation was set: racist legislation followed by Tamil resistance, followed by conciliatory government gestures, followed by Opposition rejectionism, followed by anti-Tamil riots instigated by Buddhist priests and politicians, escalating Tamil resistance, and so on – except that the mode of resistance varied and intensified with each tightening of the ethnic-cleansing screw and led to armed struggle and civil war.*[32]

As each new policy of racist discrimination was introduced, the Tamil people organised protests based on *satyagraha*, civil disobedience in the Gandhian manner. These non-violent actions were regularly crushed with repressive measures by the police and army on government orders. Tamils' socio-economic structures were also damaged by government sponsored arson, vandalism and looting.

This violence reached genocidal proportions in 1983, losing thousands of lives and property worth many millions. Since then, Tamils have suffered more of the same: abductions, torture, rape, killings, disappearances and arbitrary arrests. These abuses have been carried out with impunity by the armed forces, special task forces, police, home guards and paramilitary forces.

In 1972 a new constitution renamed Ceylon as the Republic of Sri Lanka. Buddhism was given foremost recognition. In 1976 all Tamil parties joined together to form the Tamil United Liberation Front (TULF), proposing an independent state for Tamils in the homelands of the earlier Tamil kingdoms. Frustrated by the lack of progress through politics, diplomacy and non-violent protest, Tamil youths started to form militant groups, including the Liberation Tigers of Tamil Eelam (LTTE).

Tamils targeted by UK anti-terror powers

In the name of preventing terrorism, international bans on the LTTE have helped to protect Sri Lanka's racist Sinhalese-chauvinist regime, especially its genocidal anti-Tamil war, which intensified in the years preceding the LTTE's 2009 defeat.[33] The western anti-terror framework distinguishes between acceptable and unacceptable politics among diaspora Tamils. It favours Tamils who reduce the issues to human rights, as if Sri Lanka were a normal liberal-democratic state. Those advocating Tamil self-determination are equated with the LTTE and labelled 'terrorism supporters'. This oppressive role illustrates "the securitisation of politics that the terrorism discourse entails".[34] Western bans complement the Sri Lankan strategy to construct a political dichotomy between 'the moderate and the militant/terrorist', as analysed by Sivaram, a journalist assassinated by Sri Lanka[35].

The UK Terrorism Act 2000 was the legal basis for arresting two Tamil activists, Chrishanthakumar (also known as AC Shanthan) and Goldan Lambert in June 2007. Shanthan was charged with materially supporting the LTTE. Goldan Lambert was accused of organising a Hyde Park rally in July 2006, commemorating the 1983 anti–Tamil pogrom that had provoked the war in Sri Lanka; his involvement was now treated as a crime.

The arrests came as a surprise because many Tamils had been openly supporting the LTTE for a long time. Based in the UK, Anton Balasingham had been representing the LTTE in peace negotiations around the world; his trips were financed partly by the UK and US governments. After Balasingham's death in December 2006, a greater role was played by Shanthan, who attended peace talks in Geneva. Eventually Goldan Lambert was acquitted.

Although Shanthan was convicted, the judge expressed regret and commended his efforts to send humanitarian supplies. According to the judgement, Shanthan was "a thoroughly decent man" and had been central to peace negotiations to resolve the conflict in Sri Lanka:

> *... whatever he did for the Tamils and the LTTE, he did not do it in order to assist them in war; he did them to assist in maintaining the peace process ... Shanthan was doing no more, although illegally, than the international community were doing.*[36]

Indeed, the UK's Department for International Development (DfID) had sent similar equipment to help Tamil civilians. In prosecuting Shanthan, therefore, the UK was discriminating according to the source of aid, so that the Tamil resistance would remain dependent on western states.

But why were the two Tamil activists arrested at all, and a year after the July 2006 rally? During that period, peace talks broke down, the war intensified and UK government policy changed. A couple of weeks before the June 2007 arrests, the UK Foreign Minister Kim Howells visited Sri Lanka. There he reiterated that the UK would not lift its LTTE ban until the organisation renounces terrorism. A different standard was applied to the Sri Lankan government, which was criticised simply for violating human rights, e.g. by forcibly transporting hundreds of people to dangerous areas.

In that way, anti-terror powers are used selectively as an instrument of foreign policy. The UK arrest of Tamil activists has parallels in many other countries supporting the Sri Lankan government.[37] Governments have deployed a few exemplary prosecutions, with the threat of many more, to intimidate Tamil communities into silence over the genocide.

Restrictions on charities have also been used against Tamil activists. A former leader of the LTTE, now based in London, came under pressure to dissociate himself from the organisation. After he refused, the Charities Commission ruled that he could no longer serve as trustee of a Hindu temple. He was also accused of visiting senior LTTE members, who happened to be his relatives. As these examples illustrate, the ban on association with a vaguely defined 'terrorism' is used to attack community solidarity and family relations.

The anti-terror framework has also been deployed to suppress public protest and debate. Whenever UK Tamil activists tried to book venues for public events, the Sri Lankan embassy told the venue that the organisers were LTTE supporters. The organisers were then asked to prove otherwise, and their booking was often denied or cancelled for vague 'security concerns'. Such intimidation effectively limits what it is possible to say.[38] Yet the intimidation has not stopped protest against Sri Lanka's genocidal war and the UK's complicity. An activist from the Tamil Campaign for Truth and Justice was threatened with prosecution under UK anti-terror laws, as a supposed supporter of the LTTE, yet he has continued the campaign.

Regular London protests against Sri Lanka's genocide have attracted over 100,000 Tamils. At even larger demonstrations in January 2009, thousands carried Tamil liberation flags, thus undermining the UK ban on symbols of a proscribed organisation. Tamils initiated a petition to the UK prime minister; the text concluded: "As a law-abiding citizen of this country, I demand HM's Government de-proscribes the Liberation Tigers of Tamil Eelam (LTTE) immediately." Moreover, amidst police attacks on anyone protesting in Parliament Square, a Tamil protest liberated that space, also attracting numerous Kurds to speeches and films there.

In May 2009 the war ended with large-scale massacres of both refugees and fighters by the Sir Lankan military.[39] Having annihilated the LTTE, state forces then intensified their attack on democratic freedoms. Western countries have likewise restricted liberal–democratic freedoms for Tamil activists, mainly on the pretext that they seek to promote or revive the LTTE. Tamils demanding accountability for Sri Lanka's genocide, and especially those demanding the right of self–determination, continue to be targeted by counter–terror powers, which thereby help legitimise a genocidal state. "The Sri Lankan conflict is now a transnational war against the Tamil diaspora that enables the continued repression of political aspirations both in Sri Lanka and abroad."[40]

Today Tamils remain insecure in Sri Lanka, their land is confiscated and their areas are heavily militarised, with many living in detention camps. Yet the UK government deports Tamil asylum seekers back to Sri Lanka where they face imprisonment and torture. The LTTE ban continues its role in suppressing dissent, so activists have escalated demands that the UK government lift the ban.[41]

Pre–empting 'Islamist terror'

Some UK migrant communities have been persecuted for their resistance against the oppressive regime from which they fled, as in the case of Kurds and Tamils outlined above. By contrast, Muslims have been subjected to a general suspicion of 'Islamist terrorism', indicated by various means such as political views, religious beliefs or vague associations. These indicators have been deployed for several purposes: to stigmatise individuals or groups as 'Islamist extremists', to intimidate others into disavowing any such association, to motivate pre–emptive spying, and even to justify punishment without trial.

Interning 'international terrorists'

After the 11 September attacks, anti–terror powers were expanded to include indefinite detention without trial. The Anti–Terrorism, Crime and Security Act (ATCSA) 2001 authorised internment of foreign nationals suspected of links with a vaguely defined "international terrorism". As the official rationale, this special power was directed against individuals who "threaten national security" but whose successful prosecution was unlikely.

As the basis for most detentions, the Special Immigration Appeals Tribunal (SIAC) accepted secret evidence; it was not heard in open court, and plausibly came from torturing other detainees abroad. The 'terror suspect' stigma isolated entire families and intensified fear among Muslim communities. Most detainees came from north African countries whose regimes had close relations with the UK government.

The new internment powers were opposed by a broadly-based campaign linking numerous organisations. As an initiative of Peace and Justice in East London (PJEL), SIAC hearings were regularly picketed with demands for "No detention without trial". SIAC was denounced as a 'star chamber', referencing earlier abuses of power. CAMPACC led protests at Belmarsh Prison with the slogan 'Belmarsh, Guantanamo, Abu Ghraib: Axis of Evil', thus inverting a key phrase of the 'war on terror'.

Three years after the ATCSA 2001, the Law Lords ruled that the internment powers were incompatible with human rights and unjustified by national security. As a replacement measure, the government rushed through the Prevention of Terrorism Act 2005 authorising "control orders", which keep individuals in their homes under curfew, restrict their movements and require clearance for any visitors. This system turns homes into domestic prisons. These restrictions have been only somewhat alleviated by replacing control orders with Terrorism Prevention and Investigation Measures (TPIMs), likewise based on secret evidence; they can be imposed on anyone.

Expanding 'security threats'

Frequent 'terror raids' have been carried out as spectacles, whereby the mass media reproduce disinformation from MI5 about 'al-Qaeda cells'. These operations were intensified in the run-up to the March 2003 US-UK invasion of Iraq, especially by fabricating a 'ricin conspiracy' of north African migrants.[42] Such raids serve as psychological warfare: they generate public fear, associate Islam with terrorist threats, and help justify special anti-terror powers. Facing this intimidation campaign, few Muslims attended local anti-war meetings, fearing that they may be identified by police agents, though great numbers attended London demonstrations.

In such ways, anti-terror measures have intimidated entire Muslim communities. Drawing on the experience of the Irish as a "suspect community"[43], a research project investigated comparisons with Muslims in the 'war on terror'. As the researchers note, UK counter-terror policy portrays special measures as an exceptional emergency, despite the powers being made permanent. Moreover, putative threats are identified through a vague association within suspect groups:

> *Rather than being based on a precise offence, they proceed along a logic of association, thus identifying as security threats markers of identity and behaviours that are specific to particular social groups, which could potentially become "suspect communities".*[44]

In addition to new criminal offences and special powers, the securitisation strategy was extended through the Contest programme: "Contest is intended to be a comprehensive strategy: Work on Pursue and Prevent reduces the threat from terrorism: work on Protect and Prepare reduces the UK's vulnerability to attack."[45] The government funded such efforts within local programmes, especially those officially aimed at community cohesion, which was thereby undermined through mass surveillance and community distrust. According to a study:

> *The reach of Contest was such that there was a widespread expectation upon anyone interacting with members of the Muslim community, that they should monitor the behaviour of the people they met and report any 'unusual or suspicious' behaviour. Indeed it also meant that employees of the local state could not themselves be sure whether information that they routinely gathered as part of their professional practice did not at some point get passed onto the counter intelligence agencies. Thus the securitisation of everyday life had been extensively extended through the pervasive reach of the counter-terrorism structure.*[46]

Under the Prevent Violent Extremism programme of the Home Office, a broader threat was identified as "Islamist radicalization" or "violent extremism". Vaguely defined, this could mean verbal support for resistance to oppression anywhere. Such views were cast as incompatible with "our values", as if only Muslims could support armed resistance against imperialist occupation or Zionist terror. Numerous Muslim organisations were officially engaged or even funded in an effort to counter "violent extremism". This programme was widely criticised for violating privacy, undermining professional norms of confidentiality and degrading local democracy.[47] On those grounds, many community groups and projects have declined funds from the Prevent programme.

Surveillance became more overt in the successor programme, entitled Contest 2. Promoting greater integration of policies, it blurred any distinction between domestic and foreign policy, between soft and hard power, between civilian and military approaches. Schools, youth clubs and universities were meant to monitor the views of Muslim communities.[48] For these surveillance and prevention measures, the strategy has targeted a large group of non-violent people who "create an environment in which terrorists can operate"[49], thus again blurring distinctions through a vague association.

In 2011 the prime minister broadened the threat-defence narrative: namely, the terrorist threat comes from political views, from "Islamist extremism", which has "hostility towards western democracy and liberal values".

As evidence emerges about the backgrounds of those convicted of terrorist offences, it is clear that many of them were initially influenced by what some have called 'non-violent extremists', and they then took those radical beliefs to the next level by embracing violence ... We need a lot less of the passive tolerance of recent years and a much more active, muscular liberalism to counter the non-violent and violent forms.[50]

This imperative guides the government's extension of the Prevent and Contest programmes. Participating organisations are expected to disavow 'extremism', e.g. merely verbal support for resistance to state terror abroad.

As an academic study warned, the Contest strategy is counter-productive:

... the 'terror of prevention' continuum, which ranges from the day-to-day harassment of Muslims through stop-and-search to high-profile police raids, has had a corrosive effect on the relations between Muslim communities and the police. Within this context, the conditions for radicalisation are being fomented and the 'flow of information' necessary for effective counter-terrorism policing has been jeopardised.[51]

Perhaps true, but this advice naively assumes that the UK strategy aims mainly to prevent the public from violence. A greater priority is to strengthen 'national security', equating insecurity with resistance to UK foreign policy or exposure of its crimes.

Such dissent has been the implicit target of the Prevent and Contest programmes.[52] This strategy has featured several types of punishment without trial, euphemistically called "non-prosecution civil executive actions" by the state. These powers have been officially justified to restrict the scope for "Islamist radicaliation", even by groups not advocating violence. Such measures include: house arrest, asset-freezing, travel bans, long interrogations at UK ports, long detention periods without charge, etc.[53]

As a more severe punishment, in 2002 revocation of UK citizenship was authorised for dual-national citizens if the Home Secretary believes that their presence is "not conducive to the public good". On such vague grounds, by 2013, UK governments had stripped 41 people of their UK nationality; 36 of them under the Con-Dem Coalition government, many on grounds that they had fought in Syria and would pose a threat upon their return to the UK. Long-time civil liberties solicitor Gareth Peirce denounced the process as akin to "medieval exile". Moreover, two of those individuals were subsequently assassinated in drone attacks.[54] Such punishments can deter any solidarity visits to struggles abroad, while allowing the UK government to judge which visits threaten the UK. This regime constrains the right of national self-determination, as do the bans on 'terrorist' organisations. A special target of persecution has been Moazzam Begg, a UK citizen who was detained at Guantanamo Bay for three years and subsequently campaigned for the release of other prisoners being held there. Later he became the Director of Cage, which campaigns against the UK anti-terror regime. He went on speaking tours to investigate and expose the state's complicity in kidnap and torture. When returning from such a trip to South Africa in December 2013, his passport was withdrawn on grounds that it was 'not in the public interest' for him to travel. As usual, the British state conveniently conflated the public interest with political embarrassment. Later, in February 2014, he was charged under the Terrorism Act 2000 for allegedly having provided training and fundraising in relation to Syria. This persecution turned him into a high-profile symbol of how the state uses anti-terror powers to terrorise dissent and solidarity activities. As Cage argues, it is essential "to recognise the illegitimate nature of the counter-terrorism regime that seeks to criminalise him".[55]

Previously some mosques had accepted funds from the Prevent programme; apparently this acquiescence emboldened the police to demand more. After Cage announced a 2nd March demonstration in Birmingham demanding Moazzam Begg's release, mosques there faced intimidation:

West Midlands counter-terror officers visited mosques yesterday attempting to discourage Muslims from attending a demonstration that took place today ... Mosques are scared that if they don't comply they might be seen as radical.[56]

In these ways, Moazzam Begg was turned into a symbol of the entire anti-terror regime and broader Prevent programme, where the key term 'radical' (likewise 'extremist') encompasses any dissent against the UK government.

Blackmailing and punishing Somalis

Various punishments without trial are illustrated by the persecution of British Somalis. Numerous UK Somalis have been stopped at UK ports for questioning under the Terrorism Act 2000. Through such regular stopping and questioning, visits to Somalia have been monitored and discouraged. Such intimidation reinforces the efforts to install a client regime in Somalia that is amenable to western exploitation of its mineral resources.[57]

UK Somalis are often pressurised to become informers.[58] Going beyond persuasion or bribes, MI5 has made persistent threats against those who refuse the request. For several years MI5 has intimidated many British Somalis, especially youth workers at the Kentish Town Community Organisation (KTCO). They were threatened with the label 'Islamic extremist' if they refused to become informers. MI5 warned them, "Work for us or we will say you are a terrorist" to foreign governments. Afterwards MI5 acted on the threat: some were detained as 'terror suspects' and interrogated on trips abroad.[59]

After this abuse was exposed, the local MP and council leader met Home Office officials to demand a stop to it. Although illegal, MI5 blackmail has continued and remains unaccountable. According to solicitor Gareth Peirce, "Hundreds of Somalis under suspicion of travelling to east Africa report that they have been blackmailed and harassed; this a national disgrace."[60]

A Somali-born UK citizen, Mahdi Hashi, was among the several KTCO care workers who refused to become MI5 informers in 2009. Some time later he left the UK for Somalia, where he has family members. The Home Secretary revoked his citizenship in October 2012. After leaving Somalia Mahdi disappeared. He was held at a secret detention site in Djibouti that has been notorious for extraordinary rendition[61], rendered to a New York court and accused of terrorism, on grounds that he supported the militia group al Shabaab.[62]

By revoking Mahdi's citizenship, the Home Office demonstrated its complicity in the earlier blackmail which led to the decision. As MI5 securocrats build their careers by recruiting informers, they gain co-operation from Home Office chiefs to punish those who refuse. Such decisions lack judicial accountability: "Legal protection is difficult when the decision is based on secret evidence; this is used as a cover for incompetence, corruption and outright dishonesty," declared Mahdi's solicitor.[63]

This punishment aims to frighten UK Somalis from engaging with issues affecting their communities, especially involvement in Somalia. CAMPACC organised public events in 2009 and 2012 with Somali activists, thus giving the Somali community a high-profile platform against MI5 blackmail. At the 2012 event, KTCO community worker Mohamed Nur reported many young people complaining, "If I show any form of political activism, my UK citizenship might be revoked". Somali communities have defied the intimidation by publicly exposing MI5 blackmail, in turn receiving solidarity messages from other migrant groups facing similar blackmail, especially Kurds and Tamils.[64]

Difficulties of effective protest

The anti-terror framework has been readily imposed, despite the UK's long history of campaigns for civil liberties. What have been the difficulties of effective protest? After the original Terrorism Bill was published, a May Day 2000 protest highlighted that the new powers would have criminalised famous freedom fighters and their UK supporters, but this warning gained little attention.

When the neoconservative agenda declared its 'war on terror' after the September 2001 attacks, liberalism was turned into "an ideology of total war" against a global threat, seen as "fanaticism inherent to Islam".[65] More subtly, the state's language coded anti-terror powers as targeting 'exceptional' threats, which were understood to mean migrant and Muslim populations. This focus deterred early opposition to the powers and any defence of those being targeted.

Liberals have criticised some anti-terror powers on various grounds, e.g. for unfairly targeting entire groups, undermining their trust in the authorities and thus impeding identification of 'real terrorist threats'. Such modest criticisms see exceptional powers as misguided means to protect the public, or even accept some powers as necessary for this purpose. This approach accommodates the securitisation agenda and its everyday proliferation of insecurities, thus relegating any criticism to a defensive case-by-case basis.

As the most plausible source of opposition, the UK's Stop the War Coalition denounced the entire 'war on terror'. Yet its activities focused on US-UK attacks abroad through high-profile demonstrations involving little community activity; the 'war' at home gained little attention. Muslims attended large anti-war demonstrations en masse, yet few attended local anti-war meetings, partly for fear of being identified by the police. Rarely were there solidarity actions for people being targeted by anti-terror powers. For all these reasons, the vague category 'terror suspect' has been easily broadened – to environmental activists, human rights workers and journalists – with judicial complicity.[66]

Conclusion

Securitisation has become a pervasive strategy turning political conflicts into 'insecurity' threats. Through collusion between the state and mass media, an everyday psychological warfare creates and circulates insecurities, thus warranting 'security' measures. Special powers reinforce fear of omnipresent 'terror suspects', alongside fear of danger for anyone who challenges the anti-terror regime.

Special anti-terror powers label resistance abroad as terrorism and likewise stigmatise mere verbal support at home as threats to national security. The counter-terror framework serves to legitimise oppressive regimes allied with the UK and its own global military intervention in pursuit of plunder and domination. By blurring any distinction between liberation movements and terrorism, and likewise between civil resistance and violence, the UK impedes a political route to conflict resolution abroad, while also persecuting

UK communities who oppose oppressive regimes abroad. As a key aim and effect, the anti–terror regime denies the collective right of national self–determination, especially support from abroad.

Various methods extend 'low intensity operations' from UK colonial counter–insurgency to the UK itself. Securitisation has elaborated new existential threats, defence imperatives, additional legal weapons, punishment without trial, systematic surveillance and mass intimidation. By defining terrorism (likewise 'extremism') in broad ways and targeting recalcitrant populations, special powers have turned migrants and Muslims into suspect communities, which are persecuted through various punishments without trial. In recent years the 'war on terror' slogan has been abandoned, yet the earlier 'anti–terror' powers and securitisation infrastructure have been extended through an agenda for 'countering violent extremism', even more vaguely defined than 'terrorism'. This state agenda worsens people's insecurity in the UK, while undermining efforts to pre–empt real violent threats.

To counter this state agenda, many groups have persisted in their political activities and developed communities of resistance. They have gained solidarity from each other, from fellow opponents of UK foreign policy and from civil liberties activists. This mutual support needs extending into an attack on the entire anti–terror regime, its supposed rationale, its bans on organisations, and the broad statutory definition of terrorism. Effective resistance requires a revival of political freedom and of radical political alternatives.[67]

Also needed is a Europe–wide solidarity along similar lines. Such efforts would be helped by exchanging information on a European scale, through meetings and electronic media. This exchange can help to link communities of resistance across groups and countries.

1. Campaign Against Criminalising Communities, see Biographies page 304.
2. M. Curtis, *Web Of Deceit: Britain's Real Foreign Policy: Britain's Real Role in the World* (London/NY: Vintage, 2003).
3. N. Chomsky, *World Orders, Old and New* (London: Pluto, 1994).
4. R. Falk, *On Humane Governance: Toward a New Global Politics* (Cambridge: Polity, 1995); also UNDP, *Human Development Report*, 1994.
5. Saferworld, *The Securitisation of Aid?*, 2011, http://www.saferworld.org.uk/Securitisation%20briefing%20pages.pdf.
6. The Corner House, *Energy Security For What? For Whom?*, 2012, http://www.thecornerhouse.org.uk/sites/thecornerhouse.org.uk/files/Energy%20Security%20For%20Whom%20For%20What.pdf.

7. B. Buzan, O. Wæver and J. de Wilde, *Security: A New Framework for Analysis* (Boulder: Lynne Rienner Publishers, 1998) pp. 24–25; O. Wæver, 'Securitization and desecuritization', in R. Lipschutz (ed.), *On Security* (NY: Columbia University Press, 1995) p. 51.
8. B. Evans, *Liberal Terror* (Cambridge: Polity Press, 2013).
9. J. Huysmans, 'Defining social constructivism in Security Studies: The normative dilemma of writing security', *Alternatives* 27, 2002, pp. 44, 47.
10. J. Huysmans, 'The European Union and the securitization of migration', *Journal of Common Market Studies* 38(5), 2000, pp. 751–777.
11. J. Huysmans, *The Politics of Insecurity: Fear, Migration and Asylum in the EU* (London: Routledge, 2006) p. 50.
12. T. Balzacq, 'The policy tools of securitization: Information exchange, EU foreign and interior policies', *Journal of Common Market Studies* 46 (1), 2008, pp. 76.
13. J. Huysmans, 'What's in an act? On security speech acts and little security nothings', *Security Dialogue* 42(4–5), 2011, pp. 371–83.
14. B. Hayes, *NeoConOpticon: The EU Security-Industrial Complex*, TNI/Statewatch, 2009, p. 80, http://www.statewatch.org/analyses/neoconopticon-report.pdf.
15. S. Graham, *Cities Under Siege: The New Military Urbanism* (London: Verso, 2010) pp. xviii, xx.
16. M. Foucault, *Society Must be Defended: Lectures at the College de France, 1975–76*, translated by David Macey (NY: Picador, 2003). Also at: http://en.bookfi.org/book/1064142.
17. P. Hillyard, *Suspect Community: People's Experience of the Prevention of Terrorism Acts in Britain* (London: Pluto Press, 1993).
18. F. Kitson, *Low Intensity Operations: Subversion, Insurgency, Peacekeeping* (London: Faber 1971) p. 3.
19. *ibid.*, Kitson (1971) p. 69.
20. P. Wilkinson, *Inquiry into Legislation against Terrorism*, Vol. 2, Lord Lloyd of Berwick, Cm 3420, 1996, p. 4.
21. T. Benn, Speech at meeting against the Terrorism Act 2000, Camden Town Hall, 2001.
22. G. Peirce, 'Terrorising communities', in *A Permanent State of Terror?*, pp.133–35, (London: CAMPACC with Index on Censorship, 2003) p. 74 & pp.133–35.
23. CAMPACC, Response to Home Office consultation on Schedule 7 of Terrorism Act 2000, 2012, http://www.homeoffice.gov.uk/publications/about-us/consultations/schedule-7-review.
24. A. Costello, 'Balancing security versus liberty: the wrong scales or the wrong question?', *Arches Quarterly* 1(1), 2007, p. 24, http://www.thecordobafoundation.com/attach/Arches_Q01p.pdf.
25. F. Webber, F. (2003) 'The Terrorism Act: embracing tyranny', in *A Permanent State of Terror?* (London: CAMPACC with Index on Censorship, 2003) p. 21.
26. *ibid.*, Mark Curtis (2003).
27. *ibid.*, Mark Curtis (2003).
28. MI5 (n.d.) https://www.mi5.gov.uk/home/about-us/faqs-about-mi5/does-mi5-spy-on-or-harass-muslims.html.
29. For more details and sources, see CAMPACC, 'The UK ban on the PKK: persecuting the Kurds', www.campacc.org.uk.
30. 'Hevallo says "no" to UK criminalisation', 1 November 2008, http://hevallo.blogspot.co.uk; and 'Kurds to defy and reject terrorist label', 23 April, 2009, http://hevallo.blogspot.co.uk/2009/04/defy-and-reject-terrorist-label-in.html.
31. S. Tuncel, 'The process in Turkey', *Jadaliyya*, 2013 [by MP of the Peace and Democracy Party

(BDP)], http://www.jadaliyya.com/pages/index/11590/the-process-in-turkey.

32. A. Sivanandan, 'Ethnic cleansing in Sri Lanka', 2009, http://www.irr.org.uk/2009/july/ha000021.html. See also A. Sivanandan, 'Sri Lanka: racism and the politics of underdevelopment', *Race & Class* 26(1), 1984, pp. 1–37.
33. CAMPACC, 'The Tamils of Sri Lanka – oppressed at home and persecuted in the UK', 2010, www.campacc.org.uk.
34. S. Nadarajah, 'Disciplining the diaspora? Tamil self-determination and the politics of proscription', in K. Dobb and A. Ingram (eds), *Spaces of Security and Insecurity: New Geographies of the War on Terror* (Farnham: Ashgate, 2009) pp. 109–30.
35. M. Whitaker, *Learning Politics from Sivaram: The Life and Death of a Revolutionary Tamil Journalist in Sri Lanka* (London: Pluto Press, 2007) p. 152.
36. Quoted in V. Sentas, 'Proscription on Trial: The Tamil Experience', 2009, http://campacc.org.uk/index.php?mact=News,cntnt01,detail,0&cntnt01articleid=54&cntnt01returnid=126.
37. V. Sentas, 'One more successful war? Tamil diaspora and counter-terrorism after the LTTE', in Scott Poynting and David Whyte (eds), *Counter-Terrorism and State Political Violence: The 'War on Terror' as Terror* (London: Routledge, 2012) http://www.routledge.com/books/details/9780415607209/.
38. *ibid.*, Nadarajah (2009).
39. Channel 4, *Sri Lanka's Killing Fields*, 2011, http://www.channel4.com/programmes/sri-lankas-killing-fields/4od.
40. *ibid.*, Sentas (2012).
41. Tamilnet, 'Tamils in UK protest against British role in EU ban on LTTE', 22 February 2014, http://www.tamilnet.com/art.html?catid=13&artid=37062.
42. L. Archer and F. Bawden, *Ricin! The Inside Story of the Terror Plot That Never Was* (London: Pluto, 2010).
43. *ibid.*, Hillyard (1993).
44. M.J. Hickman and L. Thomas, *'Suspect Communities'? Counter-terrorism policy, the press, and the impact on Irish and Muslim communities in Britain*, ESRC report, 2011, p. 11. Available at: http://www.londonmet.ac.uk/research-units/iset/projects/esrc-suspect-communities.cfm.
45. HM Government, *Countering International Terrorism* (London: HMSO, 2006).
46. Y. Alam and C. Husband, 'Parallel policies and contradictory practices: The case of social cohesion and counter-terrorism in the United Kingdom', University of Helsinki, 2012, p. 147. Available at: http://hdl.handle.net/10138/32365 and at: https://helda.helsinki.fi/bitstream/handle/10138/32365/011_08_alam&husband.pdf?sequence=1.
47. A. Kundnani, *Spooked: How not to prevent violent extremism* (London: IRR, 2009), http://www.irr.org.uk/news/spooked-how-not-to-prevent-violent-extremism/; see also Cage, *The Prevent Strategy: A Cradle to Grave Police-State*, 2014, http://cageuk.org/.
48. HM Government, *National Security Strategy of the United Kingdom: Security in an Interdependent World* (London: HMSO, 2008).
49. C. Farr, speech by the Director General for Security and Counter-Terrorism, Home Office, 3 October 2009.
50. D. Cameron, speech on radicalisation and Islamic extremism, Munich conference on security, 5 March 2011, http://www.number10.gov.uk/news/pms-speech-at-munich-security-conference/; Full transcript at: http://www.newstatesman.com/blogs/the-staggers/2011/02/terrorism-islam-ideology.
51. C. Pantazis and S. Pemberton, 'From the "old" to the "new" suspect community: Examining the

impacts of recent UK counter-terrorist legislation', *British Jnl of Criminology* 49, 2009, p. 662.

52. Cage, 'Grassing: the use and impact of informants in the "war on terror"', 28 December 2013, http://www.cageuk.org/article/grassing-use-and-impact-informants-war-terror [formerly Cageprisoners]; and *ibid.*, Cage (2014).
53. HM Government, *The United Kingdom's Strategy for Countering International Terrorism* (London: HMSO, 2009).
54. C. Woods, A. Ross and O. Wright, 'British terror suspects quietly stripped of citizenship... then killed by drones', *The Independent*, 28 February 2013, http://www.independent.co.uk/news/uk/crime/british-terror-suspects-quietly-stripped-of-citizenship-then-killed-by-drones-8513858.html; also see C. Woods and A. Ross, 'Medieval Exile: The 41 Britons stripped of their citizenship', Bureau of Investigative Journalism, 26 February 2014, http://www.thebureauinvestigates.com.
55. A. Qureshi, 'Martin to Moazzam: From One Birmingham to Another', 28 February 2014, http://www.cageuk.org/article/martin-moazzam-one-birmingham-another-0.
56. 5 Pillarz, 'Prevent officers approach Birmingham mosques to discourage Moazzam Begg demo', 1 March 2014, http://www.5pillarz.com/2014/03/01/birmingham-mosques-approached-by-prevent-officers-to-discourage-moazzam-begg-demo.
57. For numerous references see CAMPACC, 'Somali communities targeted by UK "counter-terror" measures: the need for solidarity', 2013, http://campacc.org.uk/uploads/CAMPACC_Somali%20briefing_v130510(1).pdf.
58. J. Osman, 'Mo Farah stopped at customs? He's not alone', Channel 4 news, 2 January 2013, http://www.channel4.com/news/mo-farah-stopped-at-customs-hes-not-alone.
59. R. Verkaik, 'How MI5 blackmails British Muslims', *The Independent*, 21 May 2009, http://www.independent.co.uk/news/uk/home-news/exclusive-how-mi5-blackmails-british-muslims-1688618.html.
60. Quoted in T. Foot, 'Terrorism suspect treatment of former Camden schoolboy', *Camden New Journal*, 24 January 2013, http://mahdihashi.net/2013/01/24/terrorism-suspect-treatment-of-mahdi-hashi-is-a-national-disgrace-claims-camden-solicitor-who-fought-for-release-of-guildford-four/.
61. Open Society Justice Initiative, 'Globalizing Torture: CIA Secret Detention and Extraordinary Rendition', 2010, pp.108-09, http://www.opensocietyfoundations.org/reports/globalizing-torture-cia-secret-detention-and-extraordinary-rendition.
62. T. Foot, 'Family are told that former Camden schoolboy is being held in US on "terror" charges', *Camden New Journal*, 28 December 2012, http://www.camdennewjournal.com/news/2012/dec/fathers-anger-family-are-told-former-camden-schoolboy-being-held-us-terror-charges; see also A. Cali, 'Mahdi Hashi and Britain's intervention in Somalia', 2013, http://cageuk.org/.
63. Quoted in *ibid.*, Foot (2013).
64. Quoted in *ibid.*, Foot (2013).
65. A. Kundnani, *The Muslims are Coming: A Critique of Counterterrorism Policy* (London: Verso, 2014).
66. See for example, S. Harrison, 'I am not a terrorist', *The Guardian*, 15 March 2014; H. Kennedy, 'A bleak day for justice', *The Guardian*, 20 February 2014 [judgement in the David Miranda case]; B. Shiban, 'Like David Miranda, I was interrogated at a British airport', *The Guardian*, 25 September 2013, http://www.theguardian.com/commentisfree/2013/sep/25/like-david-miranda-interrogated-british-airport.
67. *ibid.*, Kundnani (2014).

HOW TO EMPTY A CITY

3

Introduction

DEEPA NAIK & TRENTON OLDFIELD

Hi folks! This is the Mayor here. This is the greatest moment in the life of London for 50 years. We're welcoming more than a million people a day to our city and there is going to be huge pressure on the transport network. Don't get caught out![1]

This message was announced regularly right across London's 'public' transport system in July 2012 … until it was pulled[2], with much embarrassment, by Transport for London once it became clear London was, in fact, empty, and almost silent, in what came to feel like an induced coma. The words were spoken by US–born Alexander Boris de Pfeffel Johnson, a relative of British Queen Elizabeth Windsor (Saxe–Coburg–Gotha), a cousin of British Prime Minister David Cameron, and a member of elitist groups such as the Bullingdon Club.[3] 'Boris' also has relatives in the Swedish and Dutch 'royal' families. De Pfeffel Johnson became Mayor of London in 2008 just three years after Britain's uber–elite bid for and 'won the right to host the 2012 Summer Olympic Games'.

London has changed as a result of 'hosting' the Olympic Games. The tempo of the city was decelerated to such an extent that even a number of years on London still feels flat, significantly less interesting and less invigorating. Like someone that has suffered a stroke, it is unlikely the city will ever be quite the same again. London's mollified condition, we argue, is directly related to the processes embedded with being the host of a global mega event like the Olympics. The three papers in this chapter highlight different aspects of the passive and physical violence inflicted, and although they focus on London they can be seen as a window into similar and sometimes more problematic situations, previously for the World Cup in South Africa and currently being undertaken across 'Brazil' for the next Olympics. Globalised sporting meets nowadays are very much like social and political cyclones.

The Olympics and the processes related to 'hosting' this globalised mega event have slowly but surely flattened, hollowed out and deadened London, somehow making this deeply problematic, anxious and vigorous city feel pedestrian, mainstreamed, and every day increasingly more predictable. Just about everywhere in London now seems to have, or is in the process of developing, a bland damp pompousness that is well known in areas like Knightsbridge or South Kensington. Since the Olympics, once vigorous places have been transformed into such a smoothed-out version of themselves it now feels like they could be mothballed by museums. Perhaps a new collection will be launched by the V&A's[4] urbanist curators titled 'Early 21st Century London Neighbourhoods' where you can choose to visit or even move into new, participatory, embedded art projects. Unfortunately London now feels overwhelmingly preppy and pretentious, a city that depends on manufactured 'uppers' such as special events and meaningless dates in the calendar to pretend to be something it is not.

Britain's elite has always been tired of London, rarely if ever having more than a foothold in the capital city. Unfortunately rather than retreat they have taken to systematically hollowing London out, leaving it with a pulse barely recognisable. 'Winning' the Olympics was akin to the elite giving Londoners an unrequested shot of suspect quality, high dosage valium. From the afternoon London 'won the right to host the Olympics' the city's verve started to drain away.

Global events such as the Olympic Games are relentless in demanding high levels of conformity and blandness from the host city. Under no circumstances can there be any disruptions and there certainly should be no surprises. Within an afternoon London and Londoners were picked up and thrown down the road to 'acceptability', to becoming proper, permitted, palatable. Acceptability in these situations forces the population to 'behave', to measure themselves against and to aspire to be like the self-declared elite that illegitimately consider themselves the definition of 'acceptable and polite society'. And, when examining how London became anemic, we shouldn't underestimate the role of the fogeyish, costly and shameless 'royal' weddings[5] and the monarchy's jubilee events[6] etc., that also take place on the streets of London. These 'let them eat cake' spectacles have been very important in the pacification of London. It comes as no surprise that the International Olympic Committee (IOC) was and remains largely the preserve of European royalty. The modern Olympics founder, aristocrat Pierre de Coubertin, is long understood to have been a racist and proto-fascist. The IOC is an elitist white male organisation; it wasn't until 1981 that any women were even considered eligible to join the IOC.

For London 2012, everything and anything would be done to ensure conditions of acceptability and placidness would prevail – at any and all costs. It took less than a year, for example, for the British government to draft and gain royal assent for the deeply problematic London Olympic Games and Paralympics Games Act.[7] Of particular note are the Act's ability to create unaccountable extra-governmental organisations such as the Olympic Delivery Authority (ODA) and London Organising Committee of the Olympic Games (LOCOG), and its provisions to limit freedom of speech and ensure adherence to the IOC's demands. Some critics have suggested it is the most draconian act passed since the wartime Defense of the Realm Act (1914)[8]. Even more problematic acts have since been passed which were, in many ways, directly related to 'protecting' the Olympics – from terrorism, from protest, from ridicule and irony, and, of course, from accountability. The narrative was always insinuating a desire to do everything possible to 'preserve London's modesty', to ensure we as citizens would not be violated, deflowered. It was 'our opportunity' to show 'the watching world' an unblemished, acceptable, polite, acquiescent and consenting city.

Sugar-coated poison

This acceptability mantra was, of course, a distraction, a sideshow for something altogether more menacing – the militarisation of everyday life, the undermining of human rights, the corporatisation of the state (increasing the mass transfer of public monies into a handful of private pockets) and the practice of large-scale 'bread and circus' events as diversions, dress-rehearsal jingoism and collective brainwashing. We could think of the Games themselves as the 'arrowhead', the initial narrow part of the weapon that pierces the skin, inserts the poison and makes room for the arrow shaft carrying the broader and longer tail of new laws, corporate contracts, undermining of civil society, and so on. Or consider the Games as a Trojan horse, a gallant handsome gift that contains a concealed militia or contagious disease that will slowly but steadily undermine the rights of citizens in favour of the globalised elite.

The anemic city – pasteurised and homogenised

For seven years London was little by little, bit by bit, systematically homogenised and pasteurised to make it palatable to the widest possible audience. Palatability and the Trojan horse of laws that undermined human rights have resulted in a city and a citizenship made anemic.

The seven-year process arguably climaxed with the opening ceremony of the London 2012 Olympic Games. The subsequent weeks of sports competitions in many ways were and remain unimportant. The opening ceremony correlated with the full-scale emptying out of the city and its synchronised militarisation with over 20,000 uniformed military personnel, uncountable police, the positioning of missiles on rooftops alongside the Olympic Park and in surrounding public parks, as well armed and ready aircraft carriers in the River Thames (even though it is inconceivable that there would be any possibility of shooting down any plane over densely populated London without causing more deaths and destruction).

Before we look more broadly at how mega events such as the Olympics and G8 Summits technically and metaphorically 'empty a city', let's first look at just how stark the contrast was between Boris's hubristic public announcement and what actually transpired on London's streets during those summer weeks. Let's take the London Borough of Tower Hamlets, one of five local authorities on which the 'Olympic Park' (now Queen Elizabeth II Park) was built, as a case study. It is also the borough in which we live and where Myrdle Court Press is located.

At the time of the bid, Tower Hamlets was told by the bid organisers that the Olympic marathon would be held within the borough. The race was to start at the Tower of London, snake around the East End and, like all previous marathons, finish in the stadium at the Olympic Park.[9] However, just 12 months before the event was to be held, in quintessential British classist and racist style, the marathon was, without a sincere consultation, relocated to finish on The Mall in front of Buckingham Palace.[10] More than half of the children who live in Tower Hamlets wake up in poverty each and every day. It is London's most ethnically diverse area, has Europe's largest mosque and, as part of the East End, is mythically synonymous with dissenters and so-called free thinkers. The Olympic organisers knew very well from day one that 'in this neck of the woods' it would be more likely people would turn out to protest than to wave government-/*News-of-the World*-supplied British flags at the passing marathon runners.

In late 2011 Tower Hamlets council instituted legal proceedings against the Games organisers and pressed for a judicial review as "we have all the disruption but none of the benefits of the games".[11] Having Tower Hamlets as the backdrop to the marathon and speed walking events for many hours had been projected to provide free advertising for the borough broadcast around the world; seen by 'billions'. But there was no chance the elitist organisers were going to allow one of the most deprived, economically stratified, ethnically diverse and politically active boroughs to be seen by 'billions' on television.

In classic bait and switch tactics the premier Olympic event had been offered to Tower Hamlets early on in order to encourage local councillors to 'back the bid', so they would willingly participate and champion the global mega project. Six years later and one year before the event was to take place, it was ruthlessly and predictably snatched from under their noses. TV viewers, it was argued, should see a backdrop of appropriate, i.e. clichéd and sanitised, images of London, not council estates with brown and poor people. Hopefully that was the last time this generation of local councillors makes a decision with 'star eyes'?

The seven years of disruption, significant increases in taxes[12], the unrelenting jingoism and the siphoning of public money into private pockets were meant to be compensated and offset by a boom in local economic activity and a full-scale accumulation of cultural capital[13] caused by the Games. The much-propagated 'Olympic legacy' was meant to swash over us all in Tower Hamlets, raise all boats and even trickle down as well. This, of course, didn't happen. In fact quite the opposite occurred.

Via a Freedom of Information request we obtained Tower Hamlet's unpublished report 'Olympic Games-time Business Impacts in Tower Hamlets'.[14] It remains unpublished, we assume, as the general consensus across the governing and corporate classes is the Olympics was such a failure, measured against its own set of aims, that it has been unanimously and unequivocally declared 'a success' and everyone should just 'move on'. The post-Olympic silence is profound and it needs to be disrupted, if not for Londoners then for others around the world considering 'backing a bid' for future Games. The results of the survey should be widely known.

Remember the official mantra for seven years was how the Olympics, particularly the six weeks of the actual events, was going to be a social and economic boom for London?[15] Tower Hamlets surveyed the businesses in its borough over the six weeks of the Olympic and Para–Olympic Games and the results reveal the absolute opposite was the case. Takings and trade were predicted by business organisations like LOGOC and the Confederation of British Industry to increase by 40–60% on previous years, however:

> *Overall the survey found that the majority (80%) of local SME businesses surveyed reported negative impacts derived from the Games over the six weeks of the study. An average of 60% of businesses reported trade was badly affected. An average of 66% of businesses reported takings had decreased.*[16]

Other questions asked for the survey were to do with measuring disruption, such as difficulties travelling to work, difficulties with receiving deliveries and the like. As the city had been emptied and militarised, although businesses did experience disruption it was negligible and not even worth noting in the survey's summary document.

The truth of the lie

The Olympic Games was an unequivocal economic disaster for London. The surveyed (small and medium) businesses reveal the scale of the meltdown that occurred right across the city. Our personal experience echoes this. Even if our obtuse bail conditions hadn't prevent us from going within 100 metres of Olympic venues[17], we would never have entered any Olympic venue. We were not remotely interested in 'elite athletes' proficiently putting one foot in front of the other over and over again, but we were very interested in observing the everyday life of the host city. Our observations and conversations with shopkeepers, transport workers and the like correlate with and confirm the statistics collected by the London Borough of Tower Hamlets.

Critical Cities Volume 3 was written and edited during this time so most days we were in libraries in Holborn or Kings Cross. Central London was almost a ghost town. Simple online searches showed very high availability of hotel rooms and restaurant places. Observations of normally busy tourist attractions, such as the London Eye, Southbank, British Museum, Museum of London and Brick Lane etc., showed a city barely a skeleton of its previous self. Special venues set up for the crowds to watch the Games on big screens, such as in Victoria Park, were barely attended and, from personal observation, often completely empty except for Olympic volunteers and security staff. Reports from social and mainstream media showed that the situation was even starker in other parts of the country. There are images of the BBC's public outdoor 'live sites' completely empty. The situation was the same for government-funded 'live sites' in Newcastle, Edinburgh and Glasgow. Dorset, where Olympic sailing events were taking place, had to mount an urgent 'we are open' campaign after business was reported to be down 50% (again it had been predicted to be up 40–60%) and images were posted by the local paper of empty streets, shops, parks and venues.[18]

It was particularly problematic for special event spaces close to the Olympic sites in east London, around Silvertown Quay. A number of businesses and organisations directly related to the Olympics closed – sometimes within days of opening, particularly those set up to accommodate the 'overspill' of visitors to London – despite de Pfeffel Johnson's suggestion that companies engaging with the Olympics were doing well[19]. Secret Pleasure Gardens (SPG) was one such company and venue. Like other venues and events, SPG had received significant public funding and access to public land for an extended period. It was one of the projects that received significant press coverage in the lead up to the Summer Olympics – something of a case study of the 'regeneration ghost milk'[20] made possible via such mega events. SPG was held in particularly high esteem by the Games organisers due to its focus on popular culture, its masquerade of 18th-century pleasure gardens and contemporary set-design architecture. It was a complete flop and is reported to have cost the people of the Borough of Newham over £4 million – that's four million Great British Pounds.[21]

There were many examples where private companies went bust in this period.[22] Most event spaces, like the one in Victoria Park, stayed 'open' despite being empty as they were run and underwritten by the local authority. However businesses linked to the event spaces suffered significantly. In a story titled 'Will Games curse leave "ghost town" London out of the gold rush?', America's NBC News team interviewed Dean Houssein who had set up a coffee stall in Victoria Park, moments from the Olympic venues. In the interview he explains, "It's been like a f****** ghost town ... deader than dead, I've never seen the area like this. It's costing me money. It's really not happening."[23] The same article highlighted a tweet by Richard Bacon (@richardpbacon), who currently has 1.5 million Twitter followers, that said, "One day someone clever will explain to me the enigma of how London managed to simultaneously host the Olympics and become a ghost town."

The mainstream press reported that Westfield Shopping Centre, adjacent to the Olympic Park, was doing well 'benefiting from the Olympics'[24] but one of the people working with This Is Not A Gateway (who was also a shop assistant in one of the major retailers within the shopping centre) told us that, while people passed through the site on the way to the Olympic Park, sales were rare to non-existent. Our colleague also pointed out that there weren't even that many passing through the mall; certainly significantly less than normal and much fewer than were expected for the Games period. Numerous shop owners we spoke to elsewhere around the city were very concerned about being able to stay open. Many said they had over-hired and over-stocked (perishables were a particular concern) on the advice of government agencies that had suggested there would be huge crowds and difficulty with deliveries.

One consistently given explanation for the emptying of London is that there was a magnetic effect where everybody was actually drawn into the Olympic venues and the Olympic Park. Of course London doesn't empty like this on a Saturday afternoon when more stadiums and many more people are absorbed from the city to watch football matches in the major let alone all the other leagues. The west London Borough of Hammersmith and Fulham with its many football stadiums, exhibition centres, music venues and theatres has as many visitors each weekend as were predicted for the Olympic Park and the city doesn't suddenly empty out. It is important to note that many, if not most, of the London Olympic venues had rows upon rows of empty seats as well. The one million extra people de Pfeffel Johnson pompously proclaimed would cause 'huge pressure' certainly weren't in the Olympic Park.

If you have ever been in London over the Christmas and New Year period you will know how the city empties out. You will also be aware how dispiriting it feels as a result. For around two weeks (from 23 December to around 6 January) universities, schools and colleges are closed, public services like children's playgroups, swimming lessons etc., are halted, most businesses operate on a skeleton staff, cafés and restaurants close and absolutely everything else closes early. That same emptiness, that same stillness, that same lacklustreness and quietness was the real impact of the Olympics on London. The situation was in stark contrast to the meta-narrative, the official advice and pre-Games propaganda.

Speaking to people during the Games period that work in or own businesses in Tower Hamlets and around London we learnt the 'negative impacts' were so significant they were worried they might be forced to cease trading. It was well reported that rent and rates had also been increased year on year since the success of the bid in 2006. The six weeks in summer 2012, everyone was told, would be recompense, would shower money on everybody in and around the Olympic geography.[25] The huge pressures and changes to London's tempo as a result of the Olympic misadventure should not be underestimated and should be part of an ongoing discussion about the corruption of £24+ billion wasted and the undermining of human rights.

What is concerning is that almost everyone has relinquished any interest and few are providing critical insight on London's post-Olympic condition. It feels like those who encouraged and spurred on a street brawl, pulled in friends and passersby, but when it was finished did a quick about turn, endlessly posting on social media about this amazing event they just saw but leaving the injured on the ground, alone. It feels like it was all just a game, nothing to be bothered with now, despite it altering London and Britain in numerous problematic ways, with possible long-term consequences. If there is any criticism at all it almost entirely revolves around the Games' impact on house prices – the British obsession, particularly the invariable concern that 'not even the middle classes can afford to buy property now'.

With such grave injustices and rampant corruption one might imagine this would be a focus of many academics' work. Unfortunately academics are some of last people one can rely on for critical analysis. Academics seem to think they are BBC journalists who need to 'show both sides of the argument and be impartial'.[26] Huge effort is taken to search for and then point out the teeniest 'grey areas' and make these usually hollow examples important. They don't want to be seen to 'take a position' and generally appear preoccupied with wanting to place examples of subtlety in front of our eyes rather than undertaking thorough critical research. Despite the vast social and political space given by society to academics, along with their regular income and dedicated time to research, the vast majority produces the most risk-adverse and status-quo-supporting materials.

Given the facts of the London 2012 Olympic Games event, it should have been intellectually demolished by academics across all disciplines. Instead any academics, certainly British ones, that did bother to 'engage' seemed to be determined to not tackle the actual facts of the situation but to look at the so-called 'complexities'. They appear to care about nothing but their mortgage(s), their children's nannies and forthcoming private education, and petty bourgeois accolades and recognitions. Most do little more than hoover-up, colonise, repackage and then sell other people's work simultaneously sucking the politics, life and urgency out of whatever it is they touch. Some are outright thieves and others turn a blind eye to robbery. Like establishment vampires, feasting on the majority, they are desperate to maintain the status quo – especially their titles and social standing. Some pay lip-service to so-called 'leftist ideas' but that is evidently a red herring given the conditions of the world we are in. Very few even bother to sign a petition for a living wage and decent conditions for the people who clean their offices let alone campaign alongside them. Few people on this planet have been in a better place than academics to directly combat the rise of neo-liberalism and the violence of globalisation – and there are millions upon millions of them around the world.

To illustrate this point, for example University of East London's Emeritus Professor Phil Cohen made strenuous efforts to highlight "the complex urban processes" emphasising "Olympophiles for whom the Games can do no wrong as well as Olympophobes for whom they can do no right"[27] rather than taking a position and demonstrating the evidence of the utter social and political disaster the Games were. It is as if academics have Monty Python's absurdist song 'Always look on the bright side of life' playing on loop in their offices, as if Monty Python characters have come to life as real people in universities around the world. Academics might be 'polite and genteel society' at its very worst? Not surprisingly, 'Always look on the bright side of life' was performed in the opening ceremony of the London 2012 Olympics.

Quite unlike academics, journalists, we are told, are social pariahs; some of the least valued professional people. Journalists are as distrusted, we are told, as used car salesmen.[28] It is, however, newspapers and other news platforms rather than academics where the greatest body of knowledge to draw on when evidencing the fact London was emptied can be found. Routledge, 'the world's leading academic publisher in the Humanities and Social Sciences', hasn't considered the emptying of London as noteworthy at all. At least eight books will have been published by Routledge by the end of 2015 in which the emptiness of London may be mentioned only once in one of the forthcoming titles 'Experiencing the London 2012 Olympic Games' by Giulianotti et al, which focuses on Newham, one of the five London boroughs in which the Olympic Park was built.

The emptiness was recorded not by academics but the news platforms. They recorded photographs of near empty stadiums, photographs of empty streets, restaurants and parks, theatres and trains and buses. Although newspapers aren't able necessarily to provide critical insights, they recorded many vox-pops with a range of people. News platforms published what data was shared on the economic and social activity decline and even undertook some investigative research. The news and individual blog platforms referenced some of the erosions of human rights and the problematic laws introduced that have very much remained in place many years after the Olympics have come and gone. It is in such an archive that Londoners may be able to dig for an understanding of the impact this mega event had on themselves and the city today.

Analytical voices

In this chapter's first essay, 'The Urbanism of the G8 Summits (1999 - 2012)', Roberto Bottazzi takes a forensic look at a mega event that occurs with such regularity it has become part of the annual global media circus, alongside Wimbledon Tennis, Superbowl and Boxing Day sales. In 2014 this government-to-government meeting of the eight largest industrialised economies (France, Germany, Italy, Japan, the UK, the US, Canada, Russia and the EU) was moved at short notice from its previously agreed location in Sochi, Russia, and held in Brussels, Belgium.[29] Russia was excluded from attending. The ease with which such large events can now be moved at short notice should be considered as a reflection of our new social conditions - the ease with which laws that suppress human rights can be passed and multi-billion pound budgets allocated with little scrutiny. It reflects the way space in cities can now be reconfigured with minimal public consultation or attention, correlates with the expansion and practice of security companies, the deployment of Smart Cities technologies and the depth of everyday surveillance undertaken by governments and corporations, and shows how easily, quickly and confidently oppressive networks can now come together to further their own interests.

The paper highlights the relationship between mega events and urban environments, the growth of Smart Cities technology and rhetoric, and how mega events are testing grounds for harsher and harsher approaches to governing people. Concentrating on the spatial configurations inflicted on urban geography that reveal the harsh realities underlying the ideologies at work in a given city at a given time, it demonstrates how G8 Summits provide important case studies on the use and intensification of elements of the oppressive technologies and techniques already operating, or soon to be inserted, in our everyday urban lives.

Roberto provides significant insight into the 2001 G8 Summit in Genoa, where anti-globalisation protester Carlo Giuliani was brutally murdered by police officer Mario Placanica.[30] He outlines the scale and cost of the three-day summit: 25,000 delegates; 28,000 people living close to the summit location were removed from their homes and businesses; 18,000 police were brought in; missiles were erected alongside main transport hubs; luxury ships, isolated at sea, provided accommodation for visiting 'dignitaries'. Genoa became a performance space, an arena, where delegates had the opportunity to display their disdain and indifference – an early indicator of the methodologies they would be employing to achieve their aims in the new century. The message was clear: cities can be emptied and militarised with ease; dissent will be crushed by any means necessary; you are taking your life in your hands if you choose to protest.

Revealing the relationship of Smart Cities to mega events, Roberto's paper highlights how the definitions and understandings of 'Smart Cities' have almost entirely been provided by corporations who needed a way to market their new technologies. We learn more about the close relationship between corporations and governments, and how G8 and G20 mega events are actual laboratories for corporate Smart City technologies that by default end up being paid for out of public funds – mostly via 'security budgets'.

The second contribution, 'Fighting Gentrification and State Co-ordinated "Regeneration": Experiences from Recent London Campaigns', is a conversation between five people representing three thoughtful urban resistance campaigns that were, to varying degrees, affected by the government-corporation relationship that took advantage of the processes of homogenising and pasteurising London in time for the 2012 Olympics – Julian Cheyne from the demolished Clays Lane Housing Co-op, Mital Patel,

James Skinner and Ruth Allen from Wards Corner Community Coalition (WCC), and Charlie Charman from Save Leyton Marshes.

Clays Lane, Britain's largest purpose-built housing co-operative, was compulsorily purchased and demolished so the 'athletes village' could be built. The once mutually owned land and homes were destroyed and, with London Olympic official incompetence and corruption, the site was primed with hundreds of millions of pounds before being handed over to the Qatari royal family for what is labelled 'knock down prices'.[31] Despite this gift from the British public, just a two-bedroom very basic unfurnished apartment in what is now called 'East Village' costs over £21,000 pa to rent – just below an entire mean British salary.[32] Britain's largest housing co-operative – this once wonderful, non-conformist, anti-capitalist venture – was emptied and erased. Today East Village's website pathetically and without irony announces the launch of 'The Arty Season' "welcoming a trio of artworks to inspire locals in the lead up to Christmas".[33]

Wards Corner Community Coalition (WCC) has been running a successful campaign (for nearly a decade) to prevent the demolition of a collection of important community buildings that had been earmarked for gentrification and whitification by the local authority. Pressure from the developer and the local authority was massively ramped up using the Olympics mega event as a rallying point to push the idea because the crowds passing by on route to the Olympics would gawk at the 'dirty and neglected' site. The council and developers were suggesting WCC would bring shame on itself and on other local people by not showing the world a seemingly upbeat shiny face. WCC knew better and didn't fall for the hype and shaming attempt. Instead they organised events where community members held hands in a continuous link around the site to demonstrate community involvement and a willingness to use their bodies to defend the site. The group's argument has always been 'Better Neighbourhood, Same Neighbours'. Rather than be in a defensive position, where it can only respond, the organisation has created its own desire archive – its own community developed plan for the site.

Save Leyton Marshes formed when it was unilaterally announced that the protected green spaces would be used for basketball practice courts for the Olympic Games. The group predicted, and was right, that this would result in the militarisation of the park as well as contributing to the disintegration of democratic processes. It was also correctly argued that a precedent would be set that would eat away at the Marshes protection rights. Members and other activists used their bodies to attempt to prevent trucks from entering the park so the stadium could not be built.

The conversation calls us to pay close attention "to the chilling overarching similarities of forced evictions, displacement and the destruction of communities and livelihoods as governments and corporations work together to extract and maximise the value of land inhabited by the city's poor and ethnic minorities" around the world. It asks us to look closer at the global patterns of the Urban Industry, and to look specifically at the hand-in-hand relationship between governments and corporations. One of the core topics it addresses is how the corporations and government departments employ specialist communication companies to concoct and promote a narrative that an area is empty, derelict and in need of cleansing. This imaginary emptiness and dereliction, they argue, needs their brand of life, vigour and colour.

The final essay in this chapter is an engaging exposé of one Londoner's personal experience of the 2012 Games entitled 'The London Olympics and the State We're In'. While filming the destruction of Leyton Marshes to make way for Olympic infrastructure, Mike Wells was assaulted by one of the workers given the task of flattening the greenspace, arrested by the police, and held in prison for eight days before being released on bail. Also a resident and member of the demolished Clays Lane Housing Cooperative which became the Athletes' Village and today is East Village with its new E20 postcode, Mike reveals that this new luxury housing is on top of a newly created radioactive waste dump. Drawing together numerous seemingly disparate aspects with much humour and critical insight, Mike observes:

> *The organisational model of London 2012 is the same our government uses to manage the nation – a foundation of compacted bullshit provides a platform on which a network of well-connected vampires schmooze, positing themselves to pick up lucrative government contracts. The mainstream media, up to its neck in the same compacted bullshit, almost completely fails in its duty to monitor, investigate and inform, whilst a system of self-congratulation and industry awards is backed-up with knighthoods for the worst offenders.*

The paper highlights the entirely unfounded, over-the-top jitters (guilty conscience?) that took hold of London's elite and ricocheted across much of society in the lead up to this "once in a lifetime" sports meeting. This induced sense of vulnerability and urgency was taken advantage of at every opportunity: ushering in draconian laws, cascading public money into the pockets of corporations, demanding globalised uniformity to avoid possible embarrassment. The straightjacket placed on Londoners (often by themselves, it should be said) has left London a mollified, preppyfied and lacklustre city. The same has been said of Barcelona (1992), while Athens (2004) was famously bankrupted and opened up for global financial scavengers to pull apart. Such mega events only ever benefit the elite of a nation and are pivotal moments in the expansion and entrenchment of western-dominated globalisation.

This chapter doesn't afford the space to do justice to the processes by which London was mollified and it is our hope we will publish another book at a future date that will critically examine this, particularly the processes of whitification and 'preppyisation', and share strategies which, with hindsight, could best undermine the pantomime, the lies and the grand thefts that take place. This might provide people with irrefutable concrete evidence to ensure the elite of their city is not able to even consider bidding for a mega event. There is no cake, there is no circus, there is no trickle down, and there is no profit – just empty streets, large-scale property development and the transfer of public money into private pockets, all with the assistance of armed military personnel and a constant paternalism warning citizens not to step out of line, not to mess this one up.

It is the emptiness, the way in which the city was emptied, that we feel best communicates the false promises and deep corruption of mega events like the Olympics and the G8 summits. It throws the entire mega event into disrepute. The emptiness was an undeniable fact that is communicated powerfully through images and statistics. The emptiness might just be 'the' story that enables citizens to refute and undermine their elite's attempts at forcing the globalisation straight-jacket onto them and their city.

1. Message quoted on a number of news websites, such as *The Telegraph* (4 July 2012) and *The Atlantic*'s CityHub (4 July 2012) in the lead up to the 2012 Olympic Games. It was also part of Transport for London's press release once again warning businesses and commuters to plan for an extra 1 million people to visit London.
2. '"Hi folks! This is the Mayor here" – Boris is silenced as TFL pull Tube announcements', *The Independent*, 1 August 2012.

3. 'Revealed: how David Cameron and Boris Johnson are related', 23 April 2010 and 'Boris Johnson, the Mayor of London, is a distant relative of the Queen, it has been disclosed', 4 August 2008, www.blogs.telegraph.co.uk.
4. Victoria and Albert Museum, London.
5. William Arthur Philip Louis Mountbatten-Windsor and Kate Elizabeth Middleton married in London, UK, April 2001.
6. The Jubilee that wasn't a jubilee – Elizabeth Alexandra Mary Mountbatten Windsor's 60th year sitting on a throne. 'Jubilee' is a Jewish and then Christian biblical concept which is only meant to be celebrated every 25 years. According to Leviticus 25:8–13 debts are meant to be forgiven, slaves and prisoners set free and forgiven but, on the contrary, in Britain the series of events are estimated to have cost the British public anywhere between £1.3 and £3 billion (including lost income due to public holidays). Taxpayers are estimated by Republic to spend £300 million a year on the 'royal household' which is nine times higher than official figures. See http://www.republic.org.uk/.
7. http://www.legislation.gov.uk/ukpga/2006/12/pdfs/ukpga_20060012_en.pdf, 30 March 2006.
8. The Defence of the Realm Act was passed within days of World War I being declared (8 August 1915). The broad aim was "securing the public safety and the defence of the realm",conferring widespread powers for 'emergency' situations which were meant to cease when the war/emergency had passed. Aside from such powers, it increased the presence of the idea of emergency powers to protect the status quo.
9. Download at: http://www.towerhamlets.gov.uk/search.aspx?cx=008280465879053608327:251xeiiz6ey&cof=FORID:11;NB:1&ie=UTF-8&q=OlympicMarathonRoute.pdf.
10. See 'Tower Hamlets Taking Olympic Marathon Decision to Court – LOCOG of breaking promises made in the original bid for the Games', which Includes a map of the bid-promised and the eventual courses, http://www.lbc.co.uk/tower-hamlets-taking-olympic-marathon-decision-to-court-32339.
11. 'London 2012 Olympic marathon route a "travesty"', BBC News 5 October 2010.
12. 'Londoners will not pay any more after the government announced a rise in the Olympic budget, the mayor has said', http://news.bbc.co.uk/1/hi/england/london/6452865.stm. Tax increased by £19.76 pa for an extended period for time. Alongside this a number of Olympic sponsors are well-known tax avoiders in the UK. Furthermore companies and athletes benefitted from a temporary tax haven agreed with the IOC in the bid. They were exempt from both UK Corporation Tax and UK Income Tax. It is estimated just under £700 billion of tax was lost, according to *Ethical Consumer.*
13. 'Our Promise for 2012 – How the UK will benefit from the Olympic Games and Paralympic Games', first published 30 March 2008,https://www.gov.uk/government/publications/our-promise-for-2012-how-the-uk-will-benefit-from-the-olympic-games-and-paralympic-games.
14. Having spoken to businesses throughout Tower Hamlets at the time of the sporting event we learnt from them a survey was being done by the council. We first sought the information from the relevant department in Tower Hamlets and were told it wouldn't be published or released so we undertook a Freedom of Information Inquiry. It was finally released in June 2013.
15. 'David Cameron claims London 2012 will bring £13bn "gold for Britain"', *The Guardian*, 5 July 2012, http://www.theguardian.com/politics/2012/jul/05/david-cameron-london-2012-gold-britain. See also 'Using the Olympics to Stimulate Urban Growth',

http://www.huffingtonpost.com/mitchell-l-moss/london-olympics_b_1682584.html (updated01/10/2013) and '2012 London Olympics to regenerate one of the poorest areas of the capital', 4 April 2008, http://www.citymayors.com/sport/2012-olympics-london.html.

16. Summary from 'Olympic Games-time Business Impacts in Tower Hamlets' document.
17. 'Strict bail conditions mean Mr Oldfield has been banned from going anywhere near the Diamond Jubilee or Olympic events', 23 May 2012, http://www.bbc.co.uk/news/uk-england-london-18179494.
18. 'Blame games as traders claim business harmed by Olympics', http://www.dorsetecho.co.uk/news/9846714.Blame_games_as_traders_claim_business_harm%20ed_by_Olympics/?ref=mr; 'Olympics woe: Weymouth hoteliers fear loss of thousands during Games summer', 29 May 2012, http://www.bournemouthecho.co.uk/news/9732078.display/.
19. 'London 2012 Olympics: Boris Johnson admits Olympic effect has been "patchy"', 1 August 2012, http://www.standard.co.uk/olympics/olympic-news/london-2012-olympics-boris-johnson-admits-olympic-effect-has-been-patchy-7999276.html.
20. 'Regeneration ghost milk' is a false promise – a mirage. Every human needs milk in their infancy and ideally from their loving and selfless mother. Regeneration promises plundered and abandoned communities similar nutrients and warmth, often with a paternalistic narrative which can at first be perceived as self-sacrificing, generous and full of promise. 'Ghost milk' is the false promise, a mirage like ghosts are. This shouldn't be confused with Iain Sinclair's Ghost Milk which he describes as a secretion "CGI smears . . . Real juice from a virtual host. Embalming fluid. A soup of photographic negatives . . . The universal element in which we sink and swim." http://www.theguardian.com/books/2011/jul/15/ghost-milk-iain-sinclair-olympics.
21. 'Nothing but misery at the London Pleasure Gardens', http://www.wharf.co.uk/2013/03/nothing-but-misery-at-the-lond.html.
22. 'War of words over failure of Weymouth Bayside Festival during Olympics', 15 August 2012, http://www.dorsetecho.co.uk/news/9931258.print/.
23. 'Will Games curse leave "ghost town" London out of the gold rush?', 7 August 2012, http://worldnews.nbcnews.com/_news/2012/08/07/13146553-will-games-curse-leave-ghost-town-london-out-of-the-gold-rush.
24. 'Westfield has declared itself a winner from the 2012 Olympics after 5.5m people visited its Stratford shopping centre during the last two weeks', 5 August 2012, http://www.telegraph.co.uk/finance/newsbysector/constructionandproperty/9476894/Stratford-City-shopping-centre-attracted-5.5m-visits-during-London-2012-Olympic-Games.html.
25. Despite no evidence of any Olympic Games creating an economic boom for the people of the 'host' city (quite the opposite with huge debts in most cities) many talked themselves and others into believing it would be a gold rush. One of the most perverse was high school gossip that you could rent your property out for the period and make a fortune as "millions of Olympics visitors searching for accommodation in 2012", 8 July, 2011, http://www.theguardian.com/money/2011/jul/08/rent-your-home-olympics-visitors. The "millions of visitors" never materialised in London in 2012 nor in previous host cities.
26. "At its simplest it means not taking sides. Impartiality is about providing a breadth of view", http://www.bbc.co.uk/academy/journalism/values/article/art20130702112133788.
27. P. Cohen, *On the Wrong Side of the Track? East London and the Post Olympics* (London:Lawrence & Wishart Ltd, 2013).
28. https://www.journalism.co.uk/news/journalism-the-third-most-untrustworthy-

profession-according-to-poll/s2/a540036/.

29. http://www.aljazeera.com/video/europe/2014/03/g7-nations-suspend-russia-scrap-g8-summit-201432422400577403.html.
30. If you have access to the internet go to YouTube.com and search for the film titled *Carlo Giuliani* created and uploaded by 'TV!!! Master!!!' It is just 3 minutes and 11 seconds long but reveals much about the violence inflicted as a result of mega events. It also shows something of the scale of resistance to globalisation there was at the time - even it seems from those who have for centuries benefited from these very processes.
31. 'UK taxpayers left £275m out of pocket after deal is reached by Olympic Delivery Authority', http://www.theguardian.com/sport/2011/aug/12/olympic-village-qatari-ruling-family.
32. Rent based on a two- bedroom apartment via East Village's own lettings website www.eastvillagelondon.com (accessed 22/12/14). Mean income from HM Revenue and Customs https://www.gov.uk/government/statistics/distribution-of-median-and-mean-income-and-tax-by-age-range-and-gender-2010-to-2011 (accessed 22/12/14).
33. http://www.eastvillagelondon.co.uk/Featured/The-Arty-Season.aspx.

The Urbanism of the G8 Summits (1999-2012)

ROBERTO BOTTAZZI

Spatial organisation is a critical feature of the G8 summits that took place just before and during the first decade of this century, from Seattle in 1999 – albeit this was a WTO meeting – to Camp David in 2012. This series of global gatherings were characterised by clashes between police and protesters and levels of violence that resulted in the death of Carlo Giuliani at the 2001 summit in Genoa. Whereas many essays have examined the political and cultural aspects of the summits – covering issues such as the nature of the media images broadcast of these events[1] or denouncing the police behaviour through investigative journalism[2] – this research concentrates on space, looking at the spatial tactics employed for crowd-control and counter-strategies adopted by protesters, and at the burgeoning role that digital technology played in the temporary re-organisation of the cities involved. This is all the more urgent at a time when many cities, both in the west and other countries, advocate the introduction of digital technologies for urban management[3], under the vague label of the 'Smart City'.

The urbanism of Smart Cities utilises sensors and computers to manage a wide range of issues, from monitoring infrastructure status or usage (e.g. structural conditions of bridges or number of vehicles traversing them) and utilities' distribution (most western cities already fully rely on digital technologies for their water management), to the mapping of citizens' behaviour through CCTV cameras. The implementation of such technological apparatus takes place under the dubious agenda of efficiency, profit and control; arguments that historically have played a very marginal role in constructing rich and lively urban environments.[4] The three-day G8 summits can be seen as accelerated laboratory models in which such technologies were deployed and their effects tested.

A critical analysis of the spaces constructed at these events is not only lacking but is all the more crucial if we want to problematise how the city of the 21st century will operate. This is only superficially a western issue; even if the companies that manufacture these technologies are invariably based in the developed world, their products are utilised by cities all over the world. Masdar (United Arab Emirates) and Songdo (South Korea) are some of the cities that are built *ex-novo* on these principles, and others, like Rio de Janeiro, have equipped themselves with state of the art control rooms, a sort-of uber-police station in which data from CCTV and sensors are combined to control activities in the city. Manufactured, implemented and managed by large private corporations, all these sensors, CCTV cameras and computer centres reinforce the privatisation of the city and the ability to control and predict individual citizen behaviours. Their unquestioned implementation is becoming an urgent issue to confront.

The analysis presented here is particularly addressed to architects and urbanists; disciplines interested and consulted in the design of new cities. Extensive though not often critical debate on the role of the digital has been taking place in both disciplines since the 90s.[5] These conversations often have an optimistic, almost utopian tone that sharply contrasts with the harsh reality evidenced at the G8 summits. Unlike academic debates, the spaces of the G8 summits have had nothing abstract about them: cities did get reconfigured – sometimes permanently; people did manifest in their streets and sometimes paid a high price for doing so. The harsh, complex character of G8 events offers a healthy critique of the current largely unquestioned acceptance of Smart Cities as the inevitable or desired model for the contemporary city.

Taking an approach that considers the G8 city not as a coherent entity but as the rather tumultuous result of the implementation of strategies of diverse nature and scale, this paper aims to sharpen critical awareness of how cities are currently constructed by the stacking of digital and physical infrastructures.

Why did this spatial-political event become important?

Towards the end of the 90s a whole series of social movements that had been developing for about ten years started to make their presence visible on the streets.[6] In the realm of theory this was paralleled by increasing signs of strain vis à vis Francis Fukuyama's idea of 'the end of history'[7]. Compared to movements that developed in continental Europe around 1968 and 1977, the presence of Marxist ideology was far less noticeable in the movements of the 90s as other issues, such as global warming and globalisation, came to dominate. Their ideological foundation was perhaps best captured by Negri and Hardt's theories of globalisation and immaterial labour.[8] These two political philosophers held an ambivalent attitude towards both the notion of globalisation and the role that digital technologies played in it. On the one hand, they provided a clear critique of globalisation, condemned as a homogenising, western ideology to carpet the rest of the world. On the other, they also maintained that those same global forces also carried the potential for their overturn, a revolution from within the system. Negri and Hardt further characterised their revolutionary politics as that of 'the multitude' – a concept they derived from Spinoza – flexible, swarming constellations of groups in which individual action would not be suppressed by a hierarchical structure[9]. Their discussion on digital technologies followed a similar path, clearly acknowledging that 'the digital' was instrumental in the 'smooth' global circulation of capital but also suggesting that it carried the potential for emancipation and direct communication.[10] For these reasons, the label 'No Global' that mainstream media attributed to groups of protesters appears misleading. A more accurate description of the character and originality of these movements would highlight two elements: the lack of a central predetermined ideology (which was rejected in favour of a greater pluralism of ideas, religions and cultures) and the growing role that digital media had in connecting people and exchanging ideas as well as organising action[11].

The G8 summit provides an ideal platform for such movements to manifest public dissent since the event embodies both the notion of global governance and the control of the few – only eight countries – over the rest of the world – 178 countries. Since 1975, the year of the first G8 summit, the eight founding countries – Canada, France, Germany, Italy, Japan, Russia, United Kingdom and United States – have been meeting yearly under the stated agenda of discussing the world's governance which in reality translates as protecting and enhancing their specific western interests and agendas. Since the 1999 World Trade Organisation (WTO) ministerial summit in Seattle, a substantial amount of public resistance has mounted and expressed itself in rallies and protests during the G8 summits. As Geert Lovink and Florian Schneider point out, Seattle was also the moment when all these different groups of protesters – ranging from anarchists, communists and environmental groups to nuns[12] – clearly understood that their political action had to abandon old schemes, mostly generated from leftist movements, and embrace a new terrain on which to unfold political discussion, i.e. take the battle against globalisation to the street 'armed' with the then-emergent portable digital media[13].

From the WTO meeting in Seattle in 1999 to the 2012 gathering in Camp David, the G8 summit became a spatial laboratory in which different strategies, ideas and media were played out. From the clashes between protesters and police in Seattle to the informal conversations between national leaders wearing casual outfits in front of a fireplace in Camp David, what is important to foreground is the emergence and proliferation of a distinct spatial sensibility; one that articulates the complex relations between participation, politics and technology in cities.

A real turning point was constituted by the 2001 summit in Genoa, Italy. This is not only because of the intensity of the clashes during the event, which culminated in Carlo Giuliani's death, but also because, in Genoa, protesters' tactics involving more innovative use of media gave rise to what Lovink and Schneider label the "beta version of cyber activism"[14]. This specific event offers the most compelling account of planning strategies accompanying a G8 summit, as well as clearly setting the spatial paradigms that many other global events have been following since then. Whilst the media normally attribute much importance to the extreme violence of the clashes in Genoa, here the emphasis is rather on the planning strategies and participants' behaviour, which are instrumental in reconsidering the problematic relation between globalisation, digital technologies and urbanism. While the bibliography on the social and political issues stirred by these events is remarkably vast, no systematic urban study of this phenomenon has been carried out so far. Space does, in fact, provide a fruitful vantage point to re-examine the G8 summits because it describes a more direct though largely unconscious representation of ideologies, untainted by the manipulation of the media or the political rhetoric of conflicting groups. Space represents a sort of 'datum line' against which cultural, political and urban strategies can be observed.

The importance of space can be seen directly in different countries' choice of location for the summit: from the urban gatherings of Seattle (US, WTO 1999) or Genoa (Italy, 2001) to the touristy resort of Sea Island (US, 2004) or the remote meeting in Kananaskis (Canada, 2002). It is not perhaps a coincidence that G8 summits lost their political and media traction as soon as central sites ceased to take preference: by choosing ever more isolated locations and tightening control over public access, the G8 lost most of its *raison d'être* and virtually condemned itself to extinction. As a result, the economic G20 summits have now gained a more prominent role, the 2012 G8 was deliberately deserted by Russian President Vladimir Putin, and British Prime Minister David Cameron, who hosted the 2013 G8 meeting in Lough Erne, County Fermanagh (Northern Ireland), has already publicly expressed his doubts on the relevance of this formula[15].

The idea of the Smart City

It is useful to relate the discussion of the G8 summits to the concomitant emergence of the so-called Smart City.[16] Though there is no general consensus on a fixed definition of what a Smart City is, we can begin to frame it as the result of the extensive physical implementation of digital devices in urban environments. Posed in these terms, the Smart City is a fundamentally reactive concept as it tries to align the city with the impressive developments in the field of technology in terms of processing power, networking abilities and pervasive distribution of sensors to monitor city life.

Out of the myriads of initiatives and projects on this topic, it is possible to detect two emerging versions of Smart City – our discussion of the G8 summits can be considered as a third, actual and less reassuring version of it. The most common definition of the Smart City is the one provided by the companies that manufacture and implement the technologies underpinning it. Here the definition varies from company to company depending on levels of concern for social integration and access. Nevertheless the summary provided by Living PlanIT is one of the earnest and blunt ones: "[The Smart City is] the missing link between real estate and technology sectors."[17] This version of the Smart City emphasises control and efficiency with its spatial organisation based on control rooms. Beyond the purely metaphorical level, cities adopting these technologies also construct physical spaces – actual control rooms – in which all data available, mostly vehicular traffic, CCTV footage, weather and crime reports etc., are eventually gathered. The distributed network of processors enables the 'reading' of the city in real time, an opportunity that many municipalities across the globe are taking advantage of, and this version of the Smart City differs little between western and non-aligned countries; Rio de Janeiro, as mentioned, boasts one of the most advanced, control-room-based, Smart City infrastructures. Through joint partnerships between public and private sectors, these have come to constitute the most popular version of the Smart City.

The technology supporting this digital infrastructure is fundamentally invisible and private. CCTV cameras and smart apps literally withdraw data from individual citizens (providing reports on road traffic and their position in the city, for example) and transfer it to control centres where the data is agglomerated and mined to improve the efficiency of the city. In opposition to this, sociologist Saskia Sassen has posited a more transparent version of the Smart City in which sensing infrastructures allow citizens to see, and potentially manipulate, the data gathered.[18] Here, the model of the control room based on hiding data is reversed and distributed both physically and politically throughout the city with the aim of both stimulating citizens' appropriation and keeping data as local as possible.

The relation between control, technology and space is also central to the planning of the G8 meetings. Summits such as the one in Genoa show a complex network of technologies deployed to physically, legally and technologically alter the use of the city. The G8 summits share the fundamental cross-disciplinary nature of the Smart City definitions as well as the interweaving of space, technology and politics. They contain elements of both interpretations: the summits were both experiments on control in increasingly technological cities as well as instances of the potential for distributed behaviour and collective intelligence. Most importantly, as *ante literam* examples of the Smart City, the G8 summits were real, fully implemented 'visions' that allow us to measure the gap between theory and practice in this specific field of investigation. Despite the lack of a convincing definition of the Smart City, it is important to analyse the temporary city of the G8 summits within the

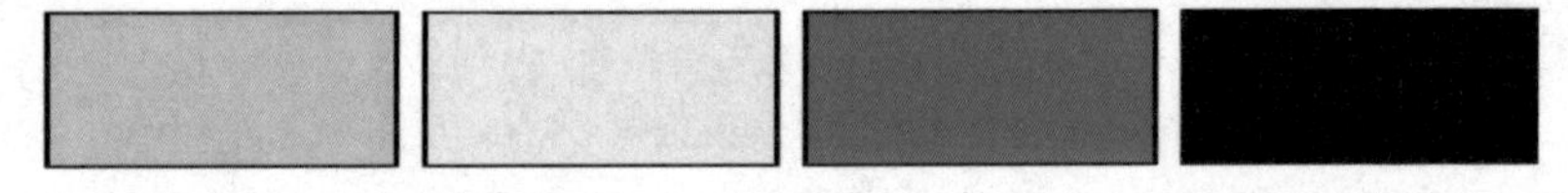

At the Genoa G8, 2001, the police classified all participants by their estimated danger: from black, most aggressive, to pink

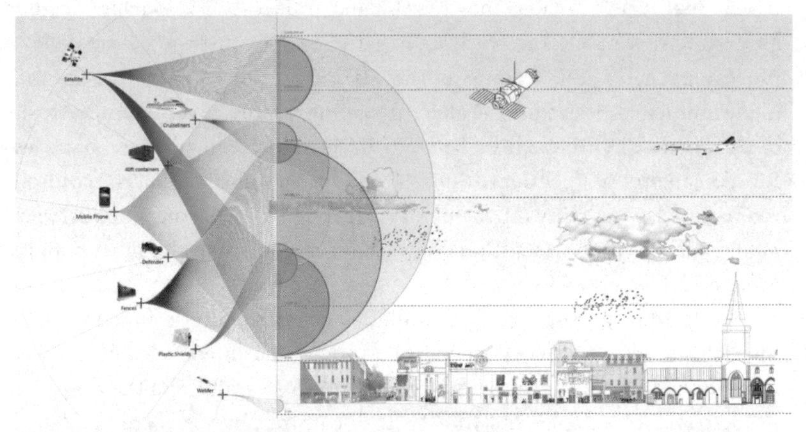

Map of all technological devices deployed at the 2001 G8 summit showing their relationship in terms of scale

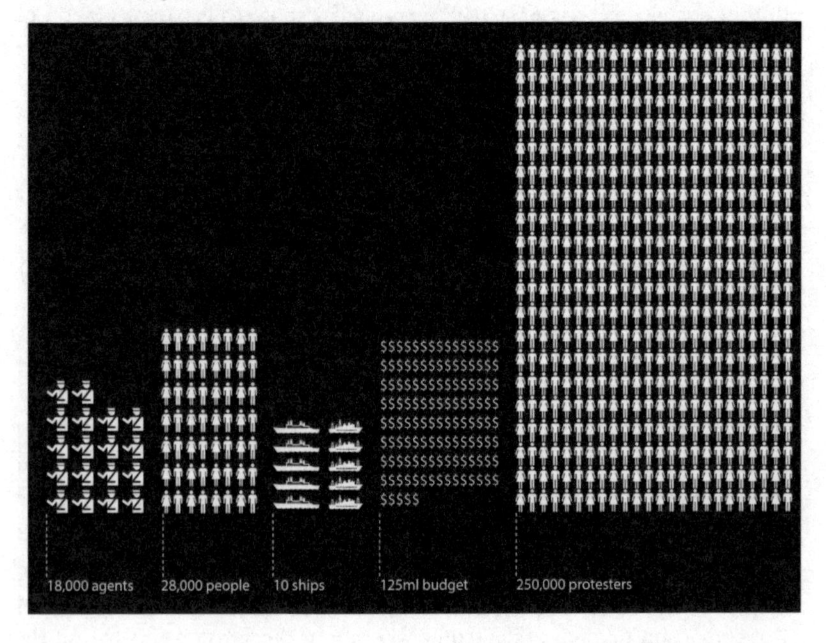

Map of the human and monetary costs of organising the 2001 G8 summit

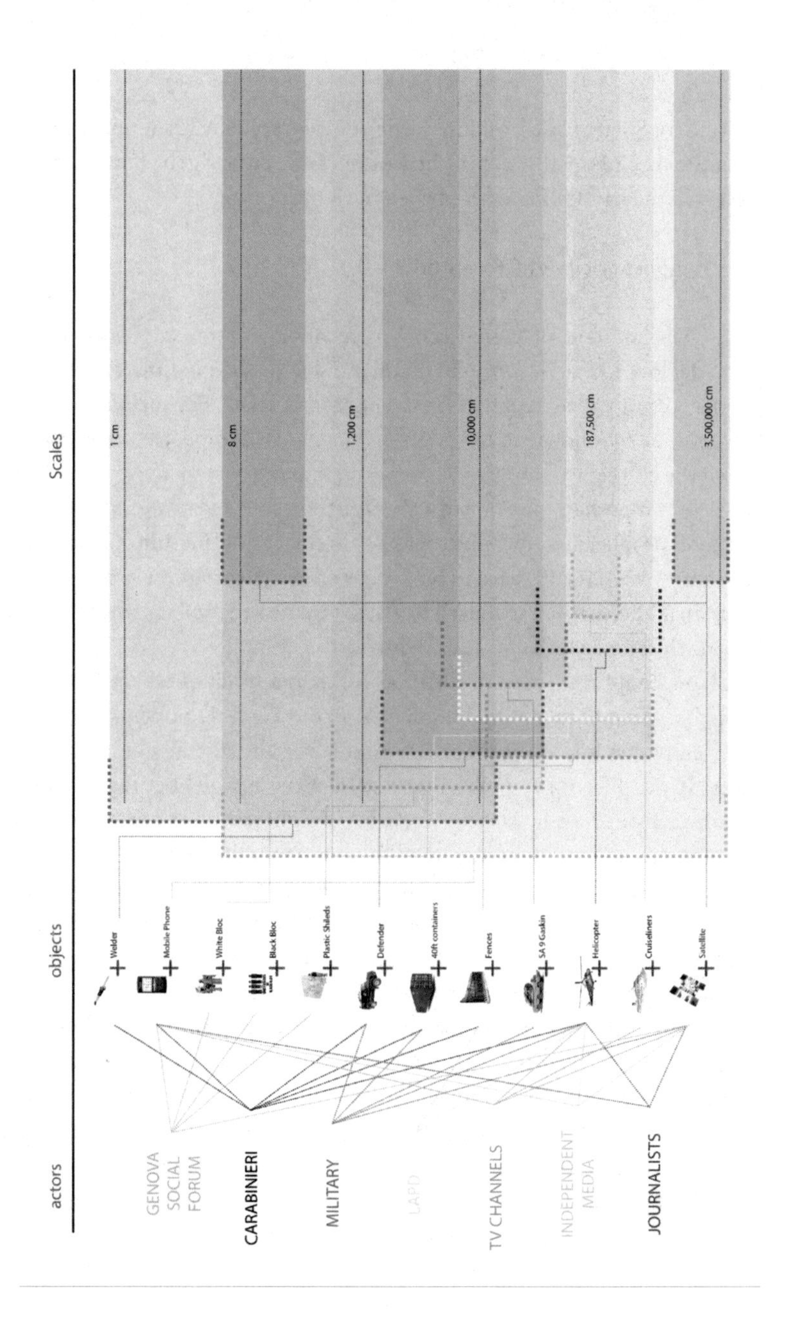

Diagram of all the actors involved in
the planning of the 2001 G8 summit in Genoa
All illustrations, 2014, Roberto Botazzi

debate on Smart Cities, and in doing so, we implicitly assume the relevance that Smart Cities will have in the future of the city, which should not be left solely in the hands of market-driven initiatives.

The temporary city of G8 summits

The sheer amount of money, bodies, technologies, objects, laws, meetings etc., deployed in a G8 summit is comparable to the investments commonly undertaken to permanently transform part of a city. For instance, in Genoa in 2001, 18,000 police agents were deployed, 28,000 people were evacuated from the city centre, 10 ships were moved into the port to house the delegates, missile ramps were positioned by main transport hubs, and approximately 250,000 people came to Genoa for the three days of the summit. The cost of the entire event is still debated but can be estimated around 125 million euros, plus an additional sum believed to also be in the range of 125 million euros to repair the damages that occurred during the event[19].

How could a three-day event be compared to cities which are artefacts based on permanence? The notion of 'event' is central to understanding both the temporary spaces of the G8 summits and the digitally enhanced Smart City. It was Pierre Levy who first outlined the parallel between events and digital information by stating, "… a bit of information is not a thing but an occurrence, an elementary event."[20] The space produced by bits of information is temporary and networked. The pervasive diffusion of digital portable devices has only increased the relevance of Levy's observation, so much so that the ephemeral experience of the city through digital devices has now become a permanent trait of the urban experience[21].

Within this framework, the G8 summits, with their mix of physical and digital participation, not only constitute a legitimate form of urbanism but actually articulate, in more complex terms, the relation between digital technologies and cities, and are therefore examples of the emerging spatiality of the 21st century. Thus the G8 summit, a 3-day long event, does not represent an exception to the normal life of a city but rather an intensification of elements that are present in the city on a daily basis.

Finally, a great deal of interest in the summits arises because they escape the recent theoretical models constructed by architects and urbanists. For instance, the work of William J. Mitchell and Derrick de Kerckhove outlines a future city in which digital technology would be smoothly implemented and have a central role in citizens' emancipation.[22] The turning point in this 'crisis' coincides with the 2001 summit in Genoa as its planning presents political, symbolic, urban, geographical and theoretical issues that demand an accurate re-assessment of what these theoreticians had initially anticipated. As we have already seen, formal readings of the city based on permanence are inadequate and so are the theories that have been accompanying the introduction of digital tools in architecture and urbanism. The digital discourse has been drawing much of its intellectual armature from French Post-Structuralism – mostly from Gilles Deleuze – applying dynamic notions, such as continuity, softness and gradient[23], to space. Devoid of the political polemic animating Deleuze's philosophy, this position has fallen short in accounting for the actual implementation of digital tools in shaping urban environments and their impact on social practices. The G8 summits describe the insertion of digital media in the urban realm as a tumultuous, incoherent phenomenon, animated by both symbolic and operational strategies, and by high and low technologies, which transform spaces both temporarily and permanently.

An urbanism of things: the urban plan of the G8 summits

What is the city of the G8 summit actually made of? At first glance, it is a type of Smart City that contains very few innovative elements. In fact, throughout the period considered, almost all technologies deployed at the summits had already been tested somewhere else, albeit at a smaller scale. The real element of novelty here was the cumulative effects that each single device, law or technology gave rise to.

The 2001 G8 summit utilised all sorts of technologies, from very primitive crowd-control techniques, such as high walls, to satellite tracking, which were deployed *ad hoc*, without any attempt to form an organic plan. The more fluid metaphor of the network can perhaps offer a more appropriate image to describe the urbanism of the G8; the notion of the comprehensive plan is substituted by a wide range of heterogeneous interventions operating at a variety of scales and which are connected *ad hoc* through both physical and immaterial means. It is only by considering the temporary, malleable network and the cumulative effects it gives rise to that we can grasp the emergence of a different kind of spatiality; one that, we argue, is paradigmatic for 21st-century urbanism.

The notion of a network allows us to navigate through the various meetings using a more appropriate framework to understand their spatial qualities and contradictions; an essential step in order to begin shaping how to operate in such conditions. Seen from above, from the zenith point of view, such space reveals very little. The traditional tools of planning still seek for cohesion, integration, whereas such space is completely fragmented, often existing at the same time in physical and digital domains as well as in local and global scale. Much more useful is to begin to describe it by looking at the complex sets of things deployed during the summits. By 'things', we not only mean what are commonly understood as finite objects, but also take a more conceptual definition of this word that allows us to include both the material and the immaterial, no longer distinguishing between the human and the non–human, and without any constraint of scale. Laws, satellite dishes, mobile phones, fences, missile ramps, emergency public control protocols, train stations, EU treaties, cruise liners, welders, temporary prisons, clothes, colours, slogans, zones of exceptions, media coverage, internet websites, political movements, tear gas, religious groups, NGOs, governments, tourist resorts, road maps, mountains, islands, embedded journalists, protesters, planning regulations and black blocks are some of the actual 'things' we are referring to.

From this vantage point, the urbanism of the G8 summits begins to expose complexity and richness – so to speak, as such urbanism is deployed to radically reduce democratic rights – that offer a fruitful counterpoint to positivist discourse underpinning the development of the Smart City.

For instance, how specific locations within hosting countries were chosen can be considered as a 'thing': in fact, this in itself contains a complex set of ideological, geographical and topographical conditions that are indicative of the kind of space generated through the summits. If, at the beginning of the period under consideration, urban locations were preferred (Seattle in 1999 and Genoa in 2001), the choice of venue moved to ever more remote sites – the case of Kananaskis in 2002, an isolated village in the Rocky Mountains, is exemplary – or to zones whose exceptional topographical conditions well suited the aim of containing dissent. Within these choices, we can observe how space becomes a vehicle and indicator of the political predisposition underpinning the organisation of a summit. We can in fact notice that, since Seattle and Genoa, hosting nations increasingly prefer to organise the summit in tourist resorts (Sea Island, USA, 2004) as their geographic position and leisure-oriented urbanism is already tailored for extra-ordinary events (i.e. holidays); they are, in other words, already zones of exception or already predisposed to be turned into one. A different but somehow complementary choice of venue is that of an emergency area: L'Aquila, 2009, a small Italian town which had been struck by a violent earthquake shortly before the announcement of the G8 summit and was, at the time of the gathering, fully preoccupied with clearing rubble and starting the reconstruction process.

In choosing such locations, space is deployed as a 'thing' and a variety of narratives, at times even conflicting ones, unfold from it. Beyond the clear and pragmatic attempt to prevent protesters from reaching the actual venues of summits, these locations also provide other, less evident statements regarding the character of protesters. By choosing resorts, for instance, protesters are implicitly considered as tourists, or, as in case of L'Aquila, the protesters' agenda is overshadowed and eventually dismissed by the gravity of the post-earthquake situation.

Planning measures are implemented at the large scale of the entire city, town or village. For instance, Genoa city centre was divided into two zones, the Red Zone and the Yellow Zone. The Red Zone, demarcated by 4-metre-high fences, was closed to the public and residents alike – an event that had never occurred in the modern history of the western city. In the Yellow Zone, though not physically demarcated, basic democratic rights, such as the right to strike, the right to manifest one's ideas and even the right to work, were suspended. The nature of these zones of exclusion has received prominent attention in the work of Italian philosopher Giorgio Agamben[24] who examines the complex nature of the spaces of the western city moved beyond binary oppositions such as inclusion/exclusion.[25]

At the 2007 summit in Heiligendamm, a 13-kilometre barrier was erected to create a buffer zone between the delegates and the general public (too often quickly labelled as protesters). Other times, it is the status of space itself or of the body entering it that is invisibly altered. For the first time since its introduction, the Schengen Treaty was suspended during the 2001 G8 summit, allowing the police to much more easily stop protesters from entering Genoa. Since the 2001 summit, European governments have taken an increasingly casual approach towards this key piece of legislation, granting its suspension much more easily, for example for the annual gathering of the European Central Bank in Barcelona in 2012, and even for events of no political relevance, such as the 2012 European Football Championship in Poland when the treaty was suspended for the entire duration of the tournament at the scale of an entire nation. This practice has become so common that in 2012 the EU was forced to ratify it *de facto,* determining that countries of the European Community are allowed to suspend their Schengen membership should they deem it necessary.

At a smaller scale, the actual fabric of the city is reconfigured. Examples in this area are numerous. In Genoa in 2001 some of the main public infrastructures connecting the city were closed: the airport (where missile ramps were installed), the port, the two main train stations, all the buses, main roads such as the famous Sopraelevata, and public buildings. All construction sites were forced to have a temporary shut down and the city was physically severed from the port, one of the city's landmarks, by a double-tier of 40-foot containers. Similarly, the 13-kilometre fence in Heiligendamm detached the city from its surroundings and, extending the analysis beyond the G8 summits, Sydney was quartered through the extensive use of metal fences for the Asia-Pacific Economic Cooperation meeting in 2007.

The complexity of the spatial organisation is further increased by how interventions at different scales interact with each other. The temporary re-coding of physical objects through temporary laws allowed the police in Genoa to transform Bolzaneto barracks into a detention centre, which also happened to be located in the Yellow Zone where constitutional rights were substantially lowered for the period of the summit. Although such practices did not originate at the G8 summits, they have become much more widely used since their G8 deployment. Compelling examples can be found during presidential campaigns in the US: first, the Republican Convention in New York in 2004[26] and then the Democratic Convention in Denver, where car parks and warehouses were temporarily re-coded as detention centres able to take up to 1,200 detainees[27].

Analysis of the complex nature of such spaces refutes the monistic nature of most architectural and urban theories. It demands different criteria that are more open and ambivalent. Acknowledging the role of 'things' allows us to grasp that this space is contradictory, disjoined and temporary – characteristics that align with Lash and Urry's definition of "disorganised capitalism"[28]. We speak of 'things' because some of the measures are deployed both for operational and symbolic reasons, despite their evident contradictory character. In Genoa, for instance, the use of anti-riot techniques seemed to serve more than one agenda: the 4-metre-high fences framing the Red Zone were allegedly erected for the purely pragmatic reason of cordoning off any unwanted person from the delegates' area, but their visual impact and presence, especially in the media coverage, was such as to overshadow any practical intention. This reading is corroborated by the curious experiment by French journalist Valerie Vie who entered the Red Zone managing to avoid any control. Once she succeeded in her demonstration, she voluntarily gave herself up, thus becoming, until 2008, the only person officially condemned and incarcerated for crimes occurring at the summit[29]. Similarly, the 13-kilometre fence put up in Heiligendamm to control the public had such a symbolic presence it became the backdrop for all sorts of demonstrations and performances.[30] Such displays of muscular power from the state can only be partially explained by the actual or anticipated violence of the events. Technologies of control are here employed for their symbolic rather than performative value; they unashamedly represent a city that is not for everybody but rather for a selected minority.

Finally, a whole series of measures operate directly at the scale of the individual human body. These include minuscule or highly ephemeral physical alterations to the city fabric as well as altogether immaterial actions without any perceivable impact whose effect is to alter the legal status of bodies. We are referring here to practices common since Seattle in 1999, ranging from boarding up shop windows and building entrances, to welding all manholes to prevent any access via the sewage system. To highlight the attention to miniscule detail, in Genoa's Red Zone the manholes were sealed with each weld being about 10 millimetres long. The cumulative effect of these discrete interventions turned all public surfaces in the city into watertight, swimming-pool-like spaces, effectively obliterating any possibility of interaction between public areas and users. At the same summit, the police employed about 6,000 tear-gas canisters during the clashes and some studies argue that the particularly toxic nature of these gases has had a long-term effect on participants' health[31]. Furthermore, all participants were classified by colour according to their estimated danger: black identified the most aggressive group, whereas blue, yellow and pink were assigned to progressively less threatening groups.

Genoa was also the first G8 gathering in which portable digital technologies began to play a substantial role, from the organisation of the protesters' actions in the months leading up to the event, to the actual tactics employed on the streets. In addition, it is important to take account of how much digital media can also achieve after the actual summit. An immense archive of images and footage of the clashes has been permanently available to the public since 2001. This has not only had tremendous importance in tracking the various crimes committed, but has also triggered several studies, including this one, and movies[32].

Conclusions

Between 1999 and 2010, the G8 summits were a laboratory to test technologies and crowd-control techniques that dramatically reduce the citizen's ability to access and use public spaces. Though this starts out as a western story, we now witness the penetration of such technologies and techniques well beyond the west.

Urbanists' attempts to create Smart Cities often rely on developments initially tested at the G8 summits. The optimistic, almost utopian theories that architects imagined would inform the penetration of digital technologies into our cities need to be re-assessed in the light of the harsh and violent tactics deployed at the G8 summits.

Unravelling the ideologies of control informing the use of digital technologies in contemporary urbanism, as well as mapping out the techniques and repressive agendas informing them, is essential not only for understanding how public space is currently constructed, but also for figuring out how we create strategies that resist them.

1. D. D. Perlmutter and G.L. Wagner, 'The Anatomy of a Photojournalistic Icon: Marginalization of Dissent in the Selection and Framing of "a death in Genoa"', *Visual Communication* 3(1), 2004, pp. 91–108. J.S. Juris, 'Violence Performed and Imagined: Militant Action, the Black Bloc and the Mass Media in Genoa', *Critique of Anthropology*, 25(4), 2005, pp. 413–32.
2. G. Chiesa, *G8/Genova* (Turin: Einaudi, 2001).
3. See paragraph on Smart Cities.
4. The large corporation Living PlanIT defines the Smart City as "...the missing link between real estate and technology sectors". See 'Living PlanIT's CEO Steve Lewis selected by the World Economic Forum as a Technology Pioneer 2012', http://living-planit.com/pr_wef_award.htm (accessed 30/04/13).
5. A case in point is the architecture magazine *AD – Architectural Design* which, since the early 90s, has dedicated numerous issues to the relation between digital technologies and architecture.

6. J. Neale, *You are the G8, We are 6 Billion: The Truth Behind the Genoa Protests* (London: Vision Paperbacks, 2002). Though narrated in the form of a personal diary, Neale provides an accurate reconstruction of the movements and main clashes from the mid-90s to the Genoa summit. A scholarly account of these issues is also provided in L.A. Fernandez, *Policing Dissent: Social Control and the Anti-Globalization Movement* (New Brunswick, New Jersey, London: Rutgers University Press, 2008).
7. F. Fukuyama, *The End of History and the Last Man* (New York: Free Press, 1992).
8. A. Negri and M. Hardt, *Empire* (Cambridge, Mass: Harvard University Press, 2000).
9. Negri and Hardt, *ibid.*, and also P. Virno, *A Grammar of the Multitude* (New York: Semiotext[e], 2004).
10. E.S. Raymond, *The Cathedral and the Bazaar: musing on linux by an accidental revolutionary* (Bejing, Cambridge, Mass: O'Reilly, 1999). G. Lovink, *Uncanny Networks* (Cambridge, Mass: MIT Press, 2002).
11. S. Baldi, 'The Internet for International Political and Social Protest: the case of Seattle' (Rome: Policy Planning Unit of the Ministry of Foreign Affairs of Italy, 2000), http://hostings.diplomacy.edu/baldi/articles/protest.htm (accessed 12/06/14).
12. The Jubilee movement participated in several G8 gatherings, most prominently the 2001 G8 in Genoa.
13. Geert Lovink and Florian Schneider, 'A Virtual world is Possible: From Tactical Media to Digital Multitudes', 2003, http://multitudes.samizdat.net/Virtual-world-is-possible-from (accessed 24/04/13).
14. Geert Lovink and Florian Schneider, *ibid.* "Both real and virtual protests risk getting stuck at the level of a global 'demo design', no longer grounded in actual topics and local situations. This means the movement never gets out of beta. At first glance, reconciling the virtual and the real seems to be an attractive rhetorical act. Radical pragmatists have often emphasised the embodiment of online networks in real-life society, dispensing with the real / virtual contradiction. Net activism, like the Internet itself, is always hybrid, a blend of old and new, haunted by geography, gender, race and other political factors. There is no pure disembodied zone of global communication, as the 90s cyber-mythology claimed."
15. P. Wintuor, 'David Cameron plans to downgrade G8 summit', *The Guardian*, 28 June 2010, http://www.guardian.co.uk/world/2010/jun/28/britain-curb-role-g8-summit (accessed 14/10/12).
16. IBM definition of Smart City: "... synchronises and analyses efforts among sectors and agencies as they happen, giving decision makers consolidated information that helps them anticipate problems [and] manage growth and development in a sustainable way that minimises disruptions and helps increase prosperity for everyone." IBM now has a Smarter City centre. See http://www-03.ibm.com/software/products/us/en/intelligent-operations-center (accessed on April 26/04/13). Cisco definition of Smart City: "... the seamless integration of public and private services, delivered across a common network infrastructure, to individuals, governments and businesses." See http://www.cisco.com/web/strategy/docs/scc/09CS2326_SCC_BrochureForWest_r3_112409.pdf (accessed 26/04/13). Siemens describes the Smart City as: "Several decades from now cities will have countless autonomous, intelligently functioning IT systems that will have perfect knowledge of users' habits and energy consumption, and provide optimum service. The goal of such a city is to optimally regulate and control resources by means of autonomous IT systems." See http://www.siemens.com/innovation/en/publikationen/publications_pof/pof_fall_2008/gebaeude/vernetzung.htm (accessed 26/04/13). Living PlanIT's Smart City is

defined as: " … a complete picture of building estate, usage, and operations … continually maintained, allowing constant optimisation of energy, resources, environment, and occupant convenience systems." They also add that the Smart City "… is the missing link between real estate and technology sectors". Of different tone is the description of the aims of the Smart City by the Institute of the Future in Palo Alto: "… harnessing sensory information for development and inclusion." See http://iftf.me/public/SR-1352_Rockefeller_Map_reader.pdf (accessed 25/05/13).

17. 'Living PlanIT's CEO Steve Lewis selected by the World Economic Forum as a Technology Pioneer 2012', http://living-planit.com/pr_wef_award.htm (accessed 30/04/13).
18. Saskia Sasssen, 'Open Source Urbanism', *Domus*, http://www.domusweb.it/en/op-ed/2011/06/29/open-source-urbanism.html (accessed 24/04/13).
19. I Commissione Permanente (Affari costituzionali, della Presidenza del Consiglio e interni) (2001), Indagine Conoscitiva sui Fatti di Genoa, http://www.g82001.altervista.org/indagine2001/01.pdf (accessed 02/07/12).
20. Pierre Levy, *Collective Intelligence: mankind's emerging world in cyberspace* (New York, London: Plenum Trade, 1997). A. Picon, *Digital Culture in Architecture: An Introduction for the Design Professions* (Basel: Birkhauser, 2010).
21. A. Picon, 'Toward a City of Events', in Neyran Turan (ed.), *New Geographies* (Boston: Harvard Press, 2009) pp. 32–43.
22. J.W. Mitchell, *Me++: The Cyborg Self and the Networked City* (Cambridge, Mass, London: MIT, 2003). D. De Keckhove, 'Global Village Square', in L. Sacchi and M. Unali, *Architettura e Cultura Digitale* (Milan: Skira, 2003).
23. Particularly, Gilles Deleuze, *The Fold: Leibniz and the Baroque* (London: Athlone, 1993) pp. 100–120.
24. G. Agamben, *State of Exception* (Chicago, London: University of Chicago Press, 2005).
25. G. Agamben, 'Metropolis', trans. Arianna Bove, Generation-Online, November 2006, www.generationonline.org/p/fpagamben4.htm (accessed 25/03/13).
26. S. Levine, *Guantanamo on the Hudson: Detained RNC Protesters Describe Prison Conditions,* http://www.democracynow.org/2004/9/2/guantanamo_on_the_hudson_detained_rnc, (accessed 27/05/2014) and '2004 Republican National Convention protest activity', http://en.wikipedia.org/wiki/2004_Republican_National_Convention_protest_activity (accessed 27/05/2014).
27. B. Finoki, *Getting Ready for a Radical Round Up in Denver,* Subtopia, 2008, http://subtopia.blogspot.co.uk/2008/08/getting-ready-for-radical-roundup-in.html (accessed 11/01/13).
28. S. Lash and J. Urry, *The End of Organised Capitalism* (Cambridge: Polity, 1987).
29. 'Processi e decisioni giudiziarie sul G8 di Genova', (2012) Wikipedia, http://it.wikipedia.org/wiki/Processi_e_decisioni_giudiziarie_sul_G8_di_Genova (accessed 13/10/12).
30. B. Cammaerts, A. Mattoni and P. McCurdy, *Mediation and Protest Movements* (Bristol, Chicago: Intellect, 2013).
31. E. Magnone and E. Mangini, *La Sindrome di Genova* (Genova: Frilli, 2002).
32. Carlo Lucarelli (dir.), *Blu notte - Il G8* (Italy: Rai TV, 2011) http://www.youtube.com/watch?v=fLtmg5ys_9A (accessed 26/05/13). Le Strade di Genova, Davide Ferrario (dir.) 2002 (Italy).

The London Olympics and the State We're In

MIKE WELLS

The case against me was the result of an unscheduled Olympic boxing match. It occurred in April 2012 at Leyton Marshes outside a construction site where basketball courts were being built for the Games. The Games were scheduled to be opened on 27 July 2012, just a few months time. Local opposition to the basketball facility was passionate because it was being erected on much loved parkland. Protesting grandmothers, dog walkers and transvestites, amongst others, had made themselves unpopular by sitting in front of construction vehicles. I was there shooting footage for my film *London Takes Gold*.[1]

I arrived at Leyton Marshes, a beautiful green space in East London, to find an excavator working in open parkland without safety measures. "Worth filming," I thought. A passing walker suddenly veered from his course and stood in front of the machine. He started yelling at the driver to stop work owing to the likelihood of crushing dogs and people with the machine's wildly swinging arm.

The digger seemed pretty dangerous to me as well and I was starting to get angry. I shouted at the driver, telling him to stop his machine because it wasn't safe. He was getting pretty agitated as well and made some sarcastic comments like 'you haven't got a job have you' and 'I'll have you' etc. I was close to the machine's cab. Suddenly its door flew open and a muddy, steel-toe-capped safety boot swung past my head. His kick missed and he leapt on me from the height of the machine, his momentum forcing me and my filmmaker's face into the ground. He struck me in the back. I couldn't see him so had no way of knowing if it was a kick or a punch. Either way it took the wind out of me and straight away I knew my ribs were broken.

I never trained in the art of pugilism and my ability to defend myself wasn't impressive. I was struggling to turn face up on the ground so I could hit the guy back, but before I could, a group of security guards who had been standing nearby dragged the unharmed driver off me. I got up off the ground. Some of the security guards were leading the driver away, others remained. There were about six of them and they forced me to the ground. They were on my back, on my freshly broken ribs. While having my face rammed into the ground for a second time, I wondered if these guys stood in front of their bedroom mirrors attempting to perfect their image: black uniform, short haircuts, wraparound sunglasses. I could barely breathe and I wondered what would happen if they inadvertently killed me. The short haircuts hauled me out of the park, then held me in an armlock. I was held captive in this way until 20 or so minutes later a car pulled up. It had a sticker on the side saying "Working for a Safer London". It was the police. Things weren't going well for me, but I could understand the chain of interests – the machine driver was working for the haircuts' client, the Olympic Delivery Authority (ODA). I was handcuffed, arrested and shoved into the back of the police car, transferred to an ambulance, and then back to the police car. Many other police cars turned up. There seemed to be uniforms everywhere, and from the back of the police car I was able to observe police officers with impressive arrays of silver insignia on their epaulettes. They seemed to be talking to each other about me. I felt pretty shaken up.

After 24 hours in a nasty cell in the ultra modern Leyton Police Station (which, rumour has it, was built especially for the Olympics – there is unfortunately surprisingly little information available in the public domain about this place), I was formally informed by the custody sergeant that I "may make mischief in relation to the Olympics if released" and they were going to keep me locked up. Hey, this was a learning process – I hadn't known they locked people up for their potential of making 'mischief'. I spent 48 hours in this fluorescent-tube-lit nightmare of a place, after which I was transported to court for a bail hearing, where it would be decided if I would be kept in prison until they put me on trial.

At the bail hearing the prosecution lawyer claimed I was part of a conspiracy against the London Olympics. He was convincing. He claimed

I'd broken an injunction making it illegal for me to film on Leyton Marshes and alleged I'd been filming with a "large camera" and had been "passing the identities of Olympic contractors to protesters for the purpose of intimidating them". All completely untrue. I was not passing anything on to anybody, and *London Takes Gold*, the film I was working on, was shot entirely on a smart phone, not a "large camera".

Feelings amongst locals towards the construction of the basketball courts ran high enough to have sent out an invite to the Occupy Movement to set up an encampment on the Marshes, which they had done, and with the world's press about to descend on London for the Olympic period, the authorities were getting twitchy over the possibility of bad publicity. The situation was escalating. The ODA's response was to seek an injunction in an attempt to prevent unruly local peasants and supporters protesting over the loss of their green space. As a journalist I had attended the High Court hearing at which the injunction came into being. A ragtag group of local residents, the same grandmothers *et al* who had sat in front of lorries, pitched themselves in a legal battle against some of the best-paid lawyers in the land. David did not give Goliath a pasting, and the authorities got their injunction. Note that an injunction can only be valid if served on named persons. The injunction hadn't been served on me and I wasn't named in it.

Meanwhile at my bail hearing, Judge Sendhimdown (I don't want to remember his face or his real name), a middle-aged man, wearing a gold-buttoned mid-blue blazer with a hanky in his top pocket, wasn't difficult to persuade, and after shouting at my lawyer, he remanded[2] me to Thameside prison. He seemed to be in a bad mood. It's not possible to know if he liked me less than I liked him.

I was quite upset about being sent to prison for allegedly assaulting someone who'd assaulted me, for having the potential to 'make mischief', for breaking an injunction that did not apply to me, and for being wrongly accused of having a "large camera".

Prison experience

In prison I got a bit paranoid as the nature of the world I had entered dawned on me and that they would most likely try and keep me in jail for months. To be honest, in the privacy of my cell there were tears – more than once. I was beginning to realise the extent of the authorities' paranoia over the Olympics and that I was being subjected to that paranoia.

My lawyer appealed the decision of the first bail hearing and eight days after my arrest, early one morning, I was transported from prison back to court for another bail hearing, where they would decide if I would be spending the coming months in prison until my trial. It was interesting seeing the system they use to transport prisoners. It was in one of those Serco prisoner transport vans I'd seen as a free man. Prisoners are handcuffed and led one by one out of the jail into the van and then into a small fibreglass cubicle within it. There was a clever system that allowed the driver and his mate to place you in the cubicle still handcuffed but then, with the door open a couple of inches, they take the cuffs off before finally locking you in your own private chicken coop. We were then taken on a tour of London police stations picking up other prisoners, and en-route, through the tinted van window, I was able to enjoy the passing spectacle of the Olympic Stadium.

Arriving at court the procedure of unloading prisoners was reversed and we were escorted into something like a dingy medieval dungeon. The cells were tiny, with paint peeling from their walls. They were just large enough for one person and empty except for a hard wooden bench wide enough to lie down on. This is where prisoners sweat until the court is ready to hear their case. Then prisoners are again handcuffed, led upstairs and put into a glass cage in the courtroom. While I waited, in the discomfort of my cell, I was able to listen to one of my fellow inmates from the prison, a fragile looking kid, lose the plot. It sounded to me as though he had slipped into a state of psychosis. I made a number of appeals to the guards to call a doctor for him.

After a few hours I was led upstairs to the courtroom by a guard who asked me what I was in for. "Murder," I replied. As he had just handcuffed himself to me I could feel him stiffen before I said, "... only joking." And he relaxed again, until I mentioned the genocide.

I now knew I could psychologically cope with prison but it seemed like a massive waste of time and there were things I wanted to do such as finish the film, and sitting in that glass enclosure I felt disempowered, anxious and apprehensive. This is when my new barrister, Tom Stevens, came onto the scene. Tom is born to perform in court, has a credibility beyond his 30 or so years, and is a master of leaning in an impressive lawyer-like way on the advocates' bench while arguing well-reasoned points of law and logic.

The judge was a white woman of around 65, with a kind face. I reckoned she bought her clothes at Marks and Spencer and looked as though she'd recently visited a quality hair salon. The young prosecution lawyer seemed new to the job. Her contribution amounted to mumbling incoherently while shuffling through bits of paper, never actually finding what she was looking for. My friends were prepared to put up money for bail and other friends gave character references. The judge listened.

I was given bail. No money was required as security and the conditions were that until my trial I didn't go near the guy who'd attacked me and didn't go within 100 metres of any Olympic venue. They didn't release me straight away though. I was led back down to my cell – the court's bureaucrats were apparently at lunch and so I spent another three hours at Her Majesty's pleasure listening to the kid continuing his descent into madness with no medical attention.

Trial

The next stage in this legal pantomime came with my trial, some nine months after the alleged incident. It was because I had a good lawyer that I hadn't been in prison for those nine months awaiting the trial for an alleged crime that carried a maximum six months' sentence. The trial wasn't disappointing – a proper drama. It would have worked well on telly, with clear hostility between the lawyers. When District Judge Reed, a grey-haired man of around 70 wearing a dark blue blazer with the compulsory hankie in his top pocket, left the courtroom to consider a disagreement between prosecution and defence, the lawyers continued their argument. There were hostile glances and some uncomfortable body language, followed by an awkward silence.

The case against me relied on one witness – also the alleged victim. Unsurprisingly, as the statements he had made were untrue, he expressed his reluctance to attend the trial. He therefore had to be summonsed to give evidence. The security guards who had witnessed the assault on me, and who had themselves forced me to the ground and sat on me, did not provide any evidence. Maybe their wraparound sunglasses were simply too dark.

My barrister, Tom Stevens, cross-examining the driver of the digger, pointed out that at every stage in the legal process he had given differing accounts of what had happened. During the 20-minute cross-examination the driver changed from an upright, confident, strutting man into a spluttering head barely visible above the witness stand. Eventually he expressed his unwillingness to give evidence, described the process as "shit", yawned frequently and failed to answer Mr Stevens' questions. Judge Reed did not throw the case out of court, but more than once, in response to groans of disapproval, he threatened to remove people from the Spectators' Gallery.

The prosecution lawyer was gifted. She alleged I was a protester with anti-Olympic sympathies and argued this was my motivation for the alleged assault on the excavator driver. She went the extra mile and also attempted to discredit witnesses called by my lawyer. Cross-examining me she made statements as to my anti-Olympic sympathies, saying, "This is why you assaulted Mr X, isn't it, Mr Wells?" I had to ask her if she was asking me questions or making statements. On about five different occasions, in a bid to portray me as using my educational advantage to mislead the court, she mentioned how well educated I am (little does she know). She was good at her job.

Before Judge Reed gave his verdict, he went through a lengthy summing up – 'on the one hand this … on the other that …' Julian Cheyne, a friend and co-contributor to Games Monitor (a website set up to monitor the London Olympics), commented that he had a feeling the judge really wanted to find me guilty. My impression was the same. In his summing up, Judge Reed rambled on saying he knew something had gone on at Leyton Marshes but couldn't tell what it was. When I gave evidence I had told the court what had happened. The judge's comments made me think he hadn't believed me. But Tom Stevens was on my side and he'd argued the case well, so well it would have been almost impossible for the judge to find me guilty. I was found innocent and was told I was free to leave court.

Protest

Some cynics have suggested my arrest, imprisonment and trial could be seen as political because, through Games Monitor and other media outlets, I have been an outspoken critic of London 2012. Also the incident occurred on the site of an Olympic construction project, which had attracted significant protest and media coverage.

I documented many protests over Olympic grievances, such as that against the demolition of the housing co-operative I used to live in (housing 500 people). The land it stood on is between what is now the Athletes' Village and the Velodrome. There have been many protests over issues connected with the Olympics, some small, some large, and as a journalist I documented most of them.

One of the protests I attended was over the destruction of my friends' allotment gardens. In 1900 these allotments were given to the gardeners of East London by an old-fashioned philanthropist, Major Villiers. There was a sweet story told by the older allotment holders that managers at a Bovril factory on the opposite side of the River Lea wrote to the Major saying they wanted to extend their factory and asked how much he would sell the allotments site for. Apparently Villiers wrote back asking how much they wanted for the factory as he wanted to extend the allotments. To me, the Major's attitude is the opposite of that which pervades the London Olympics and its so-called 'legacy'. Villiers clearly cared about the ordinary person, the small person, and about the land.

To say I have never considered violence as a means of dealing with the Olympics would not be totally honest. After our homes at the housing co-operative were demolished to make way for the Olympic 'Park', I moved onto a boat. Shortly before the London Olympics the authorities tried to impose new regulations that would have made life for our community of boat-dwellers impossible. The Olympic 'Park' is ringed by the waterways we live on. Many of our boats, though full of character, look a bit tatty. Storage space is at a premium on a boat, so often folks leave stuff on their roofs – bicycles, firewood, hosepipes, bags of coal etc. This look, this authentic display of tat, is the antithesis of the glitzy Olympic brand, which was why I thought they wanted us out of sight.

Our community fought the new regulations and, as things turned out, we were only banned from our home waterways for about three months over the Olympic period. We were apparently seen as a security threat, though strangely we were not seen as such if we paid an extra £500 for the privilege of being in this so-called Olympic exclusion zone (we already pay a licence fee to use the waterways). At the time I saw this as another Olympic blitzkrieg on a community I love, so I talked to my mates about an idea I had (this is where the 'violence' comes in): why didn't I publicly challenge Olympic boss, Sebastian Coe, to a wrestling match? He's a sporting man after all! The deal would be: he wins, and I would stop my criticism of London 2012; I win, and our community would be left alone. Surely giving Coe a good thrashing in a properly refereed bout would be a completely acceptable use of violence and probably better entertainment than the Olympics. The idea never quite clambered into the ring, and considering my not so impressive attempt to fight off the Olympic digger driver, it was probably good it never did.

I found the prosecution's suggestion that I was a protester and that this was relevant to my case unsurprising. Protest does not infer violence – in many cases it suggests the opposite. But authority doesn't like protest, and the Olympics added to their paranoia in relation to protest – a point made clear after Len McCluskey of Unite Union said that civil disobedience could be timed to disrupt the 2012 Games and the BBC reported that a spokesman for Prime Minister David Cameron called the idea "unacceptable and unpatriotic".[3]

My relationship with protest is perhaps difficult for the authorities to understand. Am I a protester with an interest in journalism? Am I a journalist with an interest in protest? Would I be better called a campaigning journalist? And if someone protests once, are they forever more a protester? In any case, the bar set to place someone on the police's Domestic Extremist list is apparently set at a much lower level than an Olympic high jump. It is likely that the grandmothers *et al* who protested the construction of the basketball courts will be on the list, and I'm pretty sure I'll be on it as well. I don't consider the grandmothers or myself extreme, and the use of the word 'extreme' in this context should be a matter of concern.

The fact is that I was not on the marshes that day to protest or to be 'extreme'. I was there to film and the case against me was, at best, flimsy. As Tom Stevens my barrister commented: "The stark feature of this case is just how little evidence there is ... Is it possible there is a very bitter irony in this case, that being the man who sits in the dock was ultimately motivated by concerns over safety of others, and yet he finds himself charged with, in effect, flagrantly disregarding people's safety?"

The case against the Olympic project

The case brought against me in many ways reminded me of the Olympic project – a job creation scheme for government employees and contractors. Costs factored into bringing a case against me should include police time, prosecution and defence costs, court costs, prisoner transport, the attendance of witnesses at court, eight days of incarceration. I did not factor into that figure the cost of feeding me during my imprisonment as the food was virtually worthless. I lost weight.

Had the case for the London Olympics been in the dock instead of me, unlike a judge and dominatrix, it would simply not have stood up in court. The most perfunctory of cross-examinations would have torn it apart. The most profound flaw in the project is that 24 days of sport simply can't be worth £24 billion[4]. How seriously the ODA took the problem of selling the defective idea of building stadia, swimming pools, horse-riding arenas and perhaps the most important venues of all, the VIP enclosures, for a mere 24 days of use, is demonstrated by the fact that 'public relations' was high enough on their agenda to support a board-level Directorship in Communications, filled by Godric Smith, who trousered £218,000 (salary £195,000, pension £23,000) in 2010-11. Mr Smith, like other senior-level staff at the ODA, has since landed other nice jobs in 'communications', as an 'Executive Director of Government Communications' and for the BBC to assist them in smoothing the Jimmy Savile sexual abuse scandal.[5]

With regard to my case, some people have suggested a conspiracy. The Oxford English Dictionary states that a conspiracy is "a secret plan by a group to do something unlawful or harmful". In relation to the charge of common assault brought against me, as I was advised by my lawyer at the police station: "no comment". As for London 2012, it was a plan by a group, and in my opinion that plan was harmful, and in some cases unlawful. There were secrets and deception right from the beginning of the project – the original cost estimate of £2.37 billion for hosting the Olympic Games was not plausible. It was already known that, just a few years before, the Athens Games had cost £9 billion and London is a more expensive city than Athens, plus there was the costly problem of attempting to decontaminate the land of the Olympic 'Park' which had, for more than a century, been a home to, and a dumping ground for, all manner of noxious industries.

Another reason I am critical of the London Olympics stems from an investigation carried out by intelligence analyst Paul Charman and myself into the issue of land contamination. Contractors working in the Olympic 'Park' excavated thousands of tonnes of soil contaminated with radioactive isotopes.[6] The origin of some of the isotopes found on the site remain a mystery, but the thorium originates from the salt used in the manufacture of gas mantles (the forerunner to the electric light bulb). The radium probably originates from the manufacture and application of glow-in-the-dark paints for luminescent watch and instrument dials.

The ODA and its contractors were clearly shaken by the problem of what to do with this material. The situation attracted careful 'communications management' and incredibly it did not turn out to be a public relations disaster.

Astonishing and completely at odds with legislation, the eventual solution was to re-bury more than a hundred tonnes of low level radioactive waste, along with thousands of tonnes of other radioactively contaminated soil, 250 metres north of the main Olympic stadium. Regulations insist this material should have been taken to the Drigg Low Level Radioactive Waste Repository in Cumbria, however, documents obtained by Charman and myself show, incredibly, that the Environment Agency told contractors they were "comfortable" with the proposal to re-bury this material in the Olympic 'Park'.[7] My theory is that there was reluctance to send this material to Drigg because, if it had been sent there, it would have been subjected to external analysis and scrutiny.

There is now a plan to build a block of flats on top of this unofficial radioactive waste repository in East London, despite ODA assurances that it would remain undisturbed.[8]

Around a third of the surface area of what is now known as the London Olympic 'Park' was formerly landfill rubbish dumps that contained domestic and industrial waste. Government documents recommend that such highly polluted sites should be investigated for radioactive contamination prior to excavation work. The ODA chose not to carry out such investigations.

From documents Charman and myself obtained under the Freedom of Information Act we learned that in 2007, months after excavation work commenced on the site, the ODA appointed radiation protection advisors. The first day they arrived on site they started finding radioactive contamination, and it was discovered contractors had been excavating material contaminated with radioactive isotopes for months .[9] Paul Charman also found evidence that dust suppression on the site was inadequate[10] and that there have been numerous complaints about dust from the Olympic construction site. The inhalation of dusts contaminated with radioactive isotopes of the sorts the Olympic 'Park' is contaminated with pose a serious risk to health. I therefore fail to see how the ODA's claim that there was "no risk" to workers or local residents[11] could be honestly made.

I believe work on the site did pose significant risk of significant harm, and independent experts should be appointed to investigate this before any further excavation work is carried out on the site in the legacy phase. The site remains highly contaminated, not just with radioactive isotopes but all manner of chemicals and biological agents.

On a recent site tour I noted and photographed excavation work which is again being carried out on the site. But, rather than an investigation, the project has benefitted from an Industry Award for Health and Safety, which to me demonstrates a consolidation and integration of nepotism, a merry-go-round of self-congratulatory 'business management', all of which must seem convincing if one hasn't had the opportunity to find out what is beneath the veneer. The number of awards pinned to chests above bloated bellies of over-OBE-ed, CBE-ed and knighted ex-personnel of the London Olympic Project is extensive and includes but is not limited to social media, architecture, planning, recruitment, construction and sustainability.[12]

Parasites and promises

In my view the relationship between host city and the Olympics is mirrored in nature – akin to that between host and parasite. The parasite embeds itself in a new host every two years (winter and summer Olympics). It sucks out £billions in resources and constructs venues that will be used for 20 or so days before moving on to its next victim. In order to persuade cities to act as hosts, the International Olympic Committee (IOC) and others engaged in the Olympic industry wildly exaggerate the benefits.

Outside a Park Lane hotel during the London Games, I filmed one of the many volunteer chauffeurs unloading shopping from the back of a large Olympic BMW (it's amazing how many designer boutique carrier bags you can get into the boot of those Beamers!). His passengers, I learned, were an IOC member and his wife. The 5-star Park Lane Hotel bedrooms provided to IOC members were paid for by the British taxpayer. To see the actual spectacle of this parasitic behaviour in front of me was fascinating – it was blatant yet banal. The London cabbies I spoke to during this time were also upset because they felt much of their business had been taken by the volunteer chauffeurs – they reported a 50% loss of earnings.

During the Olympics, we were told, London was going to be overwhelmed with people spending money – it would be a massive boost to the economy.

I interviewed business owners who, like the cabbies, typically reported a 40-50% decline in trade during the Olympic period.

Among a staggeringly long list of benefits, the London Olympics was going to provide construction jobs, but as it turns out these went mostly to foreigners. It was also going to provide homes. The Athletes' Village has already been sold to the Qatari Sovereign Wealth Fund at a huge loss to the taxpayer. True, some of the homes in the converted Athletes' Village will be 'affordable' – affordable, that is, if you earn £80,000 or more a year.

We were told London 2012 provided a "once in a lifetime opportunity to clean up this polluted area of East London".[13] What Olympic bosses don't seem to lack is a sense of ironic humour, unless of course by 'clean-up' they meant cleansing the area of its existing culture, historic buildings and community.

The main thrust of the Olympic sales pitch was that it was going to 'regenerate' an area of East London that, according to the official line, was a wasteland where nothing was happening. There was actually a lot happening there. Housing for around 1,600 people, 500 businesses employing thousands of people, and a huge, mostly African church with a Sunday congregation of around 10,000 were just a few of the things going on there.

I recently visited the ODA headquarters, which is not in the Olympic 'Park'. As I sat in the huge marble lobby waiting for an ODA member of staff, I took in the stainless-steel corporate art and unsmiling important-looking people in well-polished shoes being sucked in and out of a vortex of rotating doors. I mused on what their jobs might be, but had the feeling if they told me I wouldn't understand. I wondered if the ODA's choice of location said anything about the mindset of the organisation? They occupy two floors in the Barclays building at Canary Wharf. To me, Canary Wharf is one of the most contrived, controlled, air-conditioned and sterile places in London, with its army of private security guards sporting uniforms almost identical to the cops and who, under any other circumstances, would be arrested for impersonating police officers.

The one thing that Canary Wharf does have going for it (apart from virtual jobs in the financial sector) is the sense of history that is still felt in the dock basins and some of the few remaining historic buildings. But the ODA has demolished virtually everything that was standing in its 2.5 square kilometre domain, leaving no tangible vestige of the area's history. Somehow, of all the places in London, Canary Wharf is where I would have expected the ODA to headquarter themselves. The two territories share an ideology which has been built into their aesthetic – banks bigger than churches, money more important than people, privately owned 'public' space, private security, Perimeter Command Control Systems, CCTV, and numerous signs telling you what you can't do: no fishing, no ball games, no cycling, photography, rollerblading, etc., and in one place, no work-clothes. Both the Olympic 'Park' and Canary Wharf are, for me, despotic McDonald's/Disney dystopias, with attached shopping malls dispensing virtual happiness at a price. Interestingly, Olympic sponsor McDonald's food doesn't rot. The oldest and as yet un-decomposed McDonald's hamburgers were bought in 1999.[14] According to Natural News: "... no normal animal will perceive a McDonald's hamburger bun as food ... neither will bacteria or fungi. The reason nothing will eat a McDonald's hamburger bun (except a human) is because it's not food."[15] Is McDonald's to food, what the Olympic 'Park' is to parks?

A friend of mine, who has just been on an official visit of the Post-Olympic Olympic 'Park', comments: "Wow, the place looks like the set of a post-apocalyptic zombie type of film – bleak, and the only life is machinery digging away."

The argument that the Olympics has actually slowed down the 'regeneration' of the area is convincing. First, starting in 2006, they had to destroy what was originally in the area. They then had to build the things that were needed for 24 days (2012). Then they have to get rid of, or modify, those things ready for the so-called 'legacy' phase, which has barely started. From where I've been spectating, the benefits of London 2012 seemed to go to those high up in the Olympic industry, to an elite of corporate sponsors, and to IOC members. It looks to me pretty much like the same elite who benefit from the policies of our government.

The Olympic Games strap-line was "Inspire a Generation". Inspire them to what? I wondered. To become inventors of corporate slogans perhaps – it's a growth industry. Serco run the private prison I was locked up in. They are apparently "Bringing Service to Life". If only I'd known that while I was there, I'd have sent down for a bottle of Chablis and, as Groucho Marx said, "I'd have called room service and asked for a larger room." And G4S, in charge of the bungled security of the London Games (and infiltrated by an undercover investigative journalist friend of mine, who reported being trained by them in ways of inflicting pain without leaving marks) are apparently "Securing Your World".[16]

The Environment (strap-line: "Creating a Better Place") Agency's "comfortable" relationship with contractors dealing with the radioactive contamination problem in the Olympic 'Park' made me wonder if the parasite/host model is not now also applicable between government and its agencies and the people it is meant to serve.

Another journalist friend of mine Andy Roberson runs the blog Social Investigations and has spent years investigating parliamentarians' interests in healthcare companies. He comments:

The government appears to have morphed into one that serves corporations. Research during the process of the Health and Social Care Bill revealed over 200 parliamentarians with recent and present financial links to companies involved in healthcare. This amounts to a corporate coup and one that goes beyond the parliamentary houses and into every bureaucratic part of the system. They write the law, employ our so-called public servants, then vote on the legislation that creates new contract possibilities for their paymasters. Democracy is a brand with money and contacts.

I couldn't have put it better.

Wake-up call

My acquaintance with the Olympics has given me a learning experience money could not have bought. They say that prison is more expensive than the most exclusive private schools in the land – and yes, prison was an education, in many ways. There I met many intelligent and likeable people, a large number of whom were aged 21 or just a bit older, who had previously been in and out of young offenders' institutions before landing up, as adults, in the slammer. They had come from less than advantaged backgrounds and one thing that struck me about many of them was that jail didn't seem to bother them; they appeared to see it as a minor hazard of life. It occurred to me that this totally neutralised one of the alleged purposes for prison – a deterrent.

In prison I was forced to attend sessions that were going to help reform my fellow inmates and myself. The well-intentioned handsome black man leading the course asked the 25 tough looking guys and me what we wanted to do when we were free men. There was a universal answer – everyone wanted a job. One guy was crestfallen when he learned that working as a security guard would not be possible owing to having a criminal record. My comment: jobs not jails, but there are around 97,000 people in UK prisons. Around 55,000 are remand prisoners – in jail awaiting trial, often for months.

The prison I was banged up in is brand new. Built next to two existing prisons, it forms part of a prison industrial complex in South East London. The government has just announced plans to build a new "super prison" capable of taking more than 2,000 prisoners. These so-called Titan prisons indicate there is to be no let up in the policy of locking people up, and in fact the prison population has risen by 90% since 1993. It costs around £40,000 a year to keep a person in jail.

Experiencing the way the legal system works was interesting. The outcome of a trial clearly relies on the calibre of legal representation. Especially in the lower courts, I learned that the burden of proof is frequently not with the prosecution but rather with the defence. In other words, a complete perversion of the supposed principle of our legal system.

In my case, at both bail hearings and at the trial, in the absence of any real evidence, the judge listened to, and appeared to be influenced by, the prosecution's allegation that I was a "protester". There are two things about this that are important. Firstly, it would only be relevant insofar as it might indicate a person holds certain opinions, which raises the question, is the holding of opinions a crime? Secondly, even if there was something wrong with being a protester and holding certain opinions, in court no actual evidence of my being a protester was presented. It was simply stated by the prosecution that I was a protester. The prosecution also attempted to discredit witnesses called by my defence, claiming they were also protesters. They failed to produce any evidence of this either.

One of the things I learned from prison, which sounds like a total cliché, is that freedom is a state of mind. The oppression of my own insecurities are the opposite of freedom – they separate me from others and therefore are a form of prison.

I was released on bail, but I was apparently still seen as an enemy of the Olympics and had they caught me within 100 metres of an Olympic venue I would have been sent back to the slammer. The Olympic 'Park' has airport-style security and is completely surrounded by a 5,000-volt electric fence, yet I was still seen as a threat. As a journalist with an interest in the London

Olympics, this restriction had serious implications for me, including loss of income. The only way for me to study the Games was therefore on the TV, and I have to acknowledge that the question is, was the price tag on that 24-day TV spectacular value for money?

Amongst many stories of austerity cuts, a friend of mine, a play-worker and play-researcher, was telling me how funding for adventure playgrounds across London is being cut, causing staff layoffs and many playgrounds to close. Most of the London boroughs that hosted the Olympic Games have high indices of child deprivation, and my friend's remarks made me think of all the promises that were made to the youth of the host boroughs. Sebastian Coe went so far as to take a load of local kids to Singapore to 'big-up' the bid. The kids were there to add credibility to the bid promise of providing facilities and resources for local youth. I have to ask myself if I can see any advantage at all to the average kid in any of the host boroughs?

Actually I think the Games has had a negative impact for youth. The cost of hosting the Olympics is also put into context by cuts to the NHS, which has to shave £20 billion off its budget by 2015.

I was not the only one who fell victim to the authorities' paranoia during the Olympic period. Others served short prison sentences, were threatened with the loss of their homes through libel action and court costs etc. One hundred and eighty-two (182) people were subjected to mass arrest on the night of the opening ceremony after cycling on the Olympic Route Network. And I'm sure there were others.

A fantastic opportunity?

There were moments of comedy in jail. One of those times was when I decided to carry out a Vox Pop and ask what the other prisoners thought about the London Olympics. The first guy I asked had a one-word reply to the question: "Shit," he said. A compact and minimalist analysis of London 2012 I thought. Another prisoner I put the Olympic question to said, "It's great, it's a brilliant thing, it will bring lots of opportunities. This is a once in a lifetime opportunity." And he repeated, "Once in a lifetime opportunity." "Hang on," I thought, "that is just the sort of drivel the Olympic bullshit machine would have spewed out." I have to admit I felt disappointed. I was hoping for what I would consider a more sophisticated analysis from my fellow prisoners. Then he clarified, "Yes, it'll be a fantastic opportunity for thieving." Sorry to anyone that was robbed by this guy, but I did find it extremely funny, not only because it was such an unexpected answer but also because he was talking exactly like the Olympic spin doctors. He was a fascinating guy who told me how he enjoys thieving right under the noses of the police – he sees it as a challenge. He told me he robs from the rich and it occurred to me he is the reverse of the London Olympics that has robbed the taxpayer to give to the Olympic fat cats, and I secretly hoped he'd be out there evening the score with the IOC members staying in those swanky 5-star Park Lane hotels.

The organisational model of London 2012 is the same our government uses to manage the nation – a foundation of compacted bullshit provides a platform on which a network of well-connected vampires schmooze, positioning themselves to pick up lucrative government contracts. The mainstream mass media, up to its neck in the same compacted bullshit, almost completely fails in its duty to monitor, investigate and inform, whilst a system of self-congratulation and industry awards is backed up with knighthoods for the worst offenders. The media's collusion in the Olympic smokescreen was made apparent to me by one of the presenters of a BBC documentary focusing on people evicted for the Games. It was shot before the Games and was supposed to have ten episodes but was cut to three watered down, worthless episodes. I was told that if the BBC wanted good access during the Olympics the documentary would not rock the boat – it didn't.

This vampire capitalism, this so-called 'free market' ideology, has spiralled the cost of a secure home out of the reach of ordinary folks. Our prisons are full, and building new ones just makes more money for the well connected. A sense of insecurity pervades most work places and, most tragically, many seem pessimistic about the future. Wake up and smell the compacted bullshit – our Olympics was hijacked the same way our nation and our media is.

* I would like to thank my friends who supported me while I was in jail (I love you all), thanks also my solicitor Sashy Nathan of Bindmans, and my barrister Tom Stevens of Doughty Street Chambers. I would also like to thank the police and the ODA for an education and experiences I could not have bought.

1. The film documents a community's struggle against Olympic bosses' wish to build a parkland and also the hypocrisy behind London 2012's choice of sponsors.
2. Remand is the term used to describe the keeping of a person in prison until their trial, usually because there is a likelihood that a person may abscond before trial or because there is a likelihood that they will reoffend.
3. http://www.bbc.co.uk/news/uk-17200835.
4. An estimate given by Sky News, http://news.sky.com/story/920409/sky-investigation-olympics-bill-tops-12bn. Whatever the true cost, the figures look like phone numbers – international ones, beginning with a big fat plus sign.
5. http://www.dailymail.co.uk/news/article-2483900/BBC-pays-Tony-Blairs-spin-doctor-150k-time-PR-man.html.
6. http://www.gamesmonitor.org.uk/node/1108.
7. Email between Environment Agency and Olympic Contractor Atkins dated 28-07-2008; email obtained through Freedom of Information (FOI) by Charman and Wells.
8. https://dl.dropboxusercontent.com/u/7090098/11_90621_OUTODA-DESIGN_ACCESS_STATEMENT-180.pdf. Page 12 of this planning document shows location of proposed block of flats; page 13 shows location of radioactive waste burial.
9. Survey Reports Radiation and contamination survey reports by Olympic contractor Nukem, September 2007; obtained by Charman and Wells under FOI. See also http://www.lifeisland.org/?p=602.
10. 'Investigation into dust suppression', dated 23-04-2008, by Olympic contractor Morrison Construction; document obtained under FOI.
11. Press Release, dated 18-1-2007, posted on the 2012 Olympic website.
12. See: http://industry.shortyawards.com/category/5th_annual/olympics; http://www.mirror.co.uk/sport/other-sports/london-2012-olympic-park-to-receive-833783; https://www.gov.uk/government/news/awards-already-being-won-at-olympic-park-nine-months-before-games-begin; http://www.atkinsglobal.co.uk/en-GB/about-the-group/awards.
13. On the now shut down London 2012 website.
14. http://www.huffingtonpost.com/2013/04/23/worlds-oldest-hamburger-mcdonalds_n_3139231.html.
15. http://www.naturalnews.com/030074_Happy_Meal_decompose.html.
16. The Met Police's strap line appears to have been changed from "Working for a safer London" to "Total Policing".

Fighting Gentrification and State Co-ordinated 'Regeneration':

Experiences from Recent London Campaigns

RUTH ALLEN, CHARLIE CHARMAN, JULIAN CHEYNE,
MITAL PATEL & JAMES SKINNER

The lived experience of regeneration for those directly affected is one of forced evictions, displacement and the destruction of communities and livelihoods as governments and corporations work together to extract and maximise the value of land inhabited by the city's poor and ethnic minorities. A pattern can be seen globally, from the streets of London to Mumbai, from the informal settlements surrounding Cairo to Rio. These places are invariably contested, as people fight against the forced regeneration. Separated geographically, the specifics of each battle are different but there are some chilling overarching similarities in the way that governments and corporations together attempt to carry out these processes of urban development – these include the way they construct a false and disingenuous discourse about the place and the people living and working there, and the way they utilise or produce legal structures to wrest control of the land.

Below is an extract from a conversation between five people from three London-based campaigns working to halt evictions and defend some of the city's rapidly diminishing public spaces, independent businesses and social housing. The conversation's aim was to explore similarities in our experiences of resisting the violence of forced regeneration and to share some of the techniques we found useful in sometimes overcoming a very specific and highly tuned co-ordination between the state and global corporations.

Ruth Allen, Mital Patel and James Skinner are from the Wards Corner Community Coalition (WCC). The WCC is based in Tottenham, North London, started in 2007 and works to stop the demolition of a city block to make way for a large-scale property development project led by Grainger PLC, which comprises 200 flats and space for national retail. Wards Corner is currently home to an indoor market containing many South American, African and West Indian businesses, two streets of local independent traders, a street of affordable housing and a number of heritage buildings, including the landmark Wards Department Store which gives the site its name. The WCC are calling for a different approach, one that is led by local people, that preserves the heritage buildings and that supports and grows the existing local economy; something along the lines of 'Better Neighbourhoods, Same Neighbours'[1]. WCC developed a community plan for the site that immediately re-positioned and game changed Grainger's corporate plan. However, despite seven years of delay, victorious court battles and overwhelming local support, the site remains under threat from Grainger.

Julian Cheyne is from the Clays Lane Estate, Britain's largest purpose-built housing co-operative. Built in 1982 and housing some 450 people, the estate was quite unbelievably marked for demolition as part of the development for the London 2012 Olympic Games. Despite resistance from the residents and a public enquiry, the homes were demolished in 2007 and the residents were dispersed across London. Some residents had been wrongly told they were not eligible for rehousing and, although minimal compensation was awarded at the time, there are still ongoing arguments over individual cases.

Charlie Charman is from the Save Leyton Marsh (SLM) Campaign, a group that formed in response to plans by the Olympic Development Authority (ODA) to destroy an area of public parkland in order to build a temporary training facility for London 2012. Despite local resistance, and ignoring historic stipulations that no such development could occur, the plans were granted permission by Hackney Council. Campaigners were also concerned the development would set a precedent which would result in the public open green space being reduced little by little in future years. Soon after permission was granted and construction work began, people commenced blockading the site, halting the building work and delaying construction. A group of people from Occupy London joined the protests and formed a permanent encampment, stopping construction for two weeks. Following an injunction, the camp was violently evicted by bailiffs and the police. SLM continues to fight for the area to be restored to its original state as promised by the ODA, and now also works with other local and special interests groups dealing with the threat of further development on the marshes and in the surrounding Lea Valley.

Public authorities and private business: a lack of accountability

JS: So let's start with the role of the council in letting these plans come about. Something we've come up against a lot at Wards Corner is councillors being completely unengaged with the decisions they are making.

RA: There is an overarching sense that 'inward investment' of any kind must be good, that change that's transformative in terms of the built landscape or the built environment is just good, and that's the default position that planning officers and councillors, who are not particularly well informed, fall into. The bottom line for relatively poor Inner London boroughs is that 'inward investment is good' and everything else will be subsidiary to that.

JS: That raises interesting questions about the role of the community in engaging with councillors in that process. Something that we really felt we achieved at the last planning committee at Wards Corner was that our objection document – which is quite comprehensive and directed at councillors in terms of giving them ammunition for refusing the plan, giving them clear grounds and reasons to refuse – was being used and quoted in their questioning of the developer and in bringing up debate in the planning committee that otherwise wouldn't have been there.

JC: Yes, there are possibilities there, when a planning authority has opposition in it, because in Haringey you actually have a divided council.

CC: It is divided but the planning committee has four Labour people on it and three Lib Dem, and they always vote in blocks.

JC: Well, at Clays Lane, the second planning application, which was the one that actually counted, was dealt with by the ODA, so at that point local politicians no longer have a say. It's turned into this 'national' project. As a community there wasn't any real understanding of the planning process at all, and you're just talking about a lot of people who are living on an estate, a community which doesn't really have a particular feel about what is happening to it. So really, the planning process from Clays Lane's perspective was almost completely irrelevant in terms of anybody thinking they had anything to do with it, any say at all.

RA: There seems to be a commonality here with Wards Corner – the sense that, for the people who are going to be directly personally affected, the first thing you hear is partial, hard to understand, obscured, not presented in a way that enables the people who are going to be affected to understand it. And it is not presented to everybody who is going to be affected. There is a whole sense that you are suddenly faced with a large monster, a large kind of entity with a massive machinery behind it, that has its own internal coherence and its place in law and all the technical stuff behind it. And it arrives in front of people whose lives are going to be affected. It may be that it is about people not understanding the planning process. They don't understand the regeneration process. They don't understand how local democracy relates to other agencies or other interests. Really you just kind of get this sense of confusion initially, which quickly turns into complete outrage.

Generating legitimising narratives

JS: Often the authority or the developer have this vision that they want to implement and they use a range of tactics and approaches to justify it, perpetuating these myths about its benefits in the process. What do you think is their motivation for this and what sort of things have you come up against?

JC: With the Olympics, you have the argument that the area is derelict. So the whole area for the Olympic Park is written off as being derelict, which is not true. There was parkland, two housing estates and two travellers' sites; you have industrial areas, the Eastway Cycle Track and the allotments; all these communities that are already doing things there. These things tend to happen in what are called 'deprived' areas, so they justify it by saying this place can't help itself, it has to be helped. What is now the Olympic Park is a very valuable piece of land, extremely valuable. And this is one of the things about the Olympics, people think about it being a sporting event but actually the main point here is that it gives this opportunity to compulsorily purchase a very large piece of land. It is about property development. It's what's happening in Rio now. It's what's been happening in Sochi. It happened in Beijing. In London, it meant a deliberate deindustrialisation of the area. They wanted to get rid of all the so-called 'dirty' industry that's there, which is basically the working-class type jobs, and replace it with 'clean' creative type jobs, which again are going to be for a new population.

CC: But it may be true that the Olympics would be necessary if you think these sorts of vast master planning exercises, where you can completely redesign or clear a whole area, are a good thing, but there are a lot of arguments against.

RA: Yes absolutely, I think there is so much evidence in London, and elsewhere as well, about how with small local incremental change, where you get the right kind of combination of factors, of motivated people, and they manage to mobilise a bit of capital somehow or there is some subsidy or whatever, you start to see these changes happening and you preserve, if you like, the granularity of the city in all its diversity and in all its variation, and also things like the possibility of preserving a diverse infrastructure that can then change and develop subsequently. The thing about the sorts of developments that are proposed for Wards Corner, you obviously do away with history, but you also do away with the fabric of the site, which is very diverse and can be used, on a small scale, by lots of different people. I think the point about what vision local politicians or officers have or don't have is really important. They have a bit of a vision, they have a bit of an idea about what they want things to be, and it goes as far as saying we want a comprehensive redevelopment. They don't have the capability, or the interest, or the care, or the political will, to actually think

about a different kind of vision for that area based on what the people want or might need in the future.
CC: They argue that their approach is the most effective way of bringing economic benefits to the local community because the ultimate rhetoric, as we saw with Ken Livingstone and the Olympics, is about how to get more jobs, more housing. Basically that's the bottom line, nothing else matters, and that drives the whole process. You know, the aesthetics of it, the quality of life, all of this stuff comes after those primary considerations.

RA: At Wards Corner, they denied the economic activity that was already existing on the site – they obscured it, they ignored it – and they basically treated the place like a brownfield site. The fact that there were some 60 businesses of various sizes and types, supporting any number of families and individuals and so on, was completely ignored.

JS: Yes, there is a real struggle as to how you are defining value in that situation. Their tactic is to have a very narrow understanding of what uses of a space are of value and, in doing so, completely delegitimising anything that doesn't fit into their economic framework.

CC: And also there's this whole argument that low intensity usages are an inherently bad thing, that's the assumption. They would say that they are low quality or low intensity land uses and that's of no value.

MP: It's nonsense too, I mean the position with the markets. They're known to be high intensity. They tend to employ more people per square metre.

RA: I think it's a perverted sort of – perverted is not the right word – municipalism. It's not going to be state controlled, so it's not land or property that's going to be under state or municipal control, but you can put it en bloc under the control of a private company who will then manage it. In a way they can tell you exactly how they are going to manage it, it'll be safer, and I think it is something about civil control and a kind of appetite to move towards having large areas of geographical space and social space more controlled by somebody, by an entity, by an agency. And actually the last ten years, fifteen years, with New Labour, they've gone into partnership with those big corporations in new ways and they're the new controllers, under kind of contractual terms: 'perhaps we'll have a gloss of affluence if we give things over to this kind of modernising corporation'.

Forming and sustaining resistance

JS: So it seems there's a lot of similarity between all of the campaigns, in the way that the council and the developers present their developments, but I think there is probably quite a lot of variety in how we react and in how local resistance on the ground starts to form and gain momentum.

MP: With Wards Corner what helped in the beginning is that it was a coming together of groups that already had working relationships. So you had residents associations, you had conservation groups, you had trader groups, it really was a coming together of groups.

RA: It was a coalition of existing interest groups and all of them with a view that was loose enough to accommodate different perspectives, but always trying to be clear about some fundamental central principles. There was a bit of an ethos around it from the outset, that it would be open enough to resist becoming sluggish and ideological. It would always try and be adaptable, and flexible, and accommodating, and invite people to join. Also, leadership wasn't imbued in any individuals. People do lead on things, but they lead on them according to their abilities, interests, energy and time, and we tried to set the conditions for that to be the case.

From the outset it meant that Grainger and the council were quite confused by the type of resistance they were meeting because we didn't put an individual up as our spokesperson; we couldn't be defined as just this or that. We're not just residents, or just traders, or just conservation people, or just anything. We're seeing ourselves as about a whole idea, about a sense of place and somewhere our community might go forward.

JS: I think also, in those early stages, thinking about your organisational structures and the way you're beginning to form, it's good to avoid replicating the structures that you're opposing, and also to avoid becoming seen as this service to the people who are affected. We're not aiming to be representative. We need to work together. And if people want to see something happen we'll support them, but they have to run with it themselves.

RA: I think probably there were some co-ordinating principles, and one of them was just that the way people were being treated was deeply unfair and unjust. It was unequal, and that was very clear from the outset, and that's very difficult for public bodies not to take seriously. If you start talking about inequalities and discrimination then you can start really making the case around that, and of course it was essential to our first court case. We started to get those kinds of messages out, I think, quite early.

CC: Save Leyton Marsh (SLM) was a fresh group that started around the time the planning application was initially being heard. We too were quite loosely organised. There wasn't originally a constitution but eventually one did get drawn up, though that was in connection with the judicial review. In fact the judicial review was the main problem that we encountered; there were significant disagreements about that. The way in which the group was run was slightly fragmented, in that some people would operate quite individually and not everything got done by a group agreement. Many people would take the initiative to go and do things. People thought that the judicial review had been abandoned and that it wasn't wise to go ahead with it. But one individual did pursue it and it eventually got submitted and then that caused a lot of problems because we weren't protected against costs and there were misunderstandings about liabilities at the application stage. In the end the ODA ran up huge legal costs, over £25,000, and it then became apparent that they could seek those costs from anybody in any way associated with the group. So many people found that an extremely threatening situation. It was a unique case, because I think it was unheard of to have anybody try and claim those kinds of costs, especially as an interested party, which the ODA was. They were desperate, obviously, that this didn't get to court, even though it wouldn't stop them using the venue.

JC: In the case of SLM, you've had an occupation, you've had a lot of protests, the group is still going. I mean it has drawn together a group of very active individuals, and in that way, I think, it's the most coherent campaign that has come out of the Olympics.

CC: Yes, there has been quite an overload of work. One way that we tried to deal with that was to split it up. Instead of having lots of big meetings, we split it up into lots of groups. We had an environment group, a legal group, an events group, that concentrated on those areas according to their interests. Quite a lot of people didn't like dealing with tedious legal stuff and research. They wanted to get out there and do stuff. And there were quite a few people who were involved in comedy or music; some who wanted to do fundraising events. So it's actually quite practical to have people doing those things that they most enjoy or have connections with.

JC: At Clays Lane we had the strange situation of there not being any alliance among the groups that were affected. The businesses, the allotments, the cyclists, the Travellers, each of these groups was operating on a sort of self-defence basis. Each one was dealing with their own situation. There was no real co-ordination. What we did do was that within the community there was a kind of minority that was prepared to argue, and I think that is really the key issue, that you just have to build on what you have. We didn't have alliances outside, and we didn't have a coherent opposition inside of the community. It was down to a minority to argue, and people argued about just about everything. We argued about the compensation. They upped it, but even that didn't compensate us for the rise in rents and a lot of people spent more than the amount allowed for disturbance. We reckoned, on average, that people were going to be about £50 worse off a week, the LDA reckoned £12, and actually our figure was correct. There was a post-removal survey, and the costs were much, much higher than the LDA had estimated. We argued about moving as a community and the LDA did respond with a programme to try and find suitable sites, although in the end this came to nothing. Really it was determined individuals, who also formed small groups, who continued to argue as much as they could about everything that they could find to argue about. As a result, people are now being paid expenses which they should have been paid years ago and we are still encouraging people to put in expenses claims.

Utilising spectacle: making ourselves visible

JS: I wonder if we could talk about the role of visible public dissent and demonstrations in our campaigns. I know it played a big part at Leyton Marsh, and at Wards Corner as well. What do we think those tactics are useful for and how have they impacted on the campaigns?

CC: I think many people found it very empowering – it was great having the involvement of Occupy. It had a slight downside, in that it immediately attracted a lot of media attention and the actual specifics of the situation got lost amongst the general impact of Occupy being there and stopping an Olympics construction project. The fact that people had already been there, holding up lorries and so on, that never got reported nationally; there had been a fair bit of local press coverage but no national coverage at all. In retrospect it seemed pretty dramatic that people actually stopped construction work on an Olympic site, and it was, you know, a handful of people doing that.

The situation was actually totally predictable because they'd decided to construct this venue in the middle of a piece of parkland effectively, a large green space with no means of getting into it. So all around it was supposedly public access land. They had no particular rights to drive their vehicles into the site and force people to get out of the way. So people simply started standing in the way of vehicles and refusing to move, and the vehicles would just stop. The contractors started calling the police who'd come in and say, 'Well, there's nothing really we can do about it'. That was going on for about ten days prior to the Occupy people arriving – initially there was just local people occasionally obstructing the vehicles – but once they did, everything stopped completely. It became much more serious. They simply shut the site down for two weeks. There was then more police presence and our resistance was more robust. They got really quite involved, positioning themselves on the road in front of vehicles and there were a few arguments with site workers, and so on.

Eventually the LVRPA (Lee Valley Regional Park Authority) got an injunction to evict the campers and the ODA got an injunction to stop people obstructing vehicles. There was only two days' notice of the court case and it wasn't really possible to challenge it, so the injunctions were granted. They had also attached a potential £350,000 costs onto it – nobody then wanted to put themselves in the firing line.

RA: Can I just ask, did you want them there, Occupy?

CC: Oh yeah, they were very popular. People were very happy to go down there and give them food, and enjoyed just going round, sitting round the campfire, getting to know people. There was quite a warm relationship, and I think people really appreciated that something was happening. That was quite nice.

RA: With Wards Corner there has been a whole series of visible activities, and of course one of the key things is using artwork and films and showing those in public, both on the site and in the local area. We did a protest called 'The Big Hug' where we surrounded the site, lots of poster campaigns using professional quality imagery, and also used some advertising methods, you know using logos and branding. I think actually the branding of the WCC has been really important. We had some advice from the outset, and some really good artwork – it's never changed. Constantly making the existence of the campaign visible through imagery has been really important.

JS: I think there are also interesting consequential impacts of doing these large protests or organising events together. They really serve to build strength within your campaign, through working together, through having these often quite intense shared experiences. Especially things like protests really build strength in people's relationships and give the campaign a focus and an energy and something that everyone can get involved in that's not so technical, or legal or arduous or bureaucratic, that puts people off.There is a real inclusivity to them.

Regaining control of the story

JS: Another tactic to use to get our message out to the public is through the media. How has engaging with the press benefited or not benefited our campaigns?

JC: Well, we had the problem that basically the mainstream corporate media and most bloggers overwhelmingly supported the winning of the Olympics. There was no serious analysis of what it was going to result in. We did get some coverage when the bid was won, but it basically portrayed us only as victims, asking us where we were going to go, that kind of stuff. The moment we started talking about how actually it's not going to improve sport participation, and that there is already regeneration going on all over the area so it's not necessary ... well, they recorded it, but all you get is a little sound bite about us leaving and the rest is completely edited out. We were just these token victims. It was really manipulative and there was very little of any real substance. We had this final *Guardian* article at the end which said "they left without a struggle".[2] We had been going through judicial reviews, a CPO enquiry, arguing with these people for years – and then to be written off just like that. So sadly I can't really say the media was a great deal of use to us and I think also did the public a disservice by not exploring the issues really at stake.

JS: I think at Wards Corner we've had a similarly vexed relationship with the national media, at least, in terms of them reproducing the dominant story about the site, not one of us as victims though. We are portrayed as 'the objectors', as people who are self-interested and opposed to growth or progession. They would come and look for a story, and they would find something that was too complicated for them to reproduce so they reduced it down to this very bland narrative no matter how hard we tried to package the story for the journalists.

What I have found to be really interesting is our changing relationship with the local media. Early on the council and the developer were really controlling the media narrative around Wards Corner, and they had the upper hand in the fact that they knew when the big events would happen before anyone else. They knew when the planning application was going to go in; they knew when the planning committee was going to be. Often we'd find out about these things in the local paper and by then it was too late for us to react. So we started to get more proactive in terms of producing press releases and learning that process of how to actually write a press release that gets noticed. But still the journalists were writing articles that predominantly followed the PR information being put forward by Grainger and the council. A real turning point came at the last committee meeting, where a few of the local journalists stayed for the entire six-hour meeting and, by the end of it, clearly had had some sort of revelation. Suddenly they understood what was going on, and immediately after that we started getting much better coverage and having more control over the narrative in the local media.

MP: The only problem with the local press is the high turnover of staff. Once you build up the relationship they're gone, and suddenly you find yourself going through the same process of winning them over, or at least getting them to write a slightly more balanced and fair article where you're not portrayed as an 'objector' or someone who is stopping so-called progress.

JC: Yes, I don't want be too negative. You can achieve things and the campaign can gain attention. But I question whether that's what makes the campaign. Because without the people who are continuing to attend the meetings, continuing to argue about the planning issues, continuing to organise events, if you just have a media campaign without all the other things, you're not going to get very far, I don't think.

What is it to win?

JS: Maybe this is a good time to talk about this idea of achievement, what we feel we've achieved, or have the potential to achieve, through our campaigns?

CP: I think the most important, broader effect we've had at Leyton Marsh is making life harder for the Lee Valley Regional Park Authority. They operated completely below everyone's radar – no one knew what it was, how it operated, where it was. They were employed in this completely undemocratic fashion, and now they're finding there are a lot more people, with a lot more interest in them, asking a lot of questions.

JS: For me, one of the most exciting things about Leyton Marsh was that it was this flashpoint event that has led to the continuation of a campaign that brings people together and deals with lots of issues around the marshes.

JC: I would describe Clays Lane as a community under siege. We did force the LDA (London Development Agency) to change direction in certain ways. Although group moves weren't successful, we did manage to get that onto the agenda, and they had to devote time, energy and money to that. Following demolition, they had to go and find the people they had told they were not eligible for housing and they had to go and rehouse them. They will say they did this without our prompting, but I don't think that's true. We played a big part in that. What's more, some of the community does still exist, and particularly around the fact that we created a community move group. There was a core of people who were talking to each other all the time, and we still stay in touch, we still have meals together, and this leads out into other things, both to do with Clays Lane and other projects. I can't imagine that the GLA (Greater London Authority) would have imagined themselves saying 'oh bloody hell, we're still dealing with these people' six and a half years later, still getting letters and getting claims for expenses and things like that.

RA: I think the WCC campaign has definitely added to the development of local networks, partly because of the extensive networking that the WCC has done. I think to some extent it has changed the way the council responds to people. When we first started the level of disrespect for local people was completely off the scale. It's still nowhere near where it needs to be, but it was a crude level of disrespect and ignoring people, which I don't think they will easily repeat. But 'the riots' were an unexpected disjuncture in changing local circumstance.

MP: You can see they are reverting back to how they used to do development, bypassing local people.

JC: I suppose the riots[3] mean they can write people off?

MP: Well, actually their rhetoric is very much about community – 'we're involving the community', 'we're going to do a lot more consultation' – but actually the only people they're engaging is developers and external experts. They do these really ineffectual consultation exercises that have no relation to the plans they're forcing onto people. They're a bit better at pretending they're engaging the community, but they're not taking it seriously in any way. They also exploit the narrative around the recession by painting any critique of their processes as being against the creation of jobs and homes, against the national interest. They don't see us as an asset or even a 'resource' to draw on.

JS: For me, this shift following the protest really shows the fragility of these things. Success is defined by such a wide range of variables, so many of which are outside of your control, but you have to keep plugging away at it because you might win, and you might not. If it hadn't been for the uprising I think we'd be in a very different situation in Tottenham. There is such a strong force of community involvement and community power in Tottenham now – always has been, but now it's very united. In relation to planning, it has come out of the Wards Corner development and some other battles further down the High Road, and, on a wider scale, from the prevalence of community and voluntary sector groups in the area – we've all been saying to the council 'we are not going to go quietly along with your plans'. At the very least, the council and developers have taken notice of this and seen it as a bigger financial risk, knowing no development will go through unchallenged, but I think their willingness to engage in the issues we raise has increased too. The riots have really undermined that position. The waters have been muddied around all of those debates and they all have to be argued again.

MP: It feels like the council are exploiting the riots and using them to completely push through old plans. The Wards Corner development predated the riots, it had nothing to do with them, but now the riots are being used as justification for demolition, like physical regeneration has this magical social affect.

JS: The absurdity of their approach is that their plans for action are exactly the same as they have been for years, since long before the riots, but now they have a new angle that they feel gives them more traction in terms of doing whatever they want to do. We're in a situation now where a developer is trying to put 30% affordable housing in new build and the council is actively making them put less, because their agenda for Tottenham is to change the population. They see that the way to solve the problem of deprivation is to have richer people living in the deprived areas, not to address the needs of the people already there.

MP: For Wards Corner the most obvious thing is that Grainger thought they'd have their development built and ready by 2009, and here we are, six years after the first application and they haven't even started. I've also noticed a shift in engagement with planning issues in Tottenham, especially considering how little there was before. There are more groups and individuals actually engaging with planning and actually questioning development. And whether that gets anywhere I don't know, but people are getting more involved and more aware, and now they're starting to work together under the 'Our Tottenham' banner. It's pretty exciting.

1. Andrea Gibbons, ' A Right to the City, a Right to a Home', in *Critical Cities: Ideas, Knowledge and Agitation from Emerging Urbanists*, Volume 2 (London: Myrdle Court Press, 2010).
2. http://www.theguardian.com/society/2007/jun/21/communities.olympics2012.
3. The protests in Tottenham in 2011 following the shooting of Mark Duggan by police. For more information watch the documentary *Voice Over Riots Reframed,* Dir Fahim Alam, Voice Over Productions, 2013.

Biographies

Awqapuma Yayra Colque is an activist based in west London, who has been politically active from a very young age. She has been involved in organisations that aim to help Nican Tlaca immigrants with their English and IT skills. In 2012, under the tutelage of Olin Tezcatlipoca, Awqapuma together with Nemequene Aquiminzaque Tundama started the London Chapter of the Mexica Movement. Having already achieved a degree in sociology, she will be going to SOAS to complete a Masters and PhD in history. After her studies, she will be going back to her homeland and carrying on her work towards liberation.

Campaign Against Criminalising Communities (CAMPACC) is a growing resistance network that has opposed the entire anti-terror legislative framework, its political agenda and its exceptional powers. Since 2001 (CAMPACC) has brought together migrant groups, civil liberties campaigners, lawyers and journalists. The campaign has built solidarity with people targeted by anti-terror powers through protest actions, public meetings, petitions, seminars and submissions to consultations (e.g. by Parliamentary committees and the Home Office), meanwhile collectively developing critical analysis of the securitisation agenda. CAMPACC raised the slogan, 'We are all terror suspects', also printed on t-shirts. All these activities reinforce and build solidarity networks, which have been central to effective opposition.

For building solidarity, a crucial strength has been a long-term working relationship with numerous organisations which can bring greater resources. These include: the Haldane Society, solicitors' group practices (especially Garden Court Chambers and Birnberg Peirce), Statewatch, Cageprisoners, Cordoba Foundation, London Guantanamo Campaign, Peace in Kurdistan Campaign, Kurdish community centres, British Tamil Forum, Tamil Youth Organisation UK, London Somali Youth Forum, Hands Off Somalia, Peace and Justice in East London (PJEL), the College of Law (Birkbeck College),

State Crime Project (University of Westminster), and the National Union of Journalists. Those co-operative efforts provide the basis for our analysis of securitisation strategies and collective resistance. www.campacc.org.uk.

Charlie Charman is a Hackney resident who continues to be involved in Save Leyton Marsh.

Clara Rivas Alonso moved to Addis Ababa after an MA at Goldsmiths in postcolonial theory and globalisation. She wrote her dissertation about the branding of Istanbul whilst working for a conflict resolution organisation. She has been actively involved in movements such as Stop the War and students against cuts. She has written articles on street protests and popular uprisings in Europe and the Middle East, published in Turkey and in London. She is currently a PhD candidate at the University of Leicester working on urbanisation as a practice of social exclusion.

David Bedford is professor of political science at the University of New Brunswick. He received his PhD in political philosophy from York University, Toronto, Canada. In addition to teaching and researching in political philosophy, he has taught and published on various issues on First Nations politics. His publications include articles on First Nations voter turnout, the relation of First Nations values and ecological politics, the political issues involved in self-government, and the Iroquois Great Law of Peace as a document of international relations. He has also published a book on the relation of First Nations and the Left.

Deepa Naik is a writer, activist and co-founder of This Is Not A Gateway and Myrdle Court Press with Trenton Oldfield. Her work investigates issues of spatial justice, colonialism, resistance movements and legal systems. http://myrdlecourtpress.net.

Idle No More is an indigenous-led resistance to ongoing colonisation of indigenous peoples on Turtle Island ('Canada'); a resistance steeped in a sacred hope and dream for justice, freedom and liberation for all. The spirit of resistance instilled within Idle No More has spanned generations since Europeans arrived on the shores of indigenous lands. See: www.idlenomore.ca

James Skinner has been involved in the Wards Corner Community Coalition since 2010. He is currently training to be a nurse.

Jason Larkin is a photographer recognised for his desire to forefront subjects on the periphery of current affairs. Soon after finishing his studies, Larkin worked as a documentary photographer across the Middle East and Africa, with his work published worldwide. In 2010, he moved to Johannesburg to focus on the legacy of the mine dumps. His latest body of work *Tales from the City of Gold* has just been published both as a monograph in Europe and as a bilingual newspaper publication for Africa. Larkin is the recipient of numerous awards including, most recently the PDN Arnold Newman New Portraiture Award and a Renaissance Photography Prize. His freely distributed publication, *Cairo Divided,* was nominated for both the Deutsche Börse and Prix Pictet photography awards. Recent exhibitions include those at the Brighton Photo Biennial, Flowers Gallery, London, and a solo show at Farnsworth Art Museum, USA. In 2013 he moved from Johannesburg and is now based in London.

Julian Cheyne is a former resident at Clays Lane who now writes about Olympics for Gamesmonitor.org.uk. He helped organise counter Olympics protests and the alternative torch relay in East London in July 2012.

Kate Donington has a BA in English literature and history (2005) and an MA in art gallery and museum studies (2007) from the University of Leeds. She worked for the Imperial War Museum, London, before leaving to pursue her doctoral research. Her PhD was attached to the ESRC-funded Legacies of British Slave-ownership project at University College London. She was awarded her doctorate in 2013 and has since become a research associate on the second phase of the project. Her research examines the structures and significance of British slave-ownership in Jamaica between 1763 and 1833. For more information on the Legacies of British Slave-ownership project see: http://www.ucl.ac.uk/lbs/.

Katherine Maich is a PhD candidate in sociology at the University of California, Berkeley, with a background in labour studies. Her research analyses the racialised, gendered and classed practice of domestic work in South America and the US. She focuses on the social consequences of household worker legislation in Lima, Peru, and New York City asking when and how the law can matter when regulating a historically marginalised population of women workers, whose socially necessary labour often goes unseen and unacknowledged. Katherine is a member of the Research Network for Domestic Worker Rights and she collaborates with the International Domestic Workers Federation.

Les Levidow helped to set up the Campaign Against Criminalising Communities (CAMPACC) in early 2001. Previously he was involved in other campaigns against criminalisation, e.g. against the Prevention of Terrorism Act 1974, the Italy '79 Committee, support group for the 1984–85 miners' strike, the Free Samar and Jawad Campaign, and support for the Zapatistas in Chiapas. He also has opposed the Israeli occupation through various UK campaigns, e.g. the 'Return' petition against the Israeli Law of Return (late 1980s), Palestine Solidarity Campaign, Jews for Boycotting Israel Goods (J-BIG), and the British Committee for the Universities of Palestine (BRICUP).

Mexica Movement London Chapter is an organisation that demands the end to the genocide of the full-blood and mixed-blood Nican Tlaca (indigenous) people of Cemanahuac (falsely known as The Americas). Through education and other non-violent assertive actions they plan on bringing liberation to their people and their continent. They are fighting for the return of all that has been stolen from the Nican Tlaca people over the last 500 years through colonialism and genocide. For more information go to www.mexica-movement.org.

Mike Wells' name (along with many thousands of others) occupies a place in the databases of state computers under the heading "Domestic Extremist". According to one police file released to Wells under Access to Information legislation, the police believe him to be known as "Green Warrior". This would tend to confirm the accuracy of Groucho Marx' assertion that "military intelligence is a contradiction in terms". Wells doesn't believe in the use of violence, which would negate the "Warrior" in his alias. With reference to "Green", on the one hand Wells lives off-grid and rides a bike, on the other his friends are always upset by his poor recycling credentials. Police, if you are reading this book, Wells suggests you change his alias to Greenish-geezer-rides-a-bike-knows-how-to-use-a-camera-has-worked-hard-to-learn-to-spell-the-word-dyslexic. He and other colleagues ran and contributed to the Games Monitor website, whose remit was to monitor the London Olympics. They received no pay for this work, while their counterparts in the Communications Department at the ODA were well remunerated for creating the gigantic smokescreen behind which the whole project hid.

Mital Patel is a lifelong Tottenham resident who lives above her family business, which is threatened by the Wards Corner redevelopment plans. She has been involved in the WCC since 2008 and currently works for a disability charity.

Nemequene Aquiminzaque Tundama is an activist based in south London, who has been educating and organising the Nican Tlaca (indigenous) community through various groups for six years. Under the mentorship of Olin Tezcatlipoca, the founder and director of the Mexica Movement, Nemequene together with Awqapuma Yayra Colque started the London Chapter of the Mexica Movement. After completing his degree in social anthropology and history at SOAS, he plans to do a PhD in history. Eventually, he wants to return to his homeland and continue to work towards decolonisation.

Nicolas Draper was a research associate on the Legacies of British Slave-ownership project at University College London (UCL). He is the co-director of the second phase of the project: the Structure and Significance of British Caribbean Slave-ownership 1763–1833. Prior to joining UCL as a doctoral candidate and then a teaching fellow, Nick worked in the City for 25 years. His foundational analysis of the Slave Compensation records was published by Cambridge University Press in 2009 as *The Price of Emancipation: Slave-Ownership, Compensation and British Society at the End of Slavery.* The book was awarded the 2009 Royal Historical Society's Whitfield Prize and was short-listed for the 2011 Frederick Douglass Book Prize.

Persis Taraporevala is a researcher and trained classical dancer. She currently leads a community building project for dancers in New Delhi that focuses on issues of governance, advocacy and access to resources for dance practitioners in India. Her primary research interest has been governance and participation which she has studied through the lens of decentralised indigenous forest conservation processes in India and the theoretical underpinnings of citizenship in the urban context. She has an MPhil in Development Studies from the University of Oxford and this paper is an outcome of her dissertation during her time at Oxford.

Roberto Bottazzi is an architect, researcher and educator who studied in Italy and Canada before moving to London where he is now based. His research analyses the impact of digital technologies on architecture and urbanism. He has lectured and exhibited internationally including in the UK, USA, China, Italy and Portugal. He's research co-ordinator and master tutor at London's Royal College of Art and M.Arch lecturer at the University of Westminster.

Ruth Allen is a Tottenham resident since 1996 and involved in the inception of the Wards Corner Community Coalition resistance to the corporate plans for the centre of South Tottenham. She is a social worker in mental health by profession and also currently an NHS director.

Sakej James Ward belongs to the wolf clan. He is Mi'kmaw (Mi'kmaq Nation) from the community of Esgenoopetitj (Burnt Church First Nation, New Brunswick). Sakej went to the University of New Brunswick and immersed himself in politics and graduated from the Honours programme with a Bachelor's degree in political science with a specialisation in international relations. Sakej continued to advance his studies and attended the University of Victoria where he successfully completed the Master of Arts Degree in indigenous governance. Sakej has a long history of advocating and protecting First Nations' rights and freedoms, having spent the last 20 years fighting the government and industry. This deep desire to bring justice to all indigenous people has given Sakej experience in international relations. He spoke on behalf of the Mi'kmaq Nation at the United Nations Working Group for Indigenous Populations (WGIP). For his efforts in protecting indigenous people, freedoms and territory, he has received the National Aboriginal Achievement Award.

Saleh Mamon is currently a Visiting Research Fellow at the Goldsmith Centre of Culture Studies. He has worked as a campaigner for CAMPACC to resist the erosion of civil liberties and violation of human rights by counter-terror laws. His current research interest is evaluating the impact of counter-insurgency policy and practice across the world. He is also interested in the 'hidden' history of the so-called Third World. In the mainstream discourse the violent process of colonisation and suppression of resistance by armed force has largely been erased. He believes this needs to be challenged and alternatives explored to reveal the full experience of the colonised peoples.

Steve Rushton is a political writer, researcher and activist. He writes for Occupy News Network. More of his research is collated at www.steve-rushton.co.uk.

Sylvia McAdam Saysewahum is one of four original women behind the global Idle No More movement in defence of indigenous rights, lands and waters. She completed a degree in human justice from the University of Regina and a bachelor of laws from the University of Saskatchewan. She is a consultant and author of *Cultural Teachings: First Nations Protocols and Methodologies* (Saskatchewan Indian Cultural Centre, 2009), which brings together her research and knowledge on First Nations culture, laws and traditions.

Thomas Cheney is a PhD student at York University, Toronto, Canada, writing a dissertation on the foundations of the human-nature relation in western thought. He received his MA from University of Victoria, Canada, examining the theoretical roots of the judicial decisions regarding First Nations treaty and aboriginal rights.

Trenton Oldfield is a writer, activist and co-founder of This Is Not A Gateway and Myrdle Court Press with Deepa Naik in 2007. His research problematises 'Western' concepts of property and landownership, The Urban Industry and ongoing colonialism. http://myrdlecourtpress.net.

About Myrdle Court Press

Myrdle Court Press (MCP) advances critical, independent and rigorous inter-disciplinary work that interrogates contemporary notions and experience of 'cities'. It was established in 2009 to redress the incongruous situation that as the population, size and problems of cities are expanding, and despite the existence of many new cells of knowledge and urgent thinking, the spaces for critical public discourse are narrowing.

An independent, not-for-profit organisation that straddles the spaces between the street and the academy, Myrdle Court Press commissions, collects and publishes work that tackles pressing and political concerns without restraint. It shares the experiences, astute insights and agitation of contributors from around the world including Beirut, Zagreb, Bogota, London, Hong Kong, Johannesburg, Nicosia, Jerusalem, New York, Addis Ababa and Lavasa. Contributors come from the fields of visual arts, activism, education, property, architecture and planning, law, governmental policy, political economy, military strategy, filmmaking, philosophy and lived knowledge.

On Myrdle Court Press books:

"There is a dearth of critical commentaries examining the changes wrought by neo-liberalism. At last a multi-disciplinary collection of writing that brings together some of the best." Anna Minton, author of *Ground Control*

"This collection explicitly and honestly wears its politics on its sleeve. The exhilaration in the book lies in the stories told and in their transformative potential." Professor Jeremy Till, author of *Architecture Depends*

Select titles:

We Are Not Latino, We Are Nican Tlaca (2015)

The Queen vs Trenton Oldfield: A Prison Diary (2013)

Estate: Arts, Politics and Social Housing in Britain (2010)

Critical Cities: Ideas, Knowledge and Agitation from Emerging Urbanists, Vol 5 (2015)

Critical Cities: Ideas, Knowledge and Agitation from Emerging Urbanists, Vol 4 (2015)

Critical Cities: Ideas, Knowledge and Agitation from Emerging Urbanists, Vol 3 (2012)

Critical Cities: Ideas, Knowledge and Agitation from Emerging Urbanists, Vol 2 (2010)

Critical Cities: Ideas, Knowledge and Agitation from Emerging Urbanists, Vol 1 (2009)

Myrdle Court Press is based in London, UK. It takes a back-to-fundamentals approach to book production using design for readability, high quality ethically sourced materials, local printers and independent distribution.

www.myrdlecourtpress.net